$14.95

TRS 80™ MODEL III

PROGRAMMING AND APPLICATIONS

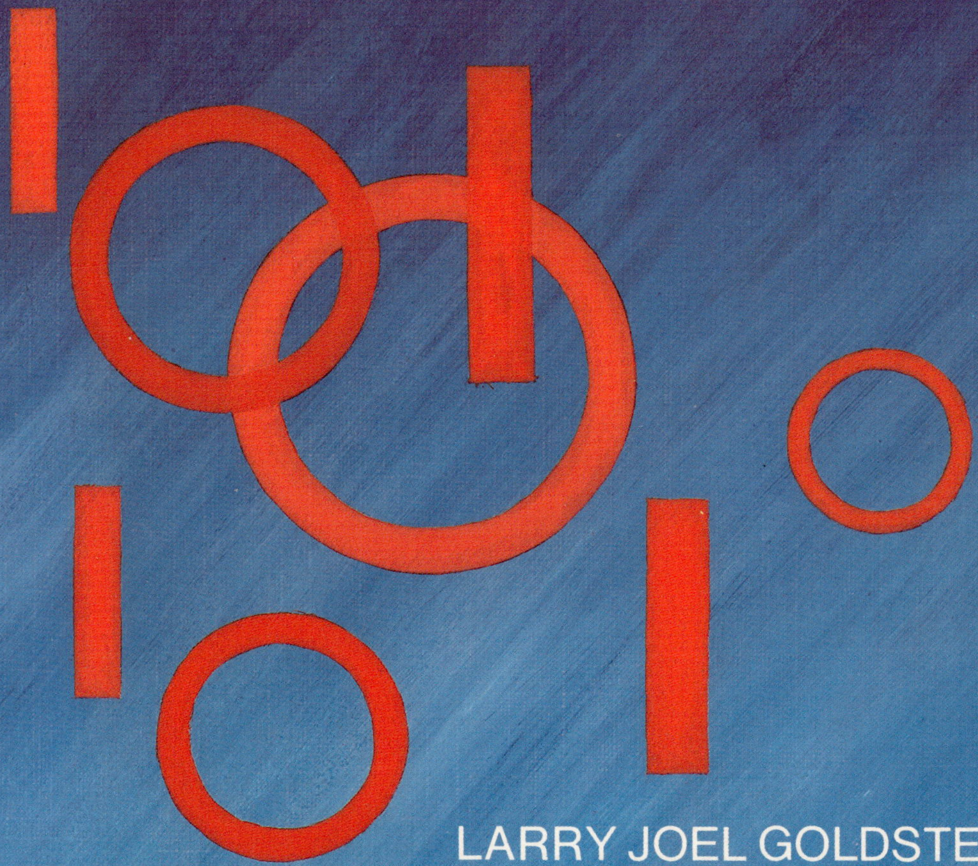

LARRY JOEL GOLDSTEIN

TRS-80 MODEL III

Executive Editor: David T. Culverwell
Production Editor: Michael J. Rogers
Art Director: Don Sellers,
Illustrator: Nancy Obloy
Typesetting by: Bi-Comp, Incorporated, York, PA
Typefaces: Zapf (display) and Optima (text)
Printed by: R. R. Donnelley & Sons Company, Harrisonburg, VA
Text designer: Michael J. Rogers
Cover design: Don Sellers

THE TRS-80 MODEL III PROGRAMMING and APPLICATIONS

Larry Joel Goldstein

University of Maryland
College Park, Maryland

Robert J. Brady Company
A Prentice-Hall Publishing and Communications Company
Bowie, Maryland 20715

The TRS-80 Model III: Programming and Applications

Library of Congress Cataloging in Publication Data

Goldstein, Larry Joel.
The TRS-80 model III.

Includes index.
1. TRS-80 (Computer) I. Title.
QA76.8.T18G64 001.64 81-21588
ISBN 0-89303-050-3 AACR2

Prentice-Hall International, Inc., London
Prentice-Hall of Australia, Pty., Ltd., Sydney
Prentice-Hall of India Private Limited, New Delhi
Prentice-Hall of Japan, Inc., Tokyo
Prentice-Hall of Southeast Asia Pte. Ltd., Singapore
Whitehall Books, Limited, Petone, New Zealand

Printed in the United States of America

82 83 84 85 86 87 88 89 90 91 92 10 9 8 7 6 5 4 3 2

CONTENTS

PREFACE

This book is designed to teach the computer novice how to use one of the most popular personal computers, the TRS-80 Model III. The development of the personal computer is one of the most exciting breakthroughs of our time. Indeed, the small, inexpensive, personal computer promises to bring the computer revolution to tens of millions of people and promises to alter the way we think, learn, work, and play. This book is an introduction to this revolution. Accordingly, it has two purposes: first, it instructs the reader in the operation of the Model III; and, second, it illustrates some of the many ways to use the TRS-80.

I have attempted to guide the reader from the moment he or she turns on the TRS-80 for the first time and discuss the rudiments of BASIC programming. Since the book is designed as a tutorial, it includes an exercise set in each section, with answers at the end of the book. Furthermore, this book may be used for self-study. In the text are questions labeled "Test Your Understanding." These questions test concepts as they are introduced and a built-in study guide. The answers to these questions are to be found at the end of the exercises for the section.

Because of my conviction that, in addition to BASIC programming, the beginner should also gain an overview of real-life applications, I have included many applied discussions, e.g., a brief look at word processing. These applications are designed to stimulate the reader's interest and can be used as preludes to further study.

Most enthusiastic personal computer users quickly upgrade their computers to include various optional equipment. Accordingly, I have included an introduction to Disk BASIC, and brief discussions of printers and communications interfaces. The book closes with possible topics for further study.

Any book owes its existence to the dedicated labors and inspirations of many people. In my case, I have been inspired by my wife, Sandy and my children, Melissa and Jonathan, who have enthusiastically joined me in applying our TRS-80 to a variety of tasks. Further inspiration has been supplied by my father, Martin Goldstein, who has come out of retirement to join the computer revolution and to assist me in researching and editing this book. My thanks to Michael Rogers, Production Editor, for the professional manner in which he managed the editing and production of this book. Finally, I would like to thank my friends Harry Gaines, President of the Brady Company, and David Culverwell, Editor-in-Chief of the Brady Company, for their continued support over the years. Their friendship has enhanced my excitement and pleasure in writing this book.

Dr. Larry Joel Goldstein
Silver Spring, Maryland
September 19, 1981

to
my father, Martin Goldstein,
always a father,
recently a collaborator

1

A First Look At Computers

1.1 INTRODUCTION

The computer age is barely thirty years old but it has already had a profound effect on all our lives. Indeed, computers are now commonplace in the office, the factory, and even the supermarket. In the last three or four years, the computer has even invaded the home, as people have purchased millions of computer games and hundreds of thousands of personal computers. Computers are in such common use today that it is hard to imagine a single day in which a computer will not somehow affect us.

In spite of the explosion of computer use in our society, most people know very little about them. People view a computer as an "electronic brain," and have no idea how a computer works, how it may be used, and the extent to which it may simplify various everyday tasks. This does not reflect a lack of interest. Most people recognize that computers are here to stay and are interested in finding out how to use them. If you are so inclined, then this is the book for you!

I have designed this book as an introduction to personal computing for the novice. You may be a student, teacher, homemaker, business person, or just a curious individual. I assume that you have had little or no previous exposure to computers and are interested in learning the fundamentals. I will guide you as you turn on your computer for the first time. (There is really nothing to it!) From there, I will lead you through the fundamentals of computer programming in the BASIC language. Throughout, we will provide exercises for you to test your understanding of the concepts presented. The approach will stress the various ways in which *you can apply your computer*. The exercises will suggest programs you can write. Many of the programs will be designed to give you insight into the workings of computers in business and industry. I will suggest a number of applications of the computer within your home. For good measure, we will build a few computer games!

What is Personal Computing?

In the early days of computing (the 1940s and 1950s), the typical computer was a huge mass of electronic components which occupied several entire rooms. In those days, it was often necessary to reinforce the floor of a computer room and install special air conditioning in order for the computer to function properly. Moreover, an early computer was likely to cost several million dollars. Over the years, the cost of computers has decreased dramatically and, thanks to micro-miniaturization, their size has shrunk quicker than their price.

A few years ago, the first "personal" computers were introduced to the marketplace. These computers were reasonably inexpensive and were designed to allow the average person to learn about the computer and to use it to solve everday problems. These personal computers proved to be incredibly popular and several hundred thousand of them were sold in only three years.

The personal computer is not a toy. It is a genuine computer which has most of the features of its big brothers, the so-called "main-frame" computers, which still cost several million dollars. A personal computer can be equipped with enough capacity to handle the accounting and inventory control tasks of most small businesses. It can perform computations for engineers and scientists. It can even be used to keep track of home finance and personal clerical chores. It would be quite impossible to give anything like a comprehensive list of the applications of personal computers. However, the following list can suggest the range of possibilities:

For the business person:
- Accounting
- Record-keeping
- Clerical chores
- Inventory
- Cash management
- Payroll
- Graph and chart preparation

For the home:
- Record-keeping
- Budget management

Investment analysis
Correspondence
Energy conservation
Home security

For the professional:
Billing
Analysis of data
Report generation
Correspondence

For recreation:
Computer games
Computer graphics
Computer art

As you can see, the list is quite comprehensive. However, your interests may not be included in any of the categories on the list. Do not worry about that. There is plenty of room for those of you who are just plain curious about computers and wish to pursue them as a hobby.

*The TRS-80 Model III**

This book will introduce you to personal computing on the TRS-80 Model III computer. This is an excellent machine with remarkable capabilities for its very modest price. Radio Shack has been one of the genuine pioneers in the personal computer movement and its Model III is a "second generation" personal computer, enjoying many more advanced features than its earlier sisters, the Model I, Levels I and II. Before we begin to discuss the features of the Model III, however, let us begin by discussing the features which are common to all computers.

1.2 WHAT IS A COMPUTER?

At the heart of every computer is a **central processing unit** (or **CPU**) which executes the commands you specify. This unit carries out arithmetic, makes logical decisions, and so forth. In essence, the CPU is the "brain" of the computer. The **memory** of a computer allows it to "remember" numbers, words, paragraphs, as well as the list of commands you wish the computer to perform. The **input unit** allows you to send information to the computer; the

---

*TRS-80 is a registered trademark of the Tandy Corporation.

output unit allows the computer to send information to you. The relationship of these four basic components of a computer are shown in Figure 1-1.

In a TRS-80 computer, the CPU is contained in a tiny circuitry chip, called a Z80 microprocessor. As a computer novice, it will not be necessary for you to know anything at all about the electronics of the CPU. For now, view the CPU as a magic device somewhere inside the case of your computer and do not give it another thought!

The input device of the TRS-80 is the computer keyboard. We will discuss the special features of the keyboard in Section Three. For now it suffices to think of the keyboard as a typewriter. By typing symbols on the keyboard, you are inputting them to the computer.

The TRS-80 has a number of output devices available. The most basic is the "TV screen" or **video display.** In addition, you may use a printer to provide output on paper. In computer jargon, such output is called **hard copy.**

There are four types of memory in a TRS-80: ROM, RAM, cassette, and disk. Each of these types of memory has its own advantages and disadvantages, so we attempt to make the memory as versatile as possible by combining the good features of each type.

ROM stands for "read only memory." This type of memory can be read by the computer (that is, the CPU), but you cannot record anything in it. The ROM is reserved for the computer language which the CPU utilizes. More

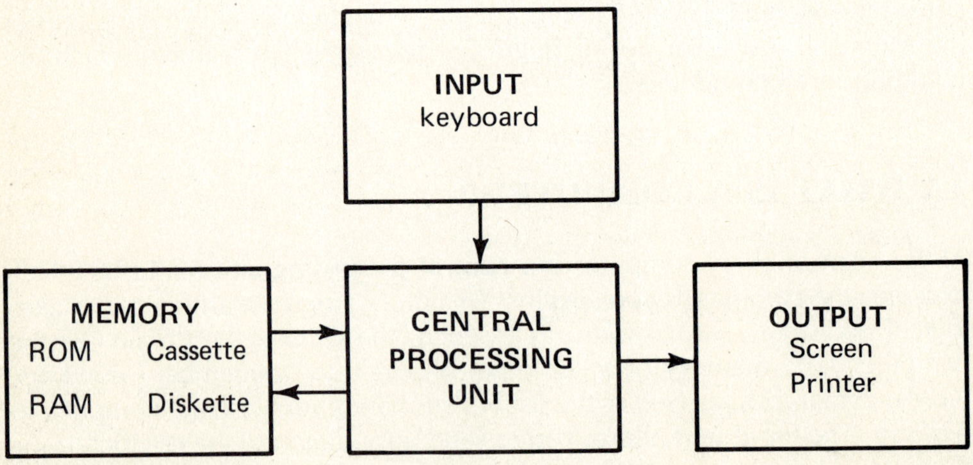

Figure 1-1.

about this language later. For now just remember that the ROM contains the information necessary for the computer to understand your commands. This information is pre-recorded in the factory and is permanently situated in the ROM. You will never need to concern yourself further with the ROM.

RAM stands for "random access memory." This is the memory into which you can write. If you type characters on the keyboard, then they are stored in RAM. Similarly, results of calculations are kept in RAM awaiting output to you. There is an extremely important feature of RAM which you should remember.

Important: If the computer is turned off, then RAM is erased.

Thus, RAM may not be used to store data in permanent form. Nevertheless, it is used as the computer's main working storage because of its great speed. It takes only about a millionth of a second to store or retrieve a piece of data from RAM.

To make permanent copies of programs and data, we may use either the cassette recorder or the disk file. The cassette recorder is just a tape recorder which allows the recording of information in a form intelligible to the computer. The recording medium is the same sort of cassette you use for musical recordings, but of a much higher quality.

A disk file records information on flexible disks which resemble phonograph records. The disks are often called "floppy disks," and can store several hundred thousand characters each! (A double-spaced typed page contains about 3,000 characters.) A disk file can provide access to information in much less time, on the average, than a cassette recorder. On the other hand, disk files are more costly than cassette recorders.

The TRS-80 Model III comes in both disk and non-disk models. Since this book is meant for novices, we will begin by assuming that you have the non-disk version. It will not make much difference which version you own until we discuss file maintenance (in Chapter 4).

1.3 MEET YOUR TRS-80

The best way to quickly master the operation of your computer is to read this book while sitting down in front of it and verifying the various statements as they come up. So why don't you have a seat in front of your TRS-80. If your computer is not conveniently available, you may refer to Figures 1-2 and 1-3.

Figure 1-2. The TRS-80 Model III.

Let us begin by examining the keyboard. Note that it is similar to a typewriter keyboard, with a few significant differences. Many typewriters use the same key for the number **1** and a lower case letter **l.** However, for the computer, spellings must not allow for any ambiguity, so there are distinct keys for these two symbols. Similarly, it is very easy to confuse the capital letter O ('oh') and the number 0 (zero). For this reason, a computer specialist usually writes zero with a slash through it: **Ø.** To prevent possible confusion, you should also adopt this convention.

Note that the keyboard has a number of specialized keys which are not on a standard typewriter keyboard. We will discuss these keys one at a time, but first let's turn the computer on. Look under the keyboard. On the right side you will find the Power-On. Push it. The computer should respond with the question:*

---

*The following discussion applies to the Model III, Levels I and II. If your computer is the disk version, then the power-on will be followed by the displayed message "Insert Diskette." In

Figure 1-3. The Model III keyboard.

CASS?

Respond by hitting the **ENTER** key. Next, the computer will ask:

MEMORY SIZE?

Hit the **ENTER** key again. (Later on we will discuss the significance of these questions.) The computer should now respond with the message:

RADIO SHACK MODEL III BASIC
(C) '80 TANDY
READY

Your computer is now awaiting your instructions! Strike a few keys just to get the feel of the keyboard. Note that as you type, the corresponding characters

---

learning to operate your computer, we recommend that you ignore the disk drives for the time being. To do so, as you turn on your computer, depress the **Break** key. This procedure causes the computer to ignore the presence of the disk files. From here on the computer will function as described above. For start-up dialog to use the disk drives and disk BASIC, see Chapter Four.

will appear on the screen. Note, also, how the small white box travels along the typing line. This box is called the **cursor.** The cursor always sits at the location where the next typed character will appear. Note also that the symbol > always sits out in the left hand margin. This symbol is called a **prompt** and indicates the current line being typed.

As you type, you should notice the similarities between the Model III keyboard and that of a typewriter. However, you should also note the differences. At the end of a typewriter line you return the carriage, either manually or, on an electric typewriter, with a carriage return key. Of course, your screen has no carriage to return. The **ENTER** key serves the same function. If you depress the **ENTER** key, the cursor will then return to the next line and position itself at the extreme left side of the screen. The **ENTER** key has another function. It signals the computer to accept the line just typed. Until you hit the **ENTER** key, the computer does not even know that the current line exists!

Keep typing until you are at the bottom of the screen. If you hit **ENTER,** the entire contents of the screen will move up by one line and the line at the top of the screen will disappear. This property of the screen is called **scrolling.**

By this time, your screen should look pretty cluttered. To clear it, push the **CLEAR** key on the right side of the keyboard. All characters on the screen are erased and only the cursor remains. The cursor is positioned in the upper left corner of the screen. See Figure 1-4.

Figure 1-4. Screen after CLEAR.

There are several other very interesting features of the Model III keyboard. Note that each of the digits 0–9 appear twice: once in the usual place at the top of the keyboard and a second time at the right hand side. The numeric keys on the right side are arranged like the keys of a calculator and are designed to facilitate typing numerical data. It makes no difference which of the sets of numerical keys you use. In fact, you may alternate them in any manner, entering a 1 from the top set, then a 5 from the right set, and so forth. The right set of keys is called the ***numeric keypad.*** Note that the numeric keypad contains an **ENTER** key. This key has the same function as the other **ENTER** key and is provided for convenience.

There are two **SHIFT** keys. They work exactly like the shift keys on a typewriter and allow the typing of capital letters (and the top characters on keys with two symbols). For example, the key in the top right corner of the keyboard has ! on top and a 1 on the bottom. To type ! strike the 1/! key while holding down the **SHIFT** key.

In most computer work it is convenient to type using only capital letters. For one thing, capitals are larger and easier to read on the screen. For another, most of the commands and statements in the BASIC language require all capital letters. You may disable the lower case letters by typing a SHIFT and Ø simultaneously. In this mode the letter keys are automatically typed as capitals. *Note, however, that the non-letter keys (such as 1 and !) still have two meanings. To type the upper symbol, you still must use the shift key.* To return from the all-capitals mode, once again hit SHIFT and Ø simultaneously.

Test Your Understanding 1.1*

(a) Type your name and address on the screen. Number the lines. (e.g. 10 NAME, 20 STREET, etc.)

(b) Erase the screen.

(c) Repeat (a) only using all capital letters.

Unless you are a superb typist (most of us are at the other extreme!), you will eventually make typing errors. So let's discover how to correct them. Type a few characters, but do not hit the **ENTER** key. Now hit the backspace key. (This is the key with the arrow pointing to the left.) Note that this key

---

*Answers to the **TEST YOUR UNDERSTANDING** questions follow the exercise set of the current section.

causes the cursor to backspace, one space at a time, erasing the characters it passes over. This is another difference between a typewriter and a computer keyboard. Note, however, that you may use the backspace to correct lines only if they have not been sent to the computer via the **ENTER** key.

If things look hopeless and you wish to start over, just push the **RESET** button at the upper right side of the keyboard. This will return the computer to the state it was in just after being turned on. Both RAM and the screen will be erased.

There are other ways to correct typing errors, but for now let us be content with the methods discussed above.

The Model III keyboard has a number of other keys but let's start using the computer and wait until later to discuss them.

EXERCISES

Type the following expressions on the screen. After each numbered exercise, clear the screen.

1. 10 Hello. I'm your new owner.
2. 10 ARITHMETIC
3. 10 PRINT 3+7
4. 20 LET A=3−5
5. 10 5% of 68
6. 10 38>−5
7. 10 Addition
   20 Subtraction
   30 Multiplication
   40 Division
8. 10 CENTRAL PROCESSING UNIT
   20 RANDOM ACCESS MEMORY
   30 READ ONLY MEMORY
9. 10 LET X=10
   20 LET Y=50.35
10. 200 Y=X*2−5
    300 PRINT Y, "Y"

Answers to Test Your Understanding 1.1

(a) Type your name, following each line with **ENTER.**

(b) Hit **CLEAR.**

(c) Hit **SHIFT** and 0 simultaneously. Now repeat (a).

2

Getting Started in BASIC

2.1 COMPUTER LANGUAGES AND PROGRAMS

In the last chapter, we learned to manipulate the keyboard and display screen of the TRS-80. Let us now take up the problem of communicating instructions to the computer.

Just as humans use languages to communicate with one another, computers use languages to communicate with other electronic devices (such as printers), human operators, and other computers. There are hundreds of computer languages in use today. However, the most common one for microcomputers is called BASIC. This is the language used by your TRS-80. BASIC is versatile and yet very easy to learn. It was developed at Dartmouth College by John Kemeny and Thomas Kurtz, especially for novices at computing. For the next few chapters, we will concentrate on learning the basics of BASIC.

Assume that you have turned on your computer and that its readiness to accept further instructions is signified by the presence of the display:

```
READY
>
```

From this point on, a typical session with your computer might go like this:

1. Type in a series of instructions in BASIC. Such a series of instructions is called a **program.**
2. Locate and correct any errors in the program.

3. Tell the computer to carry out the series of instructions in the program. This step is called **running the program.**
4. Obtain the output requested by the program.
5. Either: (a) Run the program again; or (b) repeat steps 1–4 for a new program; or (c) terminate the programming session.

To better understand what is involved in these five steps, let us consider a particular example. Suppose that you want the computer to add 5 and 7. First, you would type the following instructions:

10 PRINT 5+7
20 END

This sequence of two instructions constitutes a program to calculate 5 + 7. Note that as you type the program, the computer merely records your instructions, **but does not carry them out.** As you are typing a program, the computer provides opportunity to change, delete, and correct instruction lines. (More about how to do this later.) Once you are content with your program, you tell the computer to run it (that is, to execute the instructions) by typing the command*:

RUN

The computer will execute the program and display the desired answer:

12

If you wish the computer to run the program a second time, type **RUN** again.

Running a program does not erase it from RAM. Thus, if you wish to add instructions to the program or modify the program, you may continue typing just as if the **RUN** command had not intervened. For example, if you wish to include in your program the problem of calculating 5 − 7, we type the additional line:

15 PRINT 5−7

---

*Do not forget to follow the command with **ENTER.** Recall that the computer will not recognize lines unless they have been sent to it by hitting the **ENTER** key.

The program now consists of the three lines:

```
10 PRINT 5+7
15 PRINT 5-7
20 END
```

Note how the computer puts line 15 in proper sequence. If we now type **RUN** again, the computer will display the two answers:

```
12
-2
```

In the event that you now wish to go on to another program, type the command:

```
NEW
```

This erases the previous program from RAM and prepares the computer to accept a new program. You should always remember the following important fact:

RAM can contain only one program at a time.

Test Your Understanding 1.1

(a) Write and type in a BASIC program to calculate 12.1 + 98 + 5.32.

(b) Run the program of (a).

(c) Erase the program of (a) from RAM.

(d) Write a program to calculate 48.75 − 1.674.

(e) Type in and run the program of (d).

The TRS-80 operates in several distinct modes. In the **immediate mode,** it accepts typed program lines and commands (like **RUN** and **NEW**), used to manipulate programs. In the immediate mode, commands are executed as soon as they are given. In the **execute mode,** the computer executes a program. In execute mode, the screen is under control of the program. Finally, there is the **edit mode.** This is a special mode used to correct program lines. In this mode, the keyboard and screen work according to special rules which we will discuss in Chapter Four.

When you first turn the computer on, it is automatically in immediate mode. The immediate mode is indicated by the presence of the **READY** message on the screen. The **RUN** command puts it into execute mode. After the program has been run, the computer redisplays the **READY** message, indicating that it is back in immediate mode.

Answers to Test Your Understanding 1.1

(a) 10 PRINT 12.1+98+5.32
    20 END

(b) Type RUN

(c) Type NEW

(d) 10 PRINT 48.75−1.674
    20 END

(e) Type in program followed by RUN

2.2 ELEMENTARY BASIC PROGRAMS

In learning to use a language, you must first master the alphabet in which the language is written. Next, you must learn the vocabulary of the language. Finally, you must study the way in which words are put together into sentences. In learning the BASIC language, we will follow the progression just described. In the previous chapter, we learned about the characters of the Model III keyboard. These characters are the alphabet of BASIC. Next, let us learn some elementary vocabulary. The simplest "words" are the so-called constants.

BASIC Constants

BASIC allows us to manipulate numbers and text. Of course, the rules for manipulating numerical data differ from those for handling text, so in BASIC we distinguish between these two types of data as follows: A **numeric constant** is a number. A **string constant** is a sequence of keyboard characters, which may include letters, numbers, or any other keyboard symbols. Thus, for example, the following are examples of numeric constants:

5, −2, 3.145, 23456, 456.78345676543987, 27134566543

The following are examples of string constants:

"John", "Accounts Receivable", "$234.45 Due", "Dec. 4, 1981"

Note that string constants are always enclosed in quotation marks. In order to avoid ambiguity, quotation marks may not appear as part of a string constant. (In practice, an apostrophe ' will usually serve as an adequate substitute.) Note that although numbers may appear in a string constant, you cannot use such numbers in arithmetic operations. Only numeric constants may be used for arithmetic purposes.

For certain applications, you may wish to specify your numeric constants in *exponential format*. This will be especially helpful in the case of very large and very small numbers. For example, consider the number 15,300,000,000. It is very inconvenient to type all the zeros. It can be written in handy shorthand as 1.53E10. The 1.53 indicates the first three digits of the number. The E10 means that you move the decimal point in the 1.53 to the right 10 places. Similarly, the number −237,000 may be written in exponential format as −2.37E5. The exponential format may also be used for very small numbers. For example, the number .00000000054 may be written in exponential format as 5.4E−10. The −10 indicates that the decimal point in 5.4 is to be moved 10 places to the *left*.

Test Your Understanding 2.1

(a) Write these numbers in exponential format: .00048 , −1374.5

(b) Write these numbers in decimal format: −9.7E3, 9.7E−3, −9.7E−3

We will have more to say about constants later. For example, we will describe the number of digits of accuracy you can get, how to round off numbers, and so forth. Now, however, you know more than enough to get started. So instead of concentrating on the fine points now, let's first learn enough to make our computer **do something.**

BASIC Programs

Let us reconsider the BASIC program of the preceding section, namely:

line number

```
10 PRINT 5+7
20 END
```

end of program

This program illustrates two very important features common to all BASIC programs:

I. The instructions of a program must be numbered. Each line must start with a line number. The computer executes instructions in order of increasing line number.

II. The **END** instruction identifies the end of the program. On encountering this instruction, the computer stops execution of the program and displays **READY** and the prompt.

Note that line numbers need not be consecutive. For example, it is perfectly acceptable to have a program whose line numbers are 10,23,47, 55,100. Note also that it is not necessary to type instructions in their numerical order. You could type line 20 and then go back and type line 10. The computer will sort out the lines and rearrange them according to increasing number. This feature is especially helpful in case you accidentally omit a line while typing your program.

Here is yet another important fact about line numbering. If you type two lines having the same line number, the computer erases the first version and remembers the second version. This feature is especially useful for correcting errors: If a line has an error, just retype it!

Your TRS-80 will perform all the standard functions found on a calculator. Since most people are familiar with the operation of a calculator, let us start by writing programs to solve various arithmetic problems.

Arithmetic operations are written in customary fashion, with a few accommodations to the limited number of characters on the keyboard. Addition and subtraction are written for the computer in the usual way:

5 + 4, 9 − 8.

However, multiplication is indicated using the symbol *, which shares the ":" key. Thus, for example, the product of 5 and 3 is denoted as:

5*3

Similarly, division is denoted using /. Thus, for example, 8.2 divided by 15 is typed:

8.2/15

Example 1. Write a BASIC program to calculate the sum of 54.75, 78.83 and 548.

Solution. The sum is indicated by typing:

54.75 + 78.83 + 548

The BASIC instruction for printing data on the screen is **PRINT.** So we write our program as follows:

```
10 PRINT 54.75+78.83+548
20 END
```

BASIC carries out arithmetic operations in a special order. It scans an expression and first carries out all multiplications and divisions *in left-to-right order.* It then returns to the left side of the expression and performs addition and subtraction, also in left-to-right order. If parentheses occur, these are evaluated first, following the same rules. If parentheses occur within parentheses, then the innermost parentheses are evaluated first.

Example 2. What are the numerical values which BASIC will calculate from these expressions?

(a) (5 + 7)/2

(b) 5 + 7/2

(c) 5 + 7*3/2

(d) (5 + 7*3)/2

Solution. (a) The computer first applies its rules for the order of calculation to determine the value of the parenthesis, namely 12. Then it divides by 2 to obtain 6.

(b) The computer scans the expression from left to right performing all multiplications and divisions in the order encountered. So it does the division 7/2 to obtain 3.5. It then rescans the line and performs all additions and subtractions in order. This gives:

5 + 3.5 = 8.5.

(c) The computer first performs all multiplication and division in order:

5 + 10.5

Now it performs addition and subtraction to obtain 15.5.

(d) The computer calculates the value of all parentheses first. In this case, it computes 5 + 7*3 = 26. (Note that it does the multiplication first!) Next it rescans the line, which now looks like

26/2

It performs the division to obtain 13.

Test Your Understanding 2.2

Calculate 5 + 3/2 + 2 and (5 + 3)/(2 + 2).

Example 3. Write a BASIC program to calculate the quantity:

$$\frac{22 \times 18 + 34 \times 11 - 12.5 \times 8}{27.8}$$

Solution. Here is the program:

```
10 PRINT (22*18+34*11-12.5*8)/27.8
20 END
```

Note that we used parentheses in line 10. They tell the computer that the entire quantity in parentheses is to be divided by 27.8. If we had omitted the parentheses, the computer would divide −12.5*8 by 27.8 and add 22*18 and 34*11 to the result.

Test Your Understanding 2.3

Write BASIC programs to calculate:

(a) ((4 × 3 + 5 × 8 + 7 × 9)/(7 × 9 + 4 × 3 + 8 × 7)) × 48.7

(b) 27.8% of (112 + 38 + 42)

(c) The average of the numbers 88, 78, 84, 49, 63

Printing Words

So far, we have used the **PRINT** instruction only to display the answers to numerical problems. However, this instruction is very versatile. It also allows us to display string constants. For example, consider this instruction:

```
10 PRINT "PATIENT HISTORY"
```

During program execution, this statement will create the following display:

```
PATIENT HISTORY
```

In order to display several string constants on the same line, separate them by commas in a single **PRINT** statement. For example, consider the instruction:

10 PRINT "AGE", "SEX", "BIRTHPLACE", "ADDRESS"

It will cause four words to be printed as follows:

AGE	SEX	BIRTHPLACE	ADDRESS

Both numeric constants and string constants may appear in a single **PRINT** statement, such as:

100 PRINT "AGE", 65.43, "NO. DEPENDENTS"

Here is how the computer determines the spacing on a line. Each line is divided into **print zones,** each of which consists of 16 spaces. By placing a comma in a **PRINT** statement, you are telling the computer to start the next string of text at the beginning of the next print zone. Thus, for example, the four words above begin in columns 0,16,32,48, respectively. Note that columns are numbered beginning with 0. (See Figure. 2-1.)

Test Your Understanding 2.4

Write a program to print the following display.

	NAME		
LAST	FIRST	MIDDLE	GRADE
SMITH	JOHN	DAVID	87

Example 4. Suppose that a distributor of plumbing supplies sells 50 sinks and 5 hot water boilers. The sinks cost $39.70 each and are subject to a 30% discount. The hot water boilers cost $147.90 each and are also subject to a 30% discount. Prepare a bill for the shipment.

COLUMN

0 . . . 15	16 . . . 31	32 . . . 47	48 . . . 63
Print Zone 1	Print Zone 2	Print Zone 3	Print Zone 4

Figure 2-1. Print zones.

Solution. Let us insert four headings on our bill: Item, Quantity, Price, and Cost. We then print two lines, corresponding to the two types of items shipped. Finally, we calculate the total due.

```
10 PRINT "ITEM","QTY","PRICE","COST"
20 PRINT
30 PRINT "SINK",50,39.70,50*(39.70-.3*39.70)
40 PRINT "BOILER",5,147.90,5*(147.90-.3*147.90)
50 PRINT
60 PRINT "TOTAL DUE",,,50*(39.70-.3*39.70)+
   5*(147.90-.3*147.90)
```

Note the **PRINT** statements in lines 20 and 50. They specify that a blank line is to be printed. Also, note the series of three commas in line 60. The additional two commas move the next printing over to the beginning of the fourth print zone, which would bring the total cost directly under the column labelled **"COST"**. If we now type **RUN** (followed by **ENTER**), the screen will look like this:

```
10 PRINT "ITEM","QTY","PRICE","COST"
20 PRINT
30 PRINT "SINK","50","39.70",50*(39.70-.3*39.70)
40 PRINT "BOILER","5","147.90",5*(147.90-.3*147.90)
50 PRINT
60 PRINT "TOTAL DUE",,,50*(39.70-.3*39.70)+
   5*(147.90-.3*147.90)

RUN

ITEM          QTY           PRICE         COST

SINK          50            39.70         1389.50
BOILER        5             147.90        517.65

TOTAL DUE                                 1907.15
```

You may think that the above invoice is somewhat sloppy because the columns of figures are not properly aligned. Patience! We will learn to align the columns after we have learned a bit more programming.

Test Your Understanding 2.5

Write a computer program which creates the following display.

BUDGET-APRIL

FOOD	387.50
RENT	475.00
CAR	123.71
GAS	100.00
UTILITIES	146.00
ENTERTAINMENT	100.00
	———
TOTAL	(Calculate total)

Exponentiation

Suppose that A is a number and N is a positive integer (that is, N is one of the numbers 1,2,3,4, . . .). Then *A raised to the Nth power* is the product of A with itself N times. This quantity is usually denoted A^N, and the process of calculating it is called *exponentiation*. Thus, for example:

$2^3 = 2*2*2 = 8, \; 5^7 = 5*5*5*5*5*5*5 = 78125.$

It is possible to calculate A^N by repeated multiplication. However, if N is large, this can be tedious to type. BASIC provides a shortcut. Exponentiation is denoted by the symbol [, which is produced by hitting the key with the upward-pointing arrow. For example, 2^3 is denoted 2[3. The operation of exponentiation takes precedence over multiplication and division, as is illustrated by the following example.

Example 5. Determine the value which BASIC assigns to this expression:

20*3 − 5*2[3

Solution. The exponentiation is performed first to yield:

$$\begin{aligned} 20*3 - 5*8 &= 60 - 40 \\ &= 20. \end{aligned}$$

Test Your Understanding 2.6

Evaluate the following first manually and then by a Model III program.

(a) $2^4 \times 3^3$

(b) $2^2 \times 3^3 - 12^2/3^2 \times 2$

EXERCISES (answers on 267)

Write BASIC programs to calculate the following quantities:

1. 57 + 23 + 48
2. 57.83 × (48.27 − 12.54)
3. 127.86/38
4. $365/.005 + 1.02^5$
5. Make a table of the first, second, third, and fourth powers of the numbers 2, 3, 4, 5, and 6. Put all first powers in a column, all second powers in another column, and so forth.
6. Mrs. Anita Smith visited the doctor in connection with a broken leg. Her bill consists of 45 dollars for removal of the cast, 35 dollars for therapy, and 5 dollars for drugs. Her major medical policy will pay 80% directly to the doctor. Use the computer to prepare an invoice for Mrs. Smith.
7. A school board election is held to elect a representative for a district consisting of Wards 1, 2, 3 and 4. There are three candidates, Mr. Thacker, Ms. Hoving, and Mrs. Weatherby. The tallies by candidate and ward are as follows.

	Ward 1	Ward 2	Ward 3	Ward 4
Thacker	698	732	129	487
Hoving	148	928	246	201
Weatherby	379	1087	148	641

Write a BASIC computer program to calculate the total number of votes achieved by each candidate as well as the total number of votes cast.

Describe the output from each of these programs.

8.
```
10 PRINT 8*2-3*(2[4-10)
20 END
```

9.
```
PRINT "SILVER","GOLD","COPPER","PLATINUM"
20 PRINT 327,448,1052,2
30 END
```

10.
```
10 PRINT, "GROCERIES","MEATS","DRUGS"
20 PRINT "MON","1,245","2,348","2,531"
30 PRINT "TUE"," 248","3,459","2,148"
40 END
```

Convert the following numbers to exponential format.

11. 23,000,000
12. 175.25
13. −200,000,000
14. .00014
15. −.000000000275
16. 53,420,000,000,000,000

Convert the following numbers in exponential format to standard format.

17. 1.59E5
18. −20.3456E6
19. −7.456E−12
20. 2.39456E−18

Answers to Test Your Understanding

2.1: (a) 4.8E−4, −1.3745E3

(b) −9700, .0097, −.0097

2.2: 8.5, 2

2.3: (a)
```
10 PRINT ((4*3+5*8+7*9)/(7*9+4*3+8*7))*48.7
20 END
```

(b)
```
10 PRINT .278*(112+38+42)
20 END
```

(c)
```
10 PRINT (88+79+84+49+63)/5
20 END
```

2.4:
```
10 PRINT, "NAME"
20 PRINT
30 PRINT "LAST","MIDDLE","FIRST","GRADE"
40 PRINT
50 PRINT "SMITH","JOHN","DAVID",87
60 END
```

2.5:
```
10 PRINT, "BUDGET-APRIL"
20 PRINT "FOOD",387.50
30 PRINT "CAR",475.00
40 PRINT "GAS",123.71
50 PRINT "UTILITIES",146.00
60 PRINT "ENTERTAINMENT",100.00
70 PRINT , "____"
80 PRINT "TOTAL", 387.50+475.00+123.71+146.00+100.00
90 END
```

2.6: (a) 432

(b) 76

2.3 GIVING NAMES TO NUMBERS AND WORDS

In the examples and exercises of the preceding section, you probably noticed that you were wasting considerable time by retyping certain numbers over and over. Not only does this retyping waste time, it also is a likely source for errors. Fortunately, such retyping is unnecessary if we make use of variables.

A **variable** is a letter which represents a number. Any letter of the alphabet may be used as a variable. (There are other possible names for variables. See below.) Possible variables are A, B, C, X, Y, Z. At any given moment, a variable has a particular value. For example, the variable A might have the value 5 while B might have the value −2.137845. One method for changing the value of a variable is through use of the **LET** statement. The statement

10 LET A=7

sets the value of A equal to 7. Any previous value of A is erased. The **LET** command may be used to set the values of a number of variables simultaneously. For instance, the instruction

100 LET C=18: D=23: E=2.718

assigns C the value 18, D the value 23, and E the value 2.718.

Once the value of a variable has been set, the variable may be used throughout the program. The computer will insert the appropriate value wherever the value occurs. For instance, if A has the value 7 then the expression

A+5

is evaluated as 7 + 5 or 12. The expression

```
3*A-10
```

is evaluated 3*7 − 10 = 11. The expression 2*A[2 is evaluated

```
2*7[2=2*49=98
```

Test Your Understanding 3.1

Suppose that A has the value 4 and B has the value 3. What is the value of the expression A[2/2*B[2?

Variables may also be used in **PRINT** statements. For example, the statement

```
10 PRINT A
```

will cause the computer to print the current value of A (in the first print zone, of course!). The statement

```
20 PRINT A,B,C
```

will result in printing the current values of A, B, and C in print zones 1, 2, and 3, respectively.

Test Your Understanding 3.2

Suppose that A has the value 5. What will be the result of the instruction:

```
10 PRINT A,A[2,2*A[2
```

Example 1. Consider the three numbers 5.71, 3.23, and 4.05. Calculate their sum, their product, and the sum of their squares. (That is, the sum of their second powers; such a sum is often used in statistics.)

Solution. Introduce variables A, B, and C and set them equal, respectively, to the three numbers. Then compute the desired quantities.

```
10 LET A=5.71: B=3.23: C=4.05
20 PRINT "THE SUM IS", A+B+C
30 PRINT "THE PRODUCT IS", A*B*C
40 PRINT "THE SUM OF SQUARES IS", A[2+B[2+C[2
50 END
```

Test Your Understanding 3.3

Consider the numbers 101, 102, 103, 104, 105, 106. Write a program which calculates the product of the first 2, the first 3, the first 4, the first 5, and all 6.

The following mental imagery is often helpful in understanding how BASIC handles variables. When BASIC first encounters a variable, say A, it sets up a box (actually a memory location) which it labels "A". (See Figure 2-2.) In this box it stores the current value of A. When you request a change in the value of A, the computer throws out the current contents of the box and inserts the new value. *If you do not specify a value for a variable, BASIC will assign it the value 0.*

Note that the value of a variable need not remain the same throughout a program. At any point in the program, you may change the value of a variable (with a **LET** statement, for example). If a program is called on to evaluate an expression involving a variable, it will always use the **current** value of the variable, ignoring any previous values the variable may have had at earlier points in the program.

Test Your Understanding 3.4

Suppose that a loan for 5,000 dollars has an interest rate of 1.5% on the unpaid balance at the end of each month. Write a program to calculate the interest at the end of the first month. Suppose that at the end of the first month, you make a payment of 150.00 dollars (after the interest is added). Include in your program the balance after the payment.

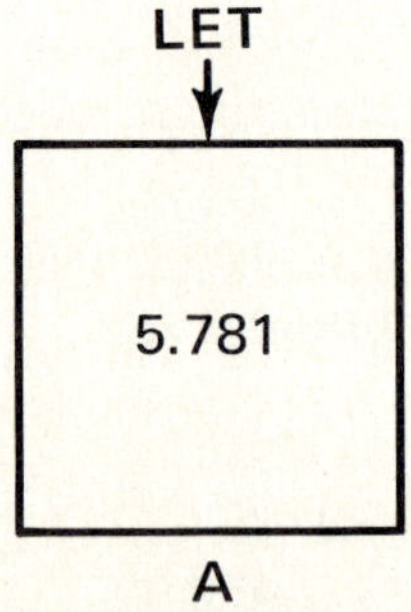

Figure 2-2. The variable A.

Example 2. What will be the output of the following computer program?

```
10 LET A=10: B=20
20 LET A=5
30 PRINT A+B+C, A*B*C
40 END
```

Solution. Note that no value for C is specified, so C = 0. Also note that the value of A is initially set to 10. However, in line 20, this value is changed to 5. So in line 30, A, B, and C have the respective values 5, 20, and 0. Therefore, the output will be:

```
25          0
```

To the computer, the statement

```
LET A=
```

means that the current value of A is to be *replaced* with whatever appears to the right of the equal sign. Thus, for example, if we write

```
LET A=A+1
```

then we are asking the computer to replace the current value of A with A + 1. So if the current value of A is 4, the value of A after performing the instruction is 4 + 1, or 5.

Test Your Understanding 3.5

What is the output of the following program?

```
10 LET A=5.3
20 LET A=A+1
30 LET A=2*A
40 LET A=A+B
50 PRINT A
60 END
```

Legal Variable Names

As we mentioned above, you may use any letter of the alphabet as a variable name. In addition, you may use a letter followed by a single digit, such as A2 or W7. Furthermore, BASIC recognizes any pair of letters, such as AA or ZR, as a legal variable name, with the following exceptions:

IF, ON, OR, TO

These letter combinations are reserved by BASIC and cannot be used as variable names. Note that the variables A, AA, and A1 are all *different* as far as the computer is concerned. Note also that a variable name must always start with a letter. In particular, 1A is *not* a legal variable name.

So far, all of our variables assume only numerical values. However, BASIC also allows variables to assume string constants as values. The variables for doing this are called *string variables* and are denoted by a variable name followed by a "$". Thus, **A$, B1$,** and **ZZ$** are all valid names of string variables. To assign a value to a string variable we use the **LET** statement, with the desired value inserted in quotation marks after the equal sign. Thus, to set A$ equal to the string "Balance Sheet", we use the statement

```
LET A$="BALANCE SHEET"
```

We may print the value of a string variable just as we print the value of a numeric variable. For example, if A$ has the value just assigned, the statement

```
PRINT A$
```

will result in the following screen output:

```
BALANCE SHEET
```

Example 3. What will be the output of the following program?

```
10 LET A$="MONTHLY RECEIPTS":B$="MONTHLY EXPENSES"
20 LET A=20373.10: B=17584.31
30 PRINT A$,B$
40 PRINT A,,B
50 END
```

Solution.

```
MONTHLY RECEIPTS        MONTHLY EXPENSES
  20373.10                17584.31
```

Note that we have used the variables A and A$ (as well as B and B$) in the same program. The variables A and A$ are considered *different* by the computer. Note also the presence of the second comma in line 40. This is due to the fact that the value of A$, namely MONTHLY RECEIPTS requires 16 spaces. Therefore, to leave a space between the two headings, we moved B$ over into the next print zone. Therefore, to correctly align the values of A and B under the appropriate headings, we must print a blank space in print zone 2 after we print the value of A. This is accomplished by the second comma. One further comment about spacing. Note that the numbers do not exactly align with the headings, but rather are offset by one space. This is because BASIC allows room for a sign (+ or −) in front of a number. In the case of positive numbers, the sign is suppressed, but the space remains.

Remarks In Programs

It is very convenient to annotate programs with remarks. For one thing, remarks make programs easier to read. For another, remarks assist in finding errors and making modifications in a program. To insert a remark in a program, we may use the **REM** statement. For example, consider the line:

```
520 REM X DENOTES THE COST BASIS
```

Since the line starts with **REM,** it will be ignored during program execution. Instead of **REM,** we may use an apostrophe as in the following example:

```
1040 ' Y IS THE TOTAL COST
```

Multiple Statements On A Single Line

It is possible to put several BASIC statements on a single line. Just separate them by a colon. For example, instead of the two statements:

```
10 LET A=5.784: B=3.571
20 PRINT A[2+B[2
```

we may use the single statement:

```
10 LET A=5.784: B=3.571: PRINT A[2+B[2
```

To insert a remark on the same line as a program statement, use a colon followed by an apostrophe (or **REM**), as in this example:

```
10 LET A=PI*R[2 : ' A IS THE AREA,R IS THE RADIUS
```

In what follows, we will sprinkle comments liberally throughout our programs so that they will be easier to understand.

Test Your Understanding 3.6

What is the result of the following program line?

```
10 LET A=7:B$="COST":C$="TOTAL":PRINT C$,B$"=",A
```

EXERCISES (answers on 268)

In Exercises 1–6, determine the output of the given program.

1.
```
10 LET A=5:B=5
20 PRINT A+B
30 END
```

2.
```
10 LET AA=5
20 PRINT AA*B
30 END
```

3.
```
10 LET A1=5
20 PRINT A1[2+5*A1
30 END
```

4.
```
10 LET A=2: B=7: C=9
20 PRINT A+B, A-C, A*C
30 END
```

5.
```
10 LET A$="JOHN JONES"
20 LET B$="AGE": C=38
30 PRINT A$, B$, C
40 END
```

6.
```
10 LET X=11, Y=19
20 PRINT 2*X
30 PRINT 3*Y
40 END
```

What is wrong with the following BASIC statements?

7. `10 LET A="YOUTH"`

8. `10 LET AA=-12`

9. `10 LET A$=57`

10. LET ZZ$=Address

11. 250 LET AAA=−9

12. 10000 LET 1A=−2.34567

13. Consider the numbers 2.3758, 4.58321, and 58.11. Write a program which computes their sum, product, and the sum of their squares.

14. A company has three divisions: Office Supplies, Computers, and Newsletters. The revenues of these three divisions for the preceding quarter were, respectively, $346,712, $459,321, and $376,872. The expenses for the quarter were $176,894, $584,837, and, $402,195, respectively. Write a program which displays this data on the screen with appropriate explanatory headings. Your program should also compute and display the net profit (loss) from each division and the net profit (loss) for the company as a whole.

Answers To Test Your Understanding

3.1: 72

3.2: It prints the display:

```
5        25        50
```

3.3:

```
10 LET A=101:B=102:C=103:D=104:E=105:F=106
20 PRINT A*B
30 PRINT A*B*C
40 PRINT A*B*C*D
50 PRINT A*B*C*D*E
60 PRINT A*B*C*D*E*F
70 END
```

3.4:

```
10 LET B=5000:I=.015:P=150.00
20 IN=I*B
30 PRINT "INTEREST EQUALS", IN
40 B=B+IN
50 PRINT "BALANCE WITH INTEREST EQUALS", B
60 B=B-P
70 PRINT "BALANCE AFTER PAYMENT EQUALS", B
80 END
```

3.5: 12.6

3.6: It creates the display:

```
TOTAL     COST     =     7
```

2.4 DOING REPETITIVE OPERATIONS

Suppose that we wish to solve 50 similar multiplication problems. It is certainly possible to type in the 50 problems one at a time and let the computer solve them. However, this is a very clumsy way to proceed. Indeed, suppose that instead of 50 problems there were 500, or even 5000. Typing the problems one at a time would not be practical. If, however, we can describe to the computer the entire class of problems we want solved, then we can instruct the computer to solve them using only a few BASIC statements. Let us consider a concrete problem. Suppose that we wish to calculate the quantities

$$1^2, 2^2, 3^2, \ldots, 10^2.$$

That is, we wish to calculate a table of squares of integers from 1 to 10. This calculation can be described to the computer as calculating J[2, where the variable J is allowed to assume, one at a time, each of the values 1,2,3, . . . ,10. Here is a sequence of BASIC statements which accomplishes the calculations:

This is the first value of J

This is the last value of J

```
10 FOR J=1 TO 10
20 PRINT J[2
30 NEXT J
40 END
```

lines 10-20-30 repeated 10 times

The sequence of statements 10,20,30 is called a **loop.** When the computer encounters the **FOR** statement, it sets J equal to 1 and continues execution of the statements. Statement 20 calls for printing J[2. Since J is equal to 1, we have J[2 = 1[2 = 1. So the computer prints a 1. Next comes statement 30, which calls for the next J. This instructs the computer to return to the **FOR** statement in 10, increase J to 2 and to repeat instructions 20 and 30. This time, J[2 = 2[2 = 4. So line 20 prints a 4. Line 30 says to go back to line 10 and increase J to 3 and so forth. Lines 10, 20 and 30 are repeated 10 times! After the computer executes line 10,20,30 with J = 10, it will leave the loop and execute line 40.

Type in the above program and give the **RUN** command. The output will look like this:

```
1
4
9
16
25
36
49
64
81
100
READY
>
```

Test Your Understanding 4.1

(a) Devise a loop which allows J to assume the values 3 to 77.

(b) Write a program which calculates J^2 for J = 3 to 77

Let's modify the above program to include on each line of output not only J[2, but also the value of J. And to make the table easier to read, let's add two column headings. The new program reads:

```
10 PRINT "J","J[2"
20 FOR J=1 TO 10
30 PRINT J,J[2
40 NEXT J
50 END
```

The output now looks like this:

```
J              J[2
1              1
2              4
3              9
4              16
5              25
6              36
7              49
```

```
8        64
9        81
10       100
READY
>
```

Test Your Understanding 4.2

What would happen if we change the number of line 10 to 25?

Let us now illustrate some of the many uses of loops by means of a series of examples.

Example 1. Write a BASIC program to calculate 1 + 2 + 3 + . . . + 100.

Solution. Let us use a variable S (for sum) to contain the sum. Let us start S at 0 and use a loop to successively add to S the numbers 1, 2, 3, . . . , 100. Here is the program.

```
10 LET S=0
20 FOR J=1 TO 100 }  These instructions
30 LET S=S+J      }  repeated 100
40 NEXT J            times
50 PRINT S
60 END
```

When we enter the loop the first time, S = 0 and J = 1. Line 30 then replaces S by S + J, or 0 + 1. Line 40 sends us back to line 20, where the value of J is now set equal to 2. In line 30, S (which is now 0 + 1) is replaced by S + J, or 0 + 1 + 2. Line 40 now sends us back to line 20, where J is now set equal to 3. Then line 30 sets S equal to 0 + 1 + 2 + 3. Finally, on the 100th time through the loop, S is replaced by 0 + 1 + 2 + . . . + 100, the desired sum. If we run the program, we derive the output

```
5050
READY
>
```

Test Your Understanding 4.3

Write a BASIC program to calculate 101 + 102 + . . . + 110.

Test Your Understanding 4.4

Write a BASIC program to calculate and display the numbers 2, 2[2, 2[3, . . . , 2[20.

Example 2. Write a program to calculate the sum

$$1 \times 2 + 2 \times 3 + 3 \times 4 + \ . \ . \ . \ + 49 \times 50.$$

Solution. We will let the sum be contained in the variable S, as in the preceding example. The quantities to be summed are just the numbers J*(J+1) for J = 1, 2, 3, . . . , 49. So here is our program:

```
10 LET S=0
20 FOR J=1 TO 49
30 LET S=S+J*(J+1)
40 NEXT J
50 PRINT S
60 END
```

Example 3. Suppose that you borrow 7000 dollars to buy a car. You finance the balance for 36 months at an interest rate of 1% per month. Your monthly payments are 232.50 dollars. Write a program which computes the amount of interest each month, the amount of the loan which is repaid and the balance owed.

Solution. Let B denote the balance owed. Then initially we have B = 7000.00 dollars. At the end of each month let us compute the interest I owed for that month, namely .01*B. For example, at the end of the first month, the interest owed is .01*7000.00 = $70.00. Let P = 232.50 denote the monthly payment, and let R denote the amount repaid out of the current payment. Then R = P − I. For example, at the end of the first month, the amount of the loan repaid is 232.50 − 70.00 = 162.50. The balance owed may then be calculated as B − R. At the end of the first month, the balance owed is 7000.00 − 162.50 = 6837.50. Here is a program which performs these calculations:

```
10 PRINT "MONTH","INTEREST","PAYMENT","BALANCE"
20 LET B=7000
25 LET P=232.50
30 FOR J=1 TO 36:   'J IS THE MONTH NUMBER
40 LET I=.01*B:   'CALCULATE INTEREST FOR MONTH
50 LET R=P-I:   'CALCULATE REPAYMENT
```

```
60 LET B=B-R:  'CALCULATE NEW BALANCE
70 PRINT J,I,R,B
80 NEXT J
90 END
```

You should attempt to run this program. You will notice that it runs, but it is pretty useless because the screen will not contain all of the output, so that most of it goes flying by before you can read it. One method for remedying this situation is to press **SHIFT** and @ simultaneously as the output is scrolling by on the screen. This will freeze the contents of the screen and pause execution of the program. To unfreeze the screen press the same pair of keys again. The output will begin to scroll again. To use this technique requires some manual dexterity. Moreover, it is not possible to guarantee where the scrolling will stop.

Test Your Understanding 4.5

RUN the program of Example 3 and practice freezing the output on the screen. It may take several runs before you are comfortable with the procedure.

Let us now describe another method of adapting the output to our screen size by printing only 12 months of data at one time. This amount of data will fit, since the screen contains 16 lines. We will use a second loop to keep track of 12 month periods. The variable for the new loop will be K and K will go from 0 to 2. The month variable will be J as before, but now J will go only from 1 to 12. The month number will now be 12*K + J (the number of years plus the number of months). Here is the revised program.

```
10 LET B=7000
15 LET P=232.50
20 FOR K=0 TO 2
30 PRINT "MONTH","INTEREST","PAYMENT","BALANCE"
40 FOR J=1 TO 12
50 LET I=.01*B
60 LET R=P-I:  'ONE 12 MONTH PERIOD
70 LET B=B-R
80 PRINT 12*K+J,I,R,B
90 NEXT J
100 STOP:  'HALTS EXECUTION
110 CLS:  'CLEARS SCREEN
120 NEXT K:  'GOES TO NEXT 12 MONTHS
130 END
```

This program utilizes several new statements. In line 100, we used the statement **STOP.** This causes the computer to stop execution of the program. However, the computer remembers where it stops and all values of variables are preserved. The **STOP** statement also leaves unchanged the contents of the screen. You can take as long as you wish to examine the data on the screen, make a copy of it, etc. When you are ready for the program to continue, type: **CONT.** The computer will resume where it left off. The first instruction it then encounters is in line 110. **CLS** clears the screen. So after being told to continue, the computer clears the screen and goes on to the next value of K—that is, the next 12 months of data. Here is a copy of the output. The underlined statements are those you type.

READY
\>

RUN

MONTH	INTEREST	PAYMENT	BALANCE
1	70	162.5	6837.5
2	68.375	164.125	6673.38
3	66.7338	165.766	6673.38
4	65.0761	167.424	6340.19
5	63.4019	169.098	6171.09
6	61.7109	170.789	6000.3
7	60.003	172.497	5827.8
8	58.278	174.222	5653.58
9	56.5358	175.964	5477.61
10	54.7761	177.724	5299.89
11	52.9989	179.501	5120.39
12	51.2039	181.296	4939.09

Break in 100
\>
CONT

MONTH	INTEREST	PAYMENT	BALANCE
13	49.3909	183.109	4755.98
14	47.5598	184.94	4571.05
15	45.7105	186.79	4384.26
16	43.8426	188.657	4195.6
17	41.956	190.544	4005.05

```
18          40.0505      192.449      3812.6
19          38.126       194.374      3618.23
20          36.1823      196.318      3421.91
21          34.2191      198.281      3223.63
22          32.2363      200.264      3023.37
23          30.2337      202.266      2821.1
24          28.211       204.289      2616.81
Break in 100
>
CONT

MONTH       INTEREST     PAYMENT      BALANCE
25          26.1681      206.332      2410.48
26          24.1048      208.395      2202.09
27          22.0209      210.479      1991.61
28          19.9161      212.584      1779.02
29          17.7902      214.71       1564.31
30          15.6431      216.857      1347.46
31          13.4746      219.025      1128.43
32          11.2843      221.216      907.216
33          9.07216      223.428      683.788
34          6.83788      225.662      458.126
35          4.58126      227.919      230.207
36          2.30207      230.198      8.92639E-03
READY
>
```

Note that the data in the output is carried out to six significant figures, even though the problem deals with dollars and cents. We will take up the problem of rounding numbers off a little later. Note also the balance listed at the end of month 36. The −03 indicates that the decimal point is to be moved three places to the left. So the number listed is just .00892639, or about .89 cents!

Using Loops to Create Delays

By using a loop, we can create a delay inside the computer. For example, consider the following sequence of instructions:

```
10 FOR J=I TO 3000
20 NEXT J
```

This loop does not do anything! However, the computer repeats instructions 10 and 20 three thousand times! This may seem like a lot of work. But not for a computer. To obtain a feel for the speed at which the computer works, you should time this sequence of instructions. Such a loop may be used as a delay. For example, when you wish to keep some data on the screen without stopping the program, just build in a delay. For example, here is a program which prints two screens of text. A delay is imposed to give a person time to read the first screen.

```
10 PRINT "THIS IS A GRAPHICS PROGRAM TO DISPLAY SALES"
20 PRINT "FOR THE YEAR TO DATE"
30 FOR J=1 TO 5000 }
40 NEXT J:         }  Delay Loop
50 CLS
60 PRINT "YOU MUST SUPPLY THE FOLLOWING PARAMETERS:"
70 PRINT "PRODUCT, TERRITORY, SALESPERSON"
80 END
```

Example 4. Use a loop to produce a blinking display for a security system.

Solution. Suppose that your security system is tied in with your computer and the system detects that an intruder is in your warehouse. Let us print out the message:

SECURITY SYSTEM DETECTS INTRUDER– ZONE 2

For attention, let us blink this message on and off by alternately printing the message and clearing the screen.

```
10 FOR J=1 TO 2000
20 PRINT "SECURITY SYSTEM DETECTS INTRUDER–ZONE 2"
30 FOR K=1 TO 50
40 NEXT K
50 CLS
60 NEXT J
70 END
```

The loop in 30–40 is a delay loop to keep the message on the screen a moment. Line 50 turns the message off, but line 10 turns it back on. The message will blink 2000 times.

Test Your Understanding 4.6

Write a program which blinks your name on the screen 500 times leaving the name on the screen for a loop of length 50 each time.

In all of our examples of loops, the loop variable increased by 1 with each repetition of the loop. However, it is possible to have the loop variable change by any amount. For example, the instructions

```
10 FOR J=1 TO 5000 STEP 2
.
.
.
1000 NEXT J
```

define a loop in which J jumps by 2 for each repetition, so J will assume the values

1, 3, 5, 7, 9, . . . , 4999

Similarly, use of STEP .5 in the above loop will cause J to advance by .5 and therefore assume the values

1, 1.5, 2, 2.5, 3, 3.5, 4, 4.5, . . . , 5000

It is even possible to have a negative step. In this case, the loop variable will run backwards. For example, the instructions

```
10 FOR J=100 TO 1 STEP -1
.
.
.
100 NEXT J
```

will "count down" from J = 100 to J = 1 one unit at a time. We will give some applications of such instructions in the Exercises.

Test Your Understanding 4.7

Write instructions to allow J to assume the following sequences of values:

(a) 95,96.7,98.4, . . . ,112

(b) 200,199.5,199, . . . ,100

EXERCISES (answers on 269)

Write BASIC programs to compute the following quantities:

1. $1^2 + 2^2 + 3^2 + \ldots + 25^2$

2. $1 + (1/2) + (1/2)^2 + \ldots + (1/2)^{10}$

3. $1^3 + 2^3 + 3^3 + \ldots + 10^3$

4. $1 + (1/2) + (1/3) + \ldots + (1/100)$

5. Write a program to compute J^2, J^3, J^4 for $J = 1, \ldots, 12$. The format of your output should be as follows:

```
J      J[2      J[3      J[4
1
2
3
.
.
.
12
```

6. Suppose that you have a car loan whose current balance is 4,000.00 dollars. The monthly payment is 125.33 dollars and the interest is 1% per month on the unpaid balance. Make a table of the interest payments and balances for the next 12 months.

7. Suppose you deposit 1,000 dollars on January 1 of each year into a savings account paying 10% interest. Suppose that the interest is computed on January 1 of each year, based on the balance for the preceding year. Calculate the balances in the account for each of the next 15 years.

8. A stock market analyst predicts that Tyro Computers, Inc. will achieve a 20% growth in sales in each of the next three years, but profits will grow at a 30% annual rate. Last year's sales were 35 million dollars and last year's profits were 5.54 million dollars. Project the sales and profits for the next three years, based on the analyst's prediction.

Answers to Test Your Understanding

4.1: (a)
```
10 FOR J=3 TO 77


100 NEXT J
```
(b)
```
10 FOR J=3 TO 77
20 PRINT J[2
30 NEXT J
40 END
```

4.2: The heading

J J[2

would be printed before each entry of the table.

4.3:
```
10 S=0
20 FOR J=101 TO 110
30 S=S+J
40 NEXT J
50 PRINT S
60 END
```

4.4:
```
10 FOR J=1 TO 20
20 PRINT 2[J
30 NEXT J
40 END
```

4.6:
```
10 FOR J=1 TO 500
20 PRINT "<YOUR NAME>"
30 FOR K=1 TO 50
40 NEXT K
50 CLS
60 NEXT J
70 END
```

4.7: (a)
```
10 FOR J=95 TO 112 STEP 1.7
```
(b)
```
20 FOR J=200 TO 100 STEP -.5
```

2.5 SOME SYSTEM COMMANDS

Thus far, most of our attention has been focused on learning statements to insert inside programs. Let us now learn a few of the commands available for manipulating programs and the computer. The **NEW** command, previously discussed, is in this category. Remember the following facts about system commands:

1. System commands are typed *without* a line number.
2. You must hit **ENTER** after typing a system command.
3. A system command may be given whenever the computer is in the immediate mode. When the computer first enters the immediate mode, it displays the READY message. The computer remains in the immediate mode until a RUN command is given (in which case the computer enters the execute mode) or an EDIT command is given (in which case the computer enters the edit mode).
4. The computer executes system commands as soon as they are received.

Listing a Program

To obtain a list of all statements of the current program in RAM, you may type the command:

LIST

For example, suppose that RAM contains the following program

```
10 PRINT 5+7,5-7
20 PRINT 5*7,5/7
30 END
```

(This program may or may not be currently displayed on the screen.) If you type **LIST,** then the above three instruction lines will be displayed, followed by the READY message.

In developing a program, you will undoubtedly find it necessary to input lines in non-consecutive order and to correct lines already input. If so, then the screen will not usually indicate the current version of the program. Typing **LIST** every so often will assist in keeping track of what has been changed. **LIST**ing is particularly helpful in checking a program or in determining why a program will not run.

Note that the Model III screen contains 16 lines so you can display only 16 program statements at one time. To **LIST** only those statements with line numbers from 1 to 16, we use the command:

LIST 1–16

In a similar fashion, we may list any collection of consecutive program lines.

There are several other variations on the **LIST** command. To list the program lines from the beginning of the program to line 75, use the command:

LIST–75

Similarly, to list the program lines from 100 to the end of the program, use the command:

LIST 100–

To list line 100, use the command:

LIST 100

Test Your Understanding 5.1

Write a command to:

(a) List line 200

(b) List lines 300–330

(c) List lines 300 to the end

Test out these commands with a program.

Deleting Program Lines

When typing a program or when revising an existing program, it is often necessary to delete lines which are already part of the program. One simple way is to type the line number followed by **ENTER.** For example,

275

(followed by **ENTER**) will delete line 275. The **DELETE** command may also by used for the same purpose. For example, we may delete line 275, using the command:

DELETE 275

The **DELETE** command has a number of variations which make it quite flexible. For example, to delete lines 200 to 500 inclusive, use the command:

DELETE 200–500

To delete all lines from the beginning of the program to 350, inclusive, use the command:

DELETE −350

Note, however, the **DELETE** command must always include a last line number to be deleted. This is to prevent ugly mishaps in which you mistakenly erase most of a program. If you wish to delete all lines from 100 to the end of the program, you must specify a deletion from 100 to the last line number. If you do not remember the last line number, **LIST** the program first, determine the final line number and then carry out the appropriate **DELETE.**

Test Your Understanding 5.2

What is wrong with the following commands?

(a) DELETE 450−

(b) LIST 450−

(c) DELETE 300−200

Saving a Program

Once you have typed a program into RAM, you may save a copy on either cassette or diskette. At any future time, you may read the cassette or diskette copy back into RAM. At that point, you may re-execute the program, modify it, or add to it. Let us describe the process of saving a program on cassette. First connect the cassette recorder and insert a cassette, as described in the Appendix to this chapter. Suppose that we have the following program in RAM:

```
10 PRINT 5+7
20 END
```

To save a copy of this program on the cassette, push the PLAY and RECORD buttons of the cassette recorder simultaneously. Next, type the command:

CSAVE "X"

The letter X is the name we have arbitrarily assigned to this program. (A program name consists of a single letter.) A copy of the program will then be written onto the cassette. (Note that the program will still be in RAM.) To read the program back into RAM, position the cassette to the beginning of the tape. Push the PLAY button on the cassette recorder and type the command:

CLOAD "X"

You should try the above sequence of commands using the given program. After recording the program onto the cassette, erase the program from RAM (by typing **NEW**). Then read the program from the cassette. When the read operation is complete, the word **READY** will be displayed. Just to check that the program has been read, you should now **LIST** it.

Test Your Understanding 5.3

Save the following program on cassette:

```
10 PRINT 5+7
20 PRINT 5-7
30 END
```

Cassettes are sometimes finicky and may result in data transmission errors to the computer. In loading a program, you may guard against such errors by using a ? after the word **CLOAD.** This variation instructs the computer to compare the program on tape with the one in RAM. Any inconsistencies are reported on the display. In case of inconsistency, the **CLOAD** operation should be repeated.

We will postpone until Chapter 4 any discussion of saving programs on diskette.

EXERCISES

Exercises 1–7 refer to the following program.

```
10 LET A=19.1,B=17.5
20 PRINT A+B,A*B
30 END
```

1. Type the above program into RAM and RUN it.
2. Erase the screen without erasing RAM. LIST the program.
3. Save the program and erase RAM.
4. Recall the program and LIST it. RUN the program again.
5. Add the following line to the program:

```
25 PRINT A[2+B[2
```

(Do not retype the entire program!) LIST the new program. RUN the new program.

6. Save the new program without destroying the old one.
7. Recall the new program. Delete line 20 and RUN the resulting program.

Answers to Test Your Understanding

5.1: (a) LIST 200
(b) LIST 300−330
(c) LIST 300−

5.2: (a) The line number of the last line to be deleted must be specified.
(b) Nothing wrong.
(c) The lower line number must come first.

2.6 LETTING YOUR COMPUTER MAKE DECISIONS

One of the principal features which makes computers useful as problem-solving tools is their ability to make decisions. The vehicle which BASIC uses to make decisions is the IF . . . THEN . . . ELSE statement. The IF part of such a statement allows us to ask a question. If the answer is YES, then the computer carries out the THEN part of the statement. If the answer is NO, then the computer carries out the ELSE portion of the statement. For example, consider the statement:

```
500 IF J=0 THEN PRINT "CALCULATION DONE" ELSE 250
```

First the computer determines if J is equal to zero. If so, it prints "CALCULA-

TION DONE" and proceeds with the next instruction after line 500. However, if J is not zero, then the computer goes to line 250 and continues program execution from that instruction.

Another possibility is for both THEN and ELSE to be followed by instructions, as in the following example:

```
600 IF A+B>=100 THEN PRINT A+B ELSE PRINT A
```

In executing this instruction,the computer will determine whether A + B is greater than or equal to 100. If so then it will print the value of A + B; if not, it will print the value of A. In both cases, execution continues with the next instruction after line 600.

After **IF,** you may insert any expression which the computer may test for truth or falsity. Here are some examples:

J=0

J>5 (J is greater than 5)

J<12.9 (J is less than 12.9)

J>=0 (J is greater than or equal to 0)

J<=−1 (J is less than or equal to −1)

J><0 (J is not equal to 0)

A+B<>C (A+B is not equal to C)

A[2+B[2<=C[2 (A^2+B^2 is less than or equal to C^2)

There is a shortened version of the **IF . . . THEN . . . ELSE** statement which has the form:

IF <expression> **THEN** <statement or line number>

In this shortened form, the computer determines if the <expression> is true. If so, it proceeds to **THEN** (it either executes the statement or goes to the indicated line number). If the <expression> is not true, then the computer proceeds to the next line. For example, consider the statements:

```
10 IF A=50 THEN END
20 LET A=A+1
```

If A equals 50 then the computer proceeds to the END of the program. If A is not equal to 50, then the computer proceeds to the next statement, namely line 20.

Test Your Understanding 6.1

Write instructions which do the following:

(a) If A is less than B, then print the value of A plus B; if not then go to the end.

(b) If $A^2 + B$ is at least 5000 then go to line 300; if not go to line 500.

(c) If J is larger than the sum of I and K then set J equal to the sum of I and K; otherwise, let J equal K.

The **IF . . . THEN** and **IF . . . THEN . . . ELSE** statements may be used to interrupt the normal sequence of execution of program lines, contingent upon the truth or falsity of some condition. In many applications, however, we will want to perform instructions out of the normal sequence, independent of any conditions. For such applications, we may use the **GOTO** instruction. (There is no typographical error! There is no space between GO and TO.) This instruction has the form:

GOTO <LINE NUMBER>

For example, the instruction

1000 GOTO 300

will send the computer back to line 300 for its next instruction.

The next examples illustrate some of the uses of the **IF . . . THEN, IF . . . THEN . . . ELSE,** and **GOTO** statements.

Example 1. A lumber supply house has a policy that credit orders may be no more than 1,000 dollars, including a 10% processing fee and 5% sales tax. A customer orders 150 2×4 studs at $1.99 each, 30 sheets of plywood at $14.00 each, 300 pounds of nails at $1.14 per pound, 2 double hung insulated windows at $187.95 each. Write a program which prepares an invoice and decides whether the order is over the credit limit.

Solution. Let's use the variables A1, A2, A3, A4 to denote, respectively, the numbers of studs, sheets of plywood, pounds of nails, and windows. Let's use the variables B1, B2, B3, B4 to denote the unit costs of these four items. The cost of the order is then computed as:

A1*B1+A2*B2+A3*B3+A4*B4.

We add 10% of this amount to cover processing and form the sum to obtain the total order. Next, we compute 5% of the last amount as tax and add it to obtain the total amount due. Finally, we determine if the total amount due is more than 1,000 dollars. If it is, we print out the message: ORDER EXCEEDS $1,000. CREDIT SALE NOT PERMITTED. Here is our program.

```
10 LET A1=150:A2=30:A3=300:A4=2
20 LET B1=1.99:B2=14:B3=1.14:B4=187.95
30 LET T=A1*B1+A2*B2+A3*B3+A4*B4
40 PRINT "TOTAL ORDER",T
50 LET P=.1*T
60 PRINT "PROCESSING FEE",P
70 LET TX=.05*(P+T)
80 PRINT "SALES TAX",TX
90 DU=T+P+TX
100 PRINT "AMOUNT DUE",DU
110 IF DU>1000 THEN 200 ELSE 300
200 PRINT "ORDER EXCEEDS $1,000"
210 PRINT "CREDIT SALE NOT PERMITTED"
220 GOTO 400
300 PRINT "CREDIT SALE OK"
400 END
```

Note the decision in line 110. If the amount due exceeds 1,000 dollars then the computer goes to line 200 where it prints out a message denying credit. In line 220, the computer is sent to line 400 which is the END of the program. On the other hand, if the amount due is less than 1,000 dollars, the computer is sent to line 300, in which case credit is approved.

Test Your Understanding 6.2

Suppose that a credit card charges 1.5% per month on any unpaid balance up to 500 dollars and 1% per month on any excess over 500 dollars.

(a) Write a program which computes the service charge and the new balance.

(b) Test your program on the unpaid balances 1300 dollars and 275 dollars.

Test Your Understanding 6.3

Consider the following sequence of instructions.

```
100 IF A>=5 THEN 200
110 IF A>=4 THEN 300
120 IF A>=3 THEN 400
130 IF A>=2 THEN 500
```

Suppose that the current value of A is 3. List the sequence of line numbers which will be executed.

Example 2. A family can afford up to 500 square feet of carpet for their dining room. They wish to patch the carpet into a circular shape. The radius of the carpet is to be an integer. What is the radius of the largest carpet they can afford? (The area of a circle of radius R is PI times R^2, where PI is the number given approximately by 3.14159.)

Solution. Let us compute the area of the circle of radius 1, 2, 3, 4, . . . and determine which of the areas are less than 500.

```
10 LET PI=3.14159
20 LET R=1:        'R IS THE RADIUS OF THE CIRCLE
30 LET A=PI*R[2:       'A IS THE AREA OF THE CIRCLE
40 IF A>=500 THEN 100:   'IF AREA IS AT LEAST 500, END
50 PRINT R:   'IF AREA IS LESS THAN 500, PRINT R
60 LET R=R+1:       'GO TO NEXT RADIUS
70 GOTO 30
100 END
```

Note that line 40 contains an **IF . . . THEN** statement. If A, as computed in line 30, is 500 or more, then the computer goes to line 100, the **END**; if A is less than 500, the computer proceeds to the next line, namely 50. It then prints out the current radius, increases the radius by 1 and goes back to line 30 to repeat the entire procedure. Note that lines 30-40-50-60-70 are repeated until the area becomes at least 500. In effect, this sequence of 5 instructions forms a loop. However, we did not use a **FOR . . . NEXT** instruction because we did not know in advance how many times we wanted to execute the loop. We let the computer decide the stopping point via the **IF . . . THEN** instruction.

Example 3. A school board race involves two candidates. The returns from the four wards of the town are as follows:

	Ward 1	Ward 2	Ward 3	Ward 4
Mr. Thompson	487	229	1540	1211
Ms. Wilson	1870	438	110	597

Calculate the total number of votes achieved by each candidate, the percentage achieved by each candidate, and decide who won the election.

Solution. Let A1, A2, A3, A4 be the totals of Mr. Thompson in the four wards; let B1 – B4 denote the corresponding numbers for Ms. Wilson. Let TA, TB denote the total votes, respectively for Mr. Thompson, and Ms. Wilson. Here is our program:

```
10 LET A1=487:A2=229:A3=1540:A4=1211
20 LET B1=1870:B2=438:B3=110:B4=597
30 LET TA=A1+A2+A3+A4:  'TOTAL FOR THOMPSON
40 LET TB=B1+B2+B3+B4:  'TOTAL FOR WILSON
50 LET T=TA+TB:  'TOTAL VOTES CAST
60 LET PA=100*TA/T:  'PERCENTAGE FOR THOMPSON
65 REM TA/T IS THE FRACTION OF VOTES FOR
   THOMPSON–MULTIPLY
66 REM BY 100 TO CONVERT TO A PERCENTAGE
70 LET PB=100*TB/T:  'PERCENTAGE FOR WILSON
110 LET A$="THOMPSON"
120 LET B$="WILSON"
130 REM 140–170 PRINT THE PERCENTAGES OF THE CANDIDATES
140 PRINT "CANDIDATE","VOTES","PERCENTAGE"
150 PRINT A$,TA,PA
160 PRINT B$,TB,PB
170 REM 180–400 DECIDE THE WINNER
180 IF TA>TB THEN 300
190 IF TA<TB THEN 400
200 PRINT A$,"AND",B$,"ARE TIED!"
210 GOTO 1000
300 PRINT A$,"WINS"
310 GOTO 1000
400 PRINT B$,"WINS"
1000 END
```

Note the logic used for deciding who won. In 180 we compare the votes TA and TB. If TA is the larger, then A (that is, Thompson) is the winner. We then go to 300, print the result and END. On the other hand, if TA > TB is *false*, then either B wins or the two are tied. According to the program, if TA > TB is false, we go to 190, where we determine if TA < TB. If this is true, then B is the winner, we go to 400, print the result and END. On the other hand, if TA < TB is false, then the only possibility left is that TA = TB. And according to the program, in this case, we go to 200, where we print the proper result, and then END.

Infinite Loops and the Break Key

As we have seen above, it is very convenient to be able to execute a loop without knowing in advance how many times the loop will be executed. However, with this convenience comes a danger. It is perfectly possible to create a loop which will be repeated an infinite number of times! For example, consider the following program:

```
10 LET J=1
20 PRINT J
30 LET J=J+1
40 GOTO 20
50 END
```

The variable J starts off at 1. We print it and then increase J by 1 (to 2), print it, increase J by 1 (to 3), print it, and so forth. This program will go on forever! Such programs should clearly be avoided. However, even an experienced programmer occasionally creates an infinite loop. When this happens, there is no need to panic. There is a way of stopping the computer. Just press the **BREAK** key. This key will interrupt the program currently in progress and will return the computer to the command level, at which point it is ready to accept a system command from the keyboard.

Test Your Understanding 6.4

Type the above program, RUN it and stop it using the BREAK key. After stopping it, RUN the program again.

The INPUT Statement

It is very convenient to have the computer request information from you while the program is actually running. This can be accomplished via the **INPUT** statement. To see how, consider the statement:

```
570 INPUT A
```

When the computer encounters this statement in the course of executing the program, it types out a ? and waits for you to respond by typing the desired value of A (followed by **ENTER**). The computer then sets A equal to the value you specified and continues execution of the program.

You may use an **INPUT** statement to specify the values of several different variables at one time. And these variables may be numeric or string variables. For example, suppose that the computer encounters the statement:

50 INPUT A,B,C$

It will type:

?

You then type in the desired values for A, B, and C$, in the same order as in the program, separated by commas. For example, suppose that you type

10.5, 11.42, BEARINGS

followed by an **ENTER.** The computer will then set

A = 10.5, B = 11.42, A$ = "BEARINGS"

If you respond to the above question mark by typing only a single number, 10.5, for example, the computer will respond with

??

to indicate that it is expecting more data. If you attempt to specify a string value for a numeric variable, the computer will respond with the message

?REDO
?

and will wait for you to repeat the **INPUT** operation.

It is helpful to include a prompting message which describes the input the computer is expecting. To do so, just put the message in quotation marks after the word **INPUT** and place a semicolon after the message and before the list of variables to be input. For example, consider the statement

175 INPUT "ENTER COMPANY, AMOUNT"; A$, B

When the computer encounters it, the dialog will be as follows:

ENTER COMPANY, AMOUNT? <u>AJAX OFFICE SUPPLIES, 2579.48</u>

The underlined portion indicates your response to the prompt. The computer will now assign the values:

A$ = "AJAX OFFICE SUPPLIES", B = 2579.48

Test Your Understanding 6.5

Write a program which allows you to set variables A and B to any desired values via an **INPUT** statement. Use the program to set A equal to 12 and B equal to 17.

The next two examples illustrate the use of the **INPUT** statement and provide further practice in using the **IF . . . THEN** statement.

Example 4. Suppose that you are a teacher compiling semester grades. Suppose that there are 4 grades for each student and that each grade is on the traditional 0 to 100 scale. Write a program which accepts the grades as input, computes the semester average and assigns grades according to the following scale:

90–100	A
80–89.9	B
70–79.9	C
60–69.9	D
<60	F

Solution. We will use an **INPUT** statement to enter the grades into the computer. Our program will allow you to compute the grades of students one after the other via a loop. You may terminate the loop by entering a negative grade. Here is our program.

```
10 PRINT "ENTER STUDENT'S 4 GRADES."
20 PRINT "SEPARATE GRADES BY COMMAS."
30 PRINT "FOLLOW LAST GRADE WITH ENTER."
40 PRINT "TO END PROGRAM, ENTER NEGATIVE GRADE."
50 INPUT A1,A2,A3,A4
60 IF A1<0 THEN END
70 IF A2<0 THEN END
80 IF A3<0 THEN END
90 IF A4<0 THEN END
100 LET A=(A1+A2+A3+A4)/4
110 PRINT "SEMESTER AVERAGE", A
120 IF A>=90 THEN PRINT "SEMESTER GRADE = A" ELSE 130
125 GOTO 200
130 IF A>=80 THEN PRINT "SEMESTER GRADE = B" ELSE 140
135 GOTO 200
140 IF A>=70 THEN PRINT "SEMESTER GRADE = C" ELSE 150
145 GOTO 200
```

```
150 IF A>=60 THEN PRINT "SEMESTER GRADE = D" ELSE 160
155 GOTO 200
160 PRINT "SEMESTER GRADE =F"
200 END
```

Note the logic for printing out the semester grades. We first compute the semester average A. In 120 we ask if A is greater than or equal to 90. If so, we assign the grade A, and go on to the next line, namely 125, which sends us to line 200, **END.** In case A is less than 90, line 120 sends us to line 130. In line 130, we ask if A is greater than or equal to 80. If so, then we assign the grade B. (The point is that the only way we can get to line 130 is for A to be less than 90. So if A is greater than or equal to 80, we know that A lies in the B range.) If not, we go to line 140, and so forth. This logic may seem a trifle confusing at first, but after repeated use, it will seem quite natural.

Example 5. Write a program to maintain your checkbook. The program should allow you to record an initial balance, enter deposits, and enter checks. It should also warn you of overdrafts.

Solution. Let the variable B always contain the current balance in the checkbook. The program will ask for the type of transaction you wish to record. A "D" will mean that you wish to record a deposit; a "C" will mean that you wish to record a check; a "Q" will mean that you are done entering transactions and wish to terminate the program. After entering each transaction, the computer will figure your new balance, report it to you, will check for an overdraft, and report any overdraft to you. In case of an overdraft, the program will allow you to cancel the preceding check!

```
10 INPUT "WHAT IS YOUR STARTING BALANCE"; B
20 INPUT "WHAT TRANSACTION TYPE (D,C,OR Q)"; A$
30 IF A$="Q" THEN END
40 IF A$="D" THEN 100 ELSE 200
100 INPUT "DEPOSIT AMOUNT"; D
110 LET B=B+D:     'ADD DEPOSIT TO BALANCE
120 PRINT "YOUR NEW BALANCE IS", B
130 GOTO 20
200 INPUT "CHECK AMOUNT"; C
210 LET B=B-C:     'DEDUCT CHECK AMOUNT
220 IF B<0 THEN 300:     'TEST FOR OVERDRAFT
230 PRINT "YOUR NEW BALANCE IS", B
240 GOTO 20
300 PRINT "LAST CHECK CAUSES OVERDRAFT"
310 INPUT "DO YOU WISH TO CANCEL CHECK(Y/N)"; E$
```

```
320 IF E$="Y" THEN 400
330 PRINT "YOUR NEW BALANCE IS", B
340 GOTO 20
400 LET B=B+C:      'CANCEL LAST CHECK
410 GOTO 20
1000 END
```

You should carefully scan this program to make sure you understand how each of the **INPUT** and **IF . . . THEN** statements are used. In addition, you should use this program to obtain a feel for the dialog between you and the computer when **INPUT** statements are used.

Example 6. Write a BASIC program which tests proficiency in addition of two digit numbers. Let the user suggest the problems and let the program keep score of the number correct out of 10.

Solution. Let us request the user of the program to suggest pairs of numbers via an **INPUT** statement. The sum will also be requested via an **INPUT** statement. An **IF . . . THEN** will be used to judge the correctness. The variable R will keep track of the number correct. We will use a loop to repeat the process 10 times.

```
10 FOR J=1 TO 10:      'LOOP TO GIVE 10 PROBLEMS
20 INPUT "TYPE TWO 2-DIGIT NUMBERS"; A,B
30 INPUT "WHAT IS THEIR SUM"; C
40 IF A+B=C THEN 200
50 PRINT "SORRY. THE CORRECT ANSWER IS",A+B
60 GO TO 500:   'GO TO THE NEXT PROBLEM
200 PRINT "YOUR ANSWER IS CORRECT! CONGRATULATIONS"
210 LET R=R+1:      'INCREASE SCORE BY 1
220 GO TO 500:      'GO TO THE NEXT PROBLEM
500 NEXT J
600 PRINT "YOUR SCORE IS",R,"CORRECT OUT OF 10"
700 PRINT "TO TRY AGAIN, TYPE RUN"
800 END
```

EXERCISES (answers on 271)

1. Write a computer program to calculate all perfect squares which are less than 45,000. (The perfect squares are the numbers 1, 4, 9, 16, 25, 36, 49, ...)

2. Write a computer program to determine all of the circles of integer radius and area less than or equal to 5,000. (The area of a circle of radius R is PI*R[2, where PI = 3.14159 approximately.)

3. Write a computer program to determine the sizes of all those boxes which are perfect cubes, have integer dimensions, and have a volume less than 175,000. (That is, find all integers X for which X^3 is less than 175,000.)

4. Modify the arithmetic testing program of Example 4 so that the operation tested is multiplication instead of addition.

5. Modify the arithmetic testing program of Example 4 so that it allows you to choose, at the beginning of each group of ten problems, from among the possible operations: addition, subtraction, or multiplication.

6. Write a program which accepts three numbers via an INPUT statement and determines the largest of the three.

7. Write a program which accepts three numbers via an INPUT statement and determines the smallest of the three.

8. Write a program which accepts a set of numbers via INPUT statements and determines the largest among them.

9. Write a program which accepts a set of numbers via INPUT statements and determines the smallest among them.

10. The following data were collected by a sociologist. Six cities experienced the following numbers of burglaries in 1980 and 1981:

City	Burglaries 1980	Burglaries 1981
A	5,782	6,548
B	4,811	6,129
C	3,865	4,270
D	7,950	8,137
E	4,781	4,248
F	6,598	7,048

For each city, calculate the increase (decrease) in the number of burglaries. Determine which had an increase of more than 500 burglaries.

11. Write a program which does the arithmetic of a cash register. That is, let it accept purchases via INPUT statements, then total the purchases, figure out the sales tax (assume 5%), and compute the total purchase. Let it ask for the amount of payment given and then let it compute the change due.

12. Write a program which analyzes cash flow. That is, let the program ask for cash on hand as well as accounts expected to be received in the next month. Let the program compute the total anticipated cash for the month. Let the program ask for the bills due in the next month and let it compute the total accounts payable during the month. By comparing the amounts to be received and to be paid out, let the program compute the net cash flow for the month and report either a surplus or a deficit.

Answers to Test Your Understanding

6.1:
```
(a) IF A<B THEN PRINT A+B ELSE END
(b) IF A[2+B>=5000 THEN 300 ELSE 500
(c) IF J>I+K THEN J=I+K ELSE J=K
```

6.2:
```
10 INPUT "UNPAID BALANCE";B
20 IF B>500 THEN 100 ELSE 200
100 LET C=B-500
110 IN=.015*500+.01*C
120 GOTO 300
200 IN=.015*B
300 PRINT "INTEREST EQUALS";IN
310 PRINT "NEW BALANCE EQUALS";B+IN
320 END
```

6.3: 100−110−120−400

6.5:
```
10 INPUT "THE VALUES OF A AND B ARE";A,B
20 END
```

2.7 SOME PROGRAMMING TIPS

Now that we have learned the most elementary BASIC commands and statements, let us discuss a few topics which will make programming easier.

Four Shortcuts

Here are four shortcuts which will save time in typing programs.

1. It is not necessary to include the word **LET** in a **LET** statement! The statement:

   10 A=5

   means the same thing to the computer as:

   10 LET A=5

2. A question mark may be used in place of the word **PRINT.** Therefore, the statement:

   10 ? A, A$

   means the same thing as the statement:

   10 PRINT A,A$

Test Your Understanding 7.1

What is the output of the following program?

```
10 A=3:B=7
20 A=2*B+3*A
30 ? A,B[2
40 END
```

3. A period may be used to refer to the current program line—that is, the line most recently sent to the computer via **ENTER.** For example, the command

   LIST.

   will display the current line. The command

   DELETE.

   will delete the current line.

4. The computer can generate program line numbers for you via the **AUTO** command. You may give this command at any stage of program

entry. The computer will begin generating line numbers as you need them. For example, if you give the command:

AUTO

the computer will generate the sequence of line numbers 10, 20, 30, 40, ... You may designate the starting line. For example, the command:

AUTO 105

will generate the sequence of line numbers 105, 115, 125, 135, ... You may even specify the difference between consecutive line numbers! For example, the command:

AUTO 50, 20

will generate the sequence of line numbers 50, 70, 90, 110, ... The **AUTO** feature may be turned off by hitting the **BREAK** key.

Using a Printer

In writing programs and analyzing their output, it is often easier to rely on written output rather than output on the screen. In computer terminology, written output is called **hard copy** and may be provided on any of a wide variety of printers. Your TRS-80 Model III may be attached to a large number of such printers, ranging from a dot-matrix thermal printer costing only a few hundred dollars to a daisy wheel printer costing several thousand dollars. As you begin to make serious use of your computer, you will find it difficult to do without hard copy. Indeed, writing programs is much easier if you can consult a hard copy listing of your program at various stages of program development. (One reason is that in printed output you are not confined to looking at your program in 16 line "snapshots.") Also, you will want to use the printer to produce output of programs, ranging from tables of numerical data to address lists and text files produced via a word processing program.

You may produce hard copy on your printer by using the BASIC statement **LPRINT.** For example, the statement

10 LPRINT A,A$

will print the current values of A and A$ on the printer, in print fields 1 and 2. (As is the case with the screen, BASIC divides the printer line into print fields which are 16 columns wide.) Moreover, the statement

20 LPRINT "CUSTOMER","CREDIT LIMIT","MOST RECENT PCHS"

will result in printing three headings in the first three print fields, namely:

CUSTOMER CREDIT LIMIT MOST RECENT PCHS

So printing on the printer proceeds very much like printing on the screen. It is important to realize, however, that in order to print on both the screen *and* the printer, it is necessary to use *both* statements **PRINT** and **LPRINT.** For example, to print the values of A and A$ on both the screen and the printer, we must give two instructions, as follows:

```
10 PRINT A,A$
20 LPRINT A,A$
```

Some Things to Check

Writing programs in BASIC is not all that difficult. However, it requires a certain amount of care and meticulous attention to detail. Each person must develop an individual programming style. However, here are a few tips which may help the novice programmer over some of the rough spots of writing those first few programs.

1. Carefully think your program through. Break up the computation into steps and outline the programming which is necessary for each of the steps.
2. Work through your program by hand, pretending that you are the computer. In doing so, do not rush. Go through your program one step at a time and check that it does what you want it to do.
3. Have you initialized all the variables with the values you want? Remember that if you do not specify the value of a variable, BASIC will automatically assign it the value 0. This may not be the value you intend!
4. Are all your loops complete? That is, have you included a **NEXT** corresponding to each **FOR?** This is an easy mistake to make but it is also easy to catch. If BASIC does not find a **NEXT** corresponding to a **FOR,** when it attempts to run the program it will report the mistake and the line number in which it occurs. This is just one of a series of checks

which BASIC makes for consistency and completeness. Later we will discuss the various other error messages which BASIC can provide.

5. Check that your **IF . . . THEN** statements do not create any infinite loops. This may be a subtle error to spot, but it is usually vulnerable to checking the program line by line and carrying it out as if you were the computer.

In the following chapters, we will present some further ideas on debugging your programs and on programming technique. For now, however, let's move on with learning to make our computer do interesting things!

Answer to Test Your Understanding

7.1: 23 49

2.8 APPENDIX—OPERATION OF THE CASSETTE RECORDER

In this Appendix, we discuss the operation of the Radio-Shack CTR 80A Computer Cassette Recorder.

Connection

There are two cables to connect. Before attempting connection, make sure your computer is unplugged.

I. Connect the cable with three plugs as follows:

   A. The end with the single plug is connected to the 'Tape' connector on the back of the Model III.

   B. Connect the three plugs to the cassette recorder:

      i. The black plug into the EAR jack.
      ii. The large gray plug into the AUX jack.
      iii. The small gray plug into the smaller MIC jack.

II. Connect the other cable to the connection marked 120V on the side of the cassette recorder. Plug the other end into a standard AC current outlet.

III. Plug the computer into the AC current outlet.

Loading a Tape

I. Use a cassette tape designed for computer use. (Standard audio tape cassettes are not of high enough quality.)

II. Start with a blank tape. The computer cannot record information directly over previously-recorded data. To erase a tape, you may use a bulk eraser. (Your Radio Shack store sells one.)

III. Press the STOP key, then the EJECT key. The cassette compartment will come open. Place the cassette in the compartment with the tape toward you. Note that tapes have two sides. The side to be played or recorded should be placed up. Rewind the tape using the REWIND button. Then press STOP. To remove the tape, press STOP, then EJECT.

Saving Programs

I. Insert tape as described above.

II. Press RECORD and PLAY together. Both keys should remain in the down position.

III. Give a command of the form **CSAVE "X",** where X is the name we have assigned to the program.

IV. When the operation is complete, the computer will display the message:

```
READY
>
```

Now press the STOP button of the cassette recorder.

Note that you may keep several programs on a single tape cassette. To do so, however, you must keep track of the position of each program using the tape counter just above the tape door. To add to a partially recorded tape, position the tape counter one unit beyond the end of the last recorded item.

Reading Programs

I. Set the volume level. In reading programs from a tape cassette, it is important to set the volume at an appropriate level. The volume setting is found on the left side of the cassette recorder. For reading tapes you have generated, set the volume in the range 5-7. For cassettes purchased from Radio Shack, set the volume in the range 4-6. For cassettes purchased elsewhere, you will probably need to experiment for the correct volume setting.

II. Position the tape to just before the start of the program or data file. Use the tape counter for positioning. Note that if you wish to load a program, you may rewind the tape using the REWIND button and give a command of the form:

CLOAD "X"

The computer will search the tape for a program saved under the name X. In case there are two such programs on the tape, the computer will read the first one encountered.

III. Press the PLAY button.

IV. Give the **CLOAD** command.

V. In the case of a **CLOAD** command, the computer will indicate the end of the operation with

READY
>

To interrupt a tape reading or writing operation, hold down the **BREAK** key until the computer responds with:

READY
>

This procedure is needed, for example, if you accidentally put the wrong tape in the cassette recorder. If the program you want is not on the tape, the computer will search the tape and wait indefinitely!

Start-up Dialog

Recall our discussion in Section 1.3 of the start-up procedure for the Model III. The computer displays the prompt

CASS?

The computer is asking for the speed of operation of the cassette recorder.

There are two possible speeds, high (H) and low (L). High speed corresponds to a data transfer rate of 190 characters per second and is automatically selected if you hit **ENTER** in response to **Cass?.** However, a tape must read at the speed at which it was recorded. And you may have some tapes which were recorded at low speed (about 63 characters per second). This might be the case, for example, with programs you purchase. For such cassettes, answer **Cass?** with

L

(followed by **ENTER**). It will probably be most convenient if you record any new tapes at high speed since the reading process will then proceed much more quickly.

3

More About BASIC

In this chapter, we will continue our introduction to programming in BASIC. As in the previous chapter, we will organize our discussion by application. Moreover, we will introduce additional system commands as appropriate applications arise.

3.1 WORKING WITH TABULAR DATA

In the preceding chapter, we introduced the notion of a variable and used variable names like:

AA, B1, CZ, W0

Unfortunately, the supply of variables available to us is not sufficient for many programs. Indeed, as we shall see in this chapter, there are relatively innocent programs which require hundreds or even thousands of variables. To meet the needs of such programs, BASIC allows the use of so-called *subscripted variables*. Such variables are suggested by the habit of mathematicians who create mathematical variables by using numbered subscripts. For instance, here is a list of 1,000 variables as might appear in a mathematical work:

$A_1, A_2, A_3, \ldots, A_{1000}$

The numbers used to distinguish the variables are called *subscripts*. Correspondingly, the BASIC language allows definition of variables distinguished by subscripts. However, since the computer has difficulty placing the numbers in the traditional position, they are placed in parentheses on the same line as the letter. For example, the above list of 1000 different variables would be written in BASIC as

A(1),A(2),A(3), . . . ,A(1000)

Please note that the variable A(1) is not the same as the variable A1. You may use both of them in the same program and BASIC will interpret them differently.

A subscripted variable is really a group of variables with a common letter identification and distinguished by different integer "subscripts." For instance, the above group of variables would constitute the subscripted variable A( ). It is often useful to view a subscripted variable as a table or array. For example, the subscripted variable A( ) considered above can be considered as providing the following table of information:

A(1)
A(2)
A(3)
.
.
.
A(1000)

That is, the subscripted variable defines a table consisting of 1,000 rows. Row number J contains a single entry, namely, the value of the variable A(J). The first row contains the value of A(1), the second the value of A(2), and so forth. Since a subscripted variable can be thought of as a table (or array), subscripted variables are often called *arrays*.

The array just considered was a table consisting of 1,000 rows and a single column. The TRS-80 allows you to consider more general arrays. For example, consider the following financial table which records the monthly income for January, February, and March from each of a chain of four dry cleaning stores:

	Store #1	Store #2	Store #3	Store #4
Jan.	1258.38	2437.46	4831.90	987.12
Feb.	1107.83	2045.68	3671.86	1129.47
March	1298.00	2136.88	4016.73	1206.34

This table has three rows and four columns. It's entries may be stored in the computer as a set of 12 of variables:

A(1,1) A(1,2) A(1,3) A(1,4)

A(2,1) A(2,2) A(2,3) A(2,4)

A(3,1) A(3,2) A(3,3) A(3,4)

This array of variables is very similar to a subscripted variable, except that there are now two subscripts. The first subscript indicates the row number and the second subscript indicates the column number. For example, the variable A(3,2) is in the third row, second column. A collection of variables such as that given above is called a *two-dimensional array* or a *doubly-subscripted* variable. Each setting of the variables of such an array defines a tabular array. For example, if we assign the values

A(1,1) = 1258.38, A(1,2) = 2437.46,

A(1,3) = 4831.90, and so forth,

then we will have the table of earnings from the dry cleaning chain.

So far, we have only considered numeric arrays—that is, arrays whose variables can assume only numerical values. However, it is possible to have arrays whose variables assume string values. (Recall that a string is a sequence of characters: letter, numeral, punctuation mark, or other printable keyboard symbol.) For example, here is an array which can contain string data:

A$(1)

A$(2)

A$(3)

A$(4)

Here each of the variables of the array is a string variable, indicated by the presence of the $. If we assign the values

A$(1) = "SLOW", A$(2) = "FAST", A$(3) = "FAST", A4(4) = "STOP"

then the array is just the table of words:

SLOW

FAST

FAST

STOP

Similarly, the employee record table

Social Security Number	Age	Sex	Marital Status
178654775	38	M	S
345861023	29	F	M
789257958	34	F	D
375486595	42	M	M
457696064	21	F	S

may be stored in an array of the form B$(I,J), where I assumes any one of the values 1,2,3,4,5 (I is the row) and J assumes any one of the values 1,2,3,4 (J = the column). For example, B$(1,1) has the value "178654775", B$(1,2) has the value "38", B$(1,3) has the value "M", and so forth.

The Model III even allows arrays which have three, four, or even more subscripts. For example, consider the dry cleaning chain array introduced above. Suppose that we had one such array for each of ten consecutive years. This collection of data could be stored in a three-dimensional array of the form C(I,J,K), where K represents the year. (K could assume the values 1, 2, 3, . . . , 10.) The only constraint on the size of an array or the number of subscripts it contains is the amount of memory available. (More about that below.)

You must inform the computer of the sizes of the arrays you plan to use in a program. This allows the computer to allocate memory space to house all of the values. To specify the size of an array, use a dimension **(DIM)** statement. For example, to define the size of the subscripted variable A(J), J = 1, . . . , 1000, we insert the statement

10 DIM A(1000)

in the program. This statement informs the computer to expect variables A(0), A(1), . . . , A(1000) in the program and therefore it should set aside memory space for 1001 variables. Note that TRS-80 BASIC begins all subscripts at 0. If you wish to use A(0), fine. If not, ignore it.

You need not use all the variables defined by a **DIM** statement. For example, in the case of the **DIM** statement above, you might actually use only the variables A(1), . . . , A(900). Do not worry about it! Just make sure that you have defined enough variables. Otherwise you could be in trouble. For example, in the case of the subscripted variable above, your program might make use of the variable A(1001). This will create an error condition. Suppose that this variable first is used in line 570. When you attempt to run the program, the computer will report:

UNDEFINED SUBSCRIPT IN LINE 570

Moreover, execution of the program will be halted. To fix the error, merely redo the **DIM** statement to accommodate the undefined subscript.

To define the size of a two-dimensional array, use a **DIM** statement of the form:

10 DIM A(5,4)

This statement defines an array A(I,J), where I can assume the values 0, 1, 2, 3, 4, 5 and J can assume the values 0, 1, 2, 3, 4. Arrays with three or more subscripts are defined similarly.

Test Your Understanding 1.1

Here is an array.

12	645.80
148	489.75
589	12.89
487	14.50

(a) Define an appropriate subscripted variable to store this data.

(b) Define an appropriate **DIM** statement.

It is possible to dimension several arrays with one **DIM** statement. For example, the dimension statement

```
10 DIM A(1000), B$(5), A(5,4)
```

defines the array A(0), . . . , A(1000), the string array B$(0), . . . , B$(5), and the two-dimensional array A(I,J), I = 0, . . . , 5; J = 0, . . . , 4.

We now know how to set aside memory space for the variables of an array. We now must take up the problem of assigning values to these variables. Of course, we could use individual **LET** statements. However, with 1,000 variables in an array, this could lead to an unmanageable number of statements. There are more convenient methods making use of loops. The next two examples illustrate two of these methods.

Example 1. Define an array A(J), J = 1, 2, . . . , 1000 and assign the following values to the variables of the array:

A(1) = 2, A(2) = 4, A(3) = 6, A(4) = 8, ...

Solution. We wish to assign each variable a value equal to twice its subscript. That is, we wish to assign A(J) the value 2*J. To do this we use a loop:

```
10 DIM A(1000)
20 FOR J=1 TO 1000
30 A(J)=2*J
40 NEXT J
50 END
```

Note that the program ignores the variable A(0). Like any variable which has not been assigned a value, it has the value 0.

Test Your Understanding 1.2

Write a program which assigns the variables A(0), . . . , A(30) the values A(0) = 0, A(1) = 1, A(2) = 4, A(3) = 9, ...

When the computer is first turned on or is reset, all variables (including those in arrays) are cleared. That is, all numeric variables are set equal to 0 and all string variables are set equal to the null string (the string with no characters in it). If you wish to return all variables to this state during the execution of a program, use the command **CLEAR.** For example, when the computer encounters the command

570 CLEAR

it will reset all the variables. (Recall from Chapter 1 that this command also clears the screen.) The **CLEAR** command can be convenient if, for example, you wish to use the same array to store two different sets of information at two different stages of the program. After the first use of the array you then could prepare for the second use by executing a **CLEAR.**

The **CLEAR** command has another important function. Namely, it allocates space for string storage. Ordinarily, the TRS-80 sets aside only enough memory space to store 50 characters of strings. If you wish to exceed this amount, you must specify the amount of string storage you will need. For example, to set aside 500 characters of string storage, you should execute the command:

10 CLEAR 500

This command resets all the variables and sets aside 500 characters of string storage. The next example illustrates how to estimate the amount of string storage you need.

Example 2. Define an array corresponding to the employee record table above. Input the values given and print the table on the screen.

Solution. Our program will print the headings of the columns and then ask for the table entries, one row at a time. We will store the entries in the array B$(I,J), where I is one of 1, 2, 3, 4, 5 and J is one of 1, 2, 3, 4. So we dimension the array as B$(5,4). Our array contains 5 × 4 or 20 entries. The length of the longest string is 9 characters. Therefore, we might need as much as 20 × 9, or 180 characters of string space. This is more than the computer automatically reserves. (This is a crude estimate. We will probably need less but it is better to be on the safe side.) Let us reserve 180 characters of string space via a **CLEAR 180** instruction.

```
1 CLEAR 180
5 DIM B$(5,4)
10 PRINT "SOC. SEC. #", "AGE", "SEX","MARITAL STATUS"
20 FOR I=1 TO 5
30 INPUT "SS #,AGE,SEX,MAR.ST.";B$(I,1),B$(I,2),B$(I,3),B$(I,4)
40 PRINT B$(I,1),B$(I,2),B$(I,3),B$(I,4)
50 NEXT I
60 END
```

In allocating string space, you should calculate the total string space needed by all string variables of your program and execute a single **CLEAR** command to reserve the total required space.

Note that it is *not* necessary to reserve space for numeric arrays. The computer takes care of this chore automatically.

Test Your Understanding 1.3

Suppose that your program will use a 9 × 2 array A$(I,J), a 9 × 1 array B$(I,J), and a 9 × 5 array C(I,J). Suppose that the strings involved are at most 10 characters in length.

(a) Write an appropriate DIM statement(s).

(b) Reserve adequate string space.

If you plan to dimension an array, you should always insert the **DIM** statement before the variable first appears in your program. Otherwise, the first time BASIC comes across the array, it will assume that the subscripts go from 0 to 10. If it subsequently comes across a **DIM** statement, it will think you are changing the size of the array in the midst of the program, something which is not allowed. If you try to change the size of an array in the middle of a program, you will get an error:

REDIMENSIONED ARRAY

EXERCISES (answers on 274)

For each of the following tables, define an appropriate array and determine the appropriate **DIM** statement.

1. 5
   2
   1.7
   4.9
   11

2. 1.1 2.0 3.5
   1.7 2.4 6.2

3. JOHN
   MARY
   SIDNEY

4. 1 2 3

5. | | |
   |---|---|
   | RENT | 575.00 |
   | UTILITIES | 249.78 |
   | CLOTHES | 174.98 |
   | CAR | 348.70 |

6. Display the following array on the screen:

RECEIPTS

	Store #1	Store #2	Store #3
1/1-1/10	57,385.48	89,485.45	38,456.90
1/11-1/20	39,485.98	76,485.49	40,387.86
1/21-1/31	45,467.21	71,494.25	37,983.38

7. Write a program that displays the array of exercise 6 along with totals of the receipts from each store.

8. Expand the program of exercise 7 so that it calculates and displays the totals of ten day periods. (Your screen will not be wide enough to display the ten day totals in a fifth column, so display them in a separate array.)

9. Devise a program which keeps track of the inventory of an appliance store chain. Store the current inventory in an array of the form

	Store #1	Store #2	Store #3	Store #4
Refrig.				
Stove				
Vacuum				
Air Cond.				
Disposal				

Your program should:

1) input the inventory corresponding to the beginning of the day,
2) continually ask for the next transaction—that is, the store number and the number of appliances of each item sold,
3) in response to each transaction, update the inventory array and redisplay it on the screen.

Answers to Test Your Understanding

1.1: (a) A(I,J), I=1,2,3,4; J=1,2 (b) DIM A(4,2)

1.2:
```
10 DIM A(30)
20 FOR J=O TO 30
30 A(J)=J[2
40 NEXT J
50 END
```

1.3: (a) DIM A$(9,2),B$(9,1),C(9,5)

(b) $(9 \times 2 + 9 \times 1) \times 10 = 270$.

Numeric arrays do not count so to reserve string space, we use CLEAR 270.

3.2 INPUTTING DATA

In the preceding section, we introduced arrays and discussed several methods for assigning values to the variables of an array. The most flexible method was via the **INPUT** statement. However, this can be a tedious method for large arrays. Fortunately, BASIC allows us an alternate method for inputting data.

A given program may need many different numbers and strings. You may store the needed data in one or more **DATA** statements. A typical data statement has the form:

10 DATA 3.457, 2.588, 11234, "WINGSPAN"

Note that this data statement consists of four data items, three numeric and one string. The data items are separated by commas. You may include as many data items in a single **DATA** statement as the line allows. Moreover, you may include any number of **DATA** statements in a program and they may be placed anywhere in the program, although a common placement is at the end of the program (just before the **END** statement). Note that we enclosed the string constant "WINGSPAN" in quotation marks. Actually this is not necessary. A string constant in a **DATA** statement does not need quotes as long as it does not contain a comma, a colon, or start with a blank.

The **DATA** statements may be used to assign values to variables and, in particular, to variables in arrays. Here's how. In conjunction with the **DATA** statements, you use one or more **READ** statements. For example, suppose that the above **DATA** statement appeared in a program. Further,suppose that you wish to assign the values:

A = 3.457, B = 2.588, C = 11234, Z$ = "WINGSPAN"

This can be accomplished via the **READ** statement:

100 READ A,B,C,Z$

More precisely, here is how the **READ** statement works. On encountering a **READ** statement, the computer will look for a **DATA** statement. It will then assign values to the variables in the **READ** statement by taking the values, in order, from the **DATA** statement. If there is insufficient data in the first **DATA** statement, the computer will continue to assign values using the data in the next **DATA** statement. If necessary, the computer will proceed to the third **DATA** statement, and so forth.

Test Your Understanding 2.1

Assign the following values: A(1) = 5.1, A(2) = 4.7, A(3) = 5.8, A(4) = 3.2, A(5) = 7.9, A(6) = 6.9.

The computer maintains an internal pointer which points to the next **DATA** item to be used. If the computer encounters a second **READ** statement, it will start reading where it left off. For example, suppose that, instead of the above

READ statement, we use the two read statements:

```
100 READ A,B
200 READ C,Z$
```

Upon encountering the first statement, the computer will look for the location of the pointer. Initially, it will point to the first item in the first **DATA** statement. So the computer will assign the values A = 3.457, B = 2.588. Moreover, the position of the pointer will be advanced to the third item in the **DATA** statement. Upon encountering the next **READ** statement, the computer will assign values beginning with the one designated by the pointer, namely: C = 11234, Z$ = "WINGSPAN".

Test Your Understanding 2.2

What values are assigned to A and B$ by the following program.

```
10 DATA 10,30,"ENGINE", "TACH"
20 READ A,B
30 READ C$,B$
40 END
```

The following example illustrates the use of **DATA** statements in assigning values to an array.

Example 1. Suppose that the monthly electricity costs of a certain family are as follows:

Jan.	$89.74	Feb.	$95.84	March	$79.42
Apr.	78.93	May	72.11	June	115.94
July	158.92	Aug.	164.38	Sep.	105.98
Oct.	90.44	Nov.	89.15	Dec.	93.97

Write a program which calculates the average monthly cost of electricity.

Solution. Let us unceremoniously dump all of the numbers given into **DATA** statements at the end of the program. Arbitrarily, let's start the **DATA** statements at line 1000, with **END** at 2000. This allows us plenty of room. To calculate the average, we must add up the numbers and divide by 12. To do this, let us first create an array A(J) , J = 1, 2, . . . , 12 and set A(J) equal to the cost of electricity in the Jth month. We do this via a loop and the **READ**

statement. We then use a loop to add all the A(J). Finally, we divide by 12 and PRINT the answer. Here is the program.

```
10 DIM A(12)
15 REM LINES 20–40 ASSIGN VALUES TO A(J)
20 FOR J=1 TO 12
30 READ A(J)
40 NEXT J
50 FOR J=1 TO 12
60 C=C+A(J):  'C ACCUMULATES THE SUM OF THE A(J)
70 NEXT J
80 C=C/12:  'DIVIDE SUM BY 12
90 PRINT "THE AVERAGE COST OF ELECTRICITY IS",C
1000 DATA 89.74, 95.84, 79.42, 78.93, 72.11, 115.94
1010 DATA 158.92, 164.38, 105.98, 90.44, 89.15, 93.97
2000 END
```

The following program could be of assistance in preparing the payroll of a small business.

Example 2. A small business has five employees. Here are their names and hourly wages.

Name	Hourly Wage
Joe Polanski	7.75
Susan Greer	8.50
Allan Cole	8.50
Betsy Palm	6.00
Herman Axler	6.00

Write a program which accepts as input hours worked for the current week and calculates the current gross pay and the amount of Social Security tax to be withheld from their pay. (Assume that the Social Security tax amounts to 6.65% of gross pay.)

Solution. Let us keep the hourly wage rates and names in two arrays, called A(J) and B$(J), respectively, where J = 1,2,3,4,5. Note that we cannot use a single two-dimensional array for this data since the names are string data and the hourly wage rates are numerical. (Recall that BASIC does not allow us to mix the two kinds of data in an array.) The first part of the program will be to assign the values to the variables in the two arrays. Next, the program will, one by one, print out tne names of the employees and ask for the number of hours worked during the current week. This data will be stored in the array C(J), J = 1,2,3,4,5. The program will then compute the gross wages as A(J)*C(J) (that is, <wage rate> times <number of hours worked>). This piece of data will be stored in the array D(J), J = 1,2,3,4,5. Next, the program will compute the amount of Social Security tax to be withheld as .0665*D(J). This piece of data will be stored in the array E(J), J = 1,2,3,4,5. Finally, all the computed data will be printed on the screen. Here is the program:

```
5 CLEAR 100
10 DIM A(5),B$(5),C(5),D(5),E(5)
20 FOR J=1 TO 5
30 READ B$(J),A(J)
40 NEXT J
50 FOR J=1 TO 5
60 PRINT "TYPE CURRENT HOURS OF", B$(J)
70 INPUT C(J)
80 D(J)=A(J)*C(J)
90 E(J)=.0665*D(J)
100 NEXT J
110 PRINT "EMPLOYEE","GROSS WAGES","SOC.SEC.TAX"
120 FOR J=1 TO 5
130 PRINT B$(J),D(J),E(J)
140 NEXT J
200 DATA JOE POLANSKI, 7.75, SUAN GREER, 8.50
210 DATA ALLAN COLE, 8.50, BETSY PALM, 6.00
220 DATA HERMAN AXLER, 6.00
1000 END
```

In certain applications, you may wish to read the same **DATA** statements more than once. To do this you must reset the pointer via the **RESTORE** statement. For example, consider the following program.

```
10 DATA 2.3, 5.7, 4.5, 7.3
20 READ A,B
30 RESTORE
40 READ C,D
50 END
```

Line 20 sets A equal to 2.3 and B equal to 5.7. The **RESTORE** statement of line 30 moves the pointer back to the first item of data, namely 2.3. The **READ** statement of line 40 then sets C equal to 2.3 and D equal to 5.7. Note that without the **RESTORE** in line 30, the **READ** statement in line 40 would set C equal to 4.5 and D equal to 7.3.

There are two common errors in using **READ** and **DATA** statements. First, you may instruct the program to **READ** more data than is present in the **DATA** statements. For example consider the following program.

```
10 DATA 1,2,3,4
20 FOR J=1 TO 5
30 READ A(J)
40 NEXT J
50 END
```

It attempts to read 5 pieces of data, but the DATA statement only has 4. In this case, you will receive an error message:

OUT OF DATA IN LINE 30

A second common error is an attempt to assign a string value to a numeric variable or vice-versa. Such an attempt will lead to a **TYPE MISMATCH** error.

EXERCISES (answers on 276)

Each of the following programs assigns values to the variables of an array. Determine which values are assigned.

1.
```
10 DIM A(10)
20 FOR J=1 TO 10
30 READ A(J)
40 NEXT J
50 DATA 2,4,6,8,10,12,14,16,18,20
100 END
```

2.
```
10 DIM A(3),B(3)
20 FOR J=0 TO 3
30 READ A(J), B(J)
40 NEXT J
50 DATA 1.1,2.2,3.3,4.4,5.5,6.6,7.7,8.8,9.9
60 END
```

3.
```
10 DIM A(3),B$(3)
20 FOR J=0 TO 3
30 READ A(J)
40 NEXT J
50 FOR J=0 TO 3
```

```
60 READ B$(J)
70 NEXT J
80 DATA 1,2,3,4,A,B,C,D
90 END
```

4.
```
10 DIM A(3), B(3)
20 READ A(0),B(0)
30 READ A(1),B(1)
40 RESTORE
50 READ A(2),B(2)
60 READ A(3),B(3)
80 DATA 1,2,3,4,5,6,7,8
90 END
```

5.
```
10 DIM A(3,4)
20 FOR I=1 TO 3
30 FOR J=1 TO 4
40 READ A(I,J)
50 NEXT J
60 NEXT I
70 DATA 1,2,3,4,5,6,7,8,9,10,11,12
80 END
```

6.
```
10 DIM A(3,4)
20 FOR J=1 TO 4
30 FOR I=1 TO 3
40 READ A(I,J)
50 NEXT I
60 NEXT J
70 DATA 1,2,3,4,5,6,7,8,9,10,11,12
80 END
```

Each of the following programs contains an error. Find it.

7.
```
10 DIM A(5)
20 FOR J=1 TO 5
30 READ A(J)
40 NEXT J
50 DATA 1,2,3,4
60 END
```

8.
```
10 DIM A(5)
20 FOR J=1 TO 5
30 READ A(J)
40 NEXT J
50 DATA 1,A,2,B
60 END
```

9. Here is a table of Federal Income Tax Withholding for weekly wages for an individual claiming one exemption. Assume that each of the employees in the business discussed in the text claims a single exemption. Modify the program given so that it correctly computed Federal Withholding and the net amount of wages. (That is, after Federal Withholding and Social Security are deducted.)

Wages at Least	But Less Than	Tax Withheld
200	210	29.10
210	220	31.20
220	230	33.80
230	240	36.40
240	250	39.00
250	260	41.60
260	270	44.20
270	280	46.80
280	290	49.40
290	300	52.10
300	310	55.10
310	320	58.10
320	330	61.10
330	340	64.10
340	350	67.10

10. Here is a set of 24 hourly temperature reports as compiled by the National Weather Service. Write a program to compute the average temperature for the last 24 hours. Let your program respond to a query concerning the temperature at a particular hour. (For example, what was the temperature at 2:00 PM?)

	AM	PM
12:00	10	38
1:00	10	39
2:00	9	40
3:00	9	40
4:00	8	42
5:00	11	38
6:00	15	33
7:00	18	27
8:00	20	22
9:00	25	18
10:00	31	15
11:00	35	12

Answers to Test Your Understanding

2.1:
```
10 DATA 5.1,4.7,5.8,3.2,7.9,6.9
20 FOR J=1 TO 6
30 READ A(J)
40 NEXT J
50 END
```

2.2: A=10, B$="TACH"

3.3 TELLING TIME WITH YOUR COMPUTER

Your TRS-80 Model III has a built-in clock (a *real-time clock* in computer jargon) which can allow you to let your programs take into account the time of day (in hours, minutes, and seconds) and the date (day, month, and year). You can use this feature for many purposes, such as keeping a computer-generated personal calendar (see Example 1 below) or timing a segment of a program (see Example 2 below). Note that the real-time clock is not present in the TRS-80 Model I.

Reading the Real-Time Clock

The TRS-80 real-time clock keeps track of six pieces of information, in the following order:

Month (01–12)

Day (00–31)

Year (00–99)

Hours (00–23)

Minutes (00–59)

Seconds (00–59).

The time is displayed in the following format:

02/15/81 14:38:27

The above display corresponds to February 15,1981, at 27 seconds after 2:38 P.M. Note that the hours are counted using a 24 hour clock, with 0 hours corresponding to midnight. So hours 0–11 correspond to A.M. and hours 12–23 correspond to P.M.

The clock is programmed to account for the number of days in a month (28, 30, or 31). However, it does not recognize leap years.

In BASIC, the time is identified as TIME$. For example, to display the current time on the screen, use the command:

10 PRINT TIME$

In order to make use of the six individual pieces of data in the clock, it is most convenient to first learn something about its internal workings. The six pieces of data are stored in six consecutive memory locations, namely:

	Memory Location
Month	16924
Day	16923
Year	16922
Hours	16921
Minutes	16920
Seconds	16919

You may read the contents of any memory location using the command **PEEK**. For example, to read the character currently stored in memory location 12047, we would use the command:

10 A=PEEK(12047)

The variable A is then set equal to a decimal number which corresponds to the character stored in memory location 12047. For example, the decimal code corresponding to E is 69 and the code corresponding to g is 103. In the case of the memory locations reserved for the clock, the decimal code returned by the **PEEK** command is the value of the corresponding piece of clock data. For example, a value of 09 for **PEEK(16924)** corresponds to the month of September.

Test Your Understanding 3.1

(a) Display the current value of the clock.

(b) Display only the minutes and seconds.

Setting the Clock

The real-time clock automatically starts when the computer is initialized. However, it is started at the value:

00/00/00 00.00.00

If you only wish to keep track of elapsed time, this may be sufficient. However, to fully utilize the clock it is necessary to set it with the correct data. This may be accomplished by using the command **POKE,** which allows you to set a location of memory to a given value. For example, the command

```
10 POKE 16924, 12
```

sets memory location 16924 (the month) to the value 12 (December). The value inserted into a memory location must be an integer between 0 and 255, inclusive.

Test Your Understanding 3.2

Write an instruction which sets the hours of the clock to 2 PM.

To set all the data of the clock, it is convenient to use a program like the following:

```
10 A=16924
20 DIM C(5)
30 INPUT "MO,DY,YR,HR,MN,SE";C(0),C(1),C(2),C(3),C(4),C(5)
40 FOR J=0 TO 5
50 POKE A-J, C(J)
60 NEXT J
70 END
```

You may wish to type in this program and store it on disk or cassette, so that it may be easily called up whenever you wish to set the time.

Test Your Understanding 3.3

Set the clock with today's date and time. Check yourself by printing out the value of the clock.

Test Your Understanding 3.4

Write a program which continually displays the correct time on the screen.

> **Important:** The clock is reset under the following circumstances: Whenever the computer is turned off, or reset; whenever cassette or disk operations take place. If any of these operations are performed and you subsequently wish to use the clock, it will be necessary to reenter the correct time and date.

Example 1. Use the real-time clock to build a computerized appointment calendar.

Solution. Let us enter appointments in **DATA** statements, with one **DATA** statement for each appointment. Let the **DATA** statements be arranged in the following format:

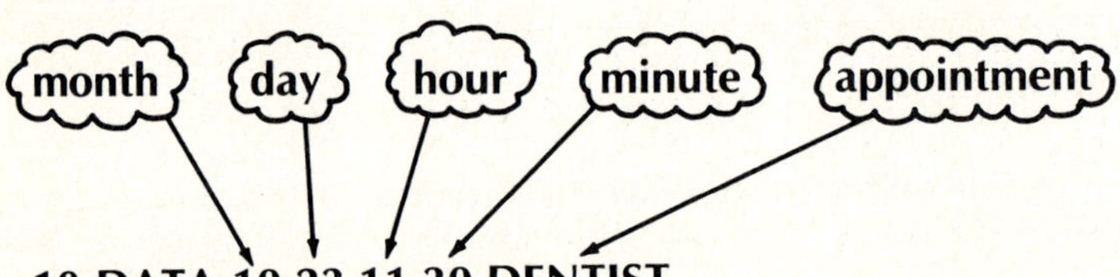

10 DATA 10,23,11,30,DENTIST

The appointments will be numbered by a variable J. For appointment J, we will store the five pieces of data in the variables A(J), B(J), C(J), D(J), E$(J), respectively. Let us allow for 300 appointments. So we dimension each of the variables for an array of size 301. (We will not use J = 0.) Moreover, we will **CLEAR** 20 characters of string space for each appointment. The program will do the following:

1. Read the various appointments in the **DATA** statements. It will stop reading when there is no more data to read.
2. Ask for the current date and time data.
3. Determine today's appointments.

Here is the program:

```
5 CLEAR 6000
10 DIM A(300),B(300),C(300),D(300),E$(300)
15 ON ERROR GOTO 100:  'IF OUT OF DATA GO TO 100
20 REM 30-60 READ THE DATA STATEMENTS IN 10000-13000
30 J=I
40 READ A(J),B(J),C(J),D(J),E$(J)
50 J=J+1:  'FINAL VALUE OF J=#APPOINTMENTS+1
60 GOTO 40
100 RESUME 110:  'END ERROR CONDITION AND GO TO 110
105 REM 110-160 ASK FOR CURRENT TIME AND DATE
110 A=16924
120 DIM F(5)
130 INPUT "MO,DY,YR,HR,MN,SE";F(0),F(1),F(2),F(3),F(4),F(5)
140 FOR K=0 TO 5
150 POKE A-K, F(K)
160 NEXT K
200 PRINT "REQUEST SCHEDULE FOR MONTH, DAY"
210 PRINT "FOR TODAY, ENTER 0,0"
220 PRINT "FOR TOMORROW ENTER -1,-1"
230 INPUT X,Y:  'X=MONTH, Y=DAY
240 IF X>0 THEN 300
245 REM IF TODAY OR TOMORROW, FIND DATE AND DAY
250 X=PEEK(16924)-X,Y=PEEK(16923)-Y
300 FOR K=1 TO J-I
310 IF A(K)=X THEN 400:  'IS APPT. FOR RIGHT MONTH?
320 GOTO 510:  'IF NOT GO TO NEXT APPT.
400 IF B(J)=Y THEN 500:  'IS APPT. FOR RIGHT DAY?
410 GOTO 510: IF NOT GO TO NEXT APPT.
500 PRINT A(K),B(K),C(K),D(K),E$(K)
510 NEXT K
10000 DATA.
10001 DATA
10002 DATA
.
.
.
10299 DATA
11000 END
```

To use the above program, just type appointments in to the data lines as you make them. You can store the current list of appointments along with the program. As new appointments are made, you can recall the program and add corresponding data lines. As appointments become obsolete, they may be removed from the list using the **DELETE** command.

A few comments are in order concerning the **ON ERROR GOTO** and **RESUME** statements. At any given moment, you have no way of knowing how many appointments are in the calendar. Therefore, you have no way of knowing in advance how many of the data lines in 10000–10299 you must read. Of course, if you attempt to read past the last data line, you will get an OUT OF DATA error. The **ON ERROR GOTO** statement allows you to handle this error when it occurs, without terminating program execution. Indeed, in the above program, we have instructed the computer to respond to an error (namely the OUT OF DATA ERROR we expect) by going to line 110. In this line, we tell the computer to **RESUME-** that is, to continue execution of the program with the next line after 110, just as if the error never occurred. This procedure allows us to read data until there is no more.

Example 2. In Example 4 of Section 2.6, we developed a program to test proficiency in the addition of two-digit numbers. Redesign this program to allow 15 seconds to answer the question.

Solution. Let us use the real-time clock. After a particular problem has been given, we will start the second portion of the clock at 0 and perform a loop which continually tests the second portion of the clock for the value 15. When this value is encountered, the program will print out "TIME'S UP. WHAT IS YOUR ANSWER?" Here is the program. Lines 50–60 contain the loop.

```
10 FOR J=1 TO 10:  'LOOP TO GIVE 10 PROBLEMS
20 INPUT "TYPE TWO 2–DIGIT NUMBERS"; A,B
30 PRINT "WHAT IS THEIR SUM?"
40 POKE 16919,0:  'SET SECONDS TO 0
50 IF PEEK(16919)=15 THEN GOTO 100:  'COUNT 15 SECONDS
60 GOTO 50
100 INPUT "TIME'S UP! WHAT IS YOUR ANSWER";C
120 IF A+B=C THEN 200
130 PRINT "SORRY. THE CORRECT ANSWER IS",A+B
140 GO TO 500:  'GO TO THE NEXT PROBLEM
200 PRINT "YOUR ANSWER IS CORRECT! CONGRATULATIONS"
210 LET R=R+1:  'INCREASE SCORE BY 1
220 GO TO 500:  'GO TO THE NEXT PROBLEM
500 NEXT J
600 PRINT "YOUR SCORE IS",R,"CORRECT OUT OF 10"
700 PRINT "TO TRY AGAIN, TYPE RUN"
800 END
```

Test Your Understanding 3.5

Modify the above program so that it allows you to take as much time as you like to solve a problem, but keeps track of elapsed time (in seconds) and prints out the number of seconds used.

EXERCISES (answers on 277)

1. Set the clock with today's date and the current time.
2. Print out the current time on the screen.
3. Write a program which prints out the date and time at one second intervals.
4. Write a program which prints out the date and time at one minute intervals.
5. Set up the appointment program of Example 1 and use it to enter a week's worth of appointments.
6. Modify the appointment program of Example 1 so that it prints out the appointments on a per hour basis.
7. Modify the addition tester program so that it allows a choice of four levels of speed: Easy (2 minutes), Moderate (30 seconds), Hard (15 seconds), and Whiz Kid (8 seconds).
8. Write a program which can be run for an entire day and at the start of each hour prints out the appointments for that hour. (Such a program would be useful in a doctor's or dentist's office.)

Answers to Test Your Understanding

3.1: (a)

```
10 PRINT TIME$
20 END
RUN
```

(b)

```
10 PRINT PEEK(16920), "MINUTES"
20 PRINT PEEK(16919), "SECONDS
30 END
```

3.2:

```
10 POKE(16921), 14
```

3.4:

```
10 PRINT TIME$
20 CLS
30 GOTO 10
40 END
```

Note: This program is an infinite loop and will need to be terminated via the BREAK key.

3.5: Delete lines 50–60. Add lines:

```
40 POKE 16920,0:   'Set minutes to 0
100 INPUT "WHAT IS YOUR ANSWER";C
110 X=PEEK(16920):Y=PEEK(16919)
115 PRINT "YOU TOOK", 60*X+Y, "SECONDS"
```

3.4 ADVANCED PRINTING

In this section, we will discuss the various ways in which you can format output on the screen and on the printer. Model III BASIC is quite flexible in the form in which you can cast output. You have control over the size of the letters on the screen, placement of output on the line, degree of accuracy to which calculations are displayed, and so forth. Let us begin by reviewing what we have already learned about printing.

The Model III screen is 64 characters across (at least in terms of characters of normal size. See below.) This gives 64 print positions in each line. These are divided into four print zones of 16 characters each. To start printing at the beginning of the next print zone, insert a comma between the items to be printed. To avoid any space between items, separate them in the PRINT statement by a semicolon. For example, the following program

```
10 A=5
20 PRINT "THE VALUE OF A IS EQUAL TO";A
30 END
```

will result in the following screen display:

```
THE VALUE OF A IS EQUAL TO 5
```

Note that the second print item (namely the value of A, which is 5) is not at the beginning of the next print zone. Instead, there is a single blank space separating the first print item from the 5. Actually, the semicolon tells the computer to begin printing in the next space. The blank arises because BASIC ordinarily prints all positive numbers with a blank in front (in place of a +). So the blank space in front of the 5 actually belongs to the 5. To print the same program with 5 replaced by −5, we would modify the above program as follows:

```
10 A=-5
20 PRINT "THE VALUE OF A IS EQUAL TO ";A
30 END
```

Note that the string in quotation marks includes a blank at the end. BASIC will print this blank and will begin the −5 in the first print position after the string. However, for negative numbers, BASIC does not insert an initial blank, so the screen would look like this:

THE VALUE OF A IS EQUAL TO −5

Test Your Understanding 4.1

Write a program which allows you to input two numbers. The program should then display them as an addition problem in the form: 5+7=12.

Horizontal Tabbing

You may begin a print item in any print position. To do this, use the **TAB** command. The print positions are numbered from 1 to 64, going from left to right. The statement TAB(7) means to move to print position 7. **TAB** is always used in conjunction with a **PRINT** statement. For example, the print statement

```
50 PRINT TAB(7) A
```

will print the value of the variable A, beginning in print position 7. It is possible to use more than one **TAB** per **PRINT** statement. For example, the statement

```
100 PRINT TAB(5) A; TAB(15) B
```

will print the value of A beginning in print position 5 and the value of B beginning in print position 15. Note the semicolon between the two **TAB** instructions.

In typing a **PRINT** statement, you may run out of room on the line. To get around this problem, end the **PRINT** statement with a semicolon and continue the list of print items in another **PRINT** statement on the next line. For example, consider the pair of statements:

```
100 PRINT "INVENTORY OF MEN'S SHOES";
110 PRINT, "INVENTORY OF LADIES SHOES"
```

The first line has a single print item. The semicolon indicates continued printing on the same line. The comma which begins the second **PRINT** statement moves printing to the beginning of the next print zone, where the string in line 110 is printed. Here is what the output looks like:

INVENTORY OF MEN'S SHOES   INVENTORY OF LADIES SHOES

Test Your Understanding 4.2

Write an instruction which prints the value of A in column 25 and the value of B seven columns further to the right.

Formatting Numbers

Model III BASIC has rather extensive provisions for formatting numerical output. Here are some of the things you may specify with regard to printing a number:

> Number of digits of accuracy
> Alignment of columns (one's column, ten's column, hundred's column, etc.)
> Display and positioning of initial dollar sign
> Display of comma in large numbers (as in 1,000,000)
> Display and positioning of + and − signs

All of these formatting options may be requested with the **PRINT USING** statement. Roughly speaking, you describe to the computer what you wish your number to look like by specifying a "prototype." For example, suppose you wish to print the value of the variable A with 4 digits to the left of the decimal point and two digits to the right. This could be done via the instruction:

```
10 PRINT USING ####.##; A
```

Here, each # stands for a digit and the period stands for the decimal point. If, for example, A was equal to 5432.381, this instruction would round the value of A to the specified two decimal places and would print the value of A as:

```
5432.38
```

On the other hand, if the value of A was 932.547, then the computer would print the value as:

```
 932.55
```

In this case, the value is printed with a leading blank space, since the format specified four digits to the right of the decimal point. This sort of printing is especially useful in aligning columns of figures like:

```
  367.1
 1567.2
29573.3
    2.4
```

The above list of numbers could be printed using the following program:

```
10 DATA 367.1, 1567.2, 29573.3, 2.4
20 FOR J=1 TO 4
30 READ A(J)
40 PRINT USING #####.#;A(J)
50 NEXT J
60 END
```

Test Your Understanding 4.3

Write an instruction which prints the number 456.75387 rounded to two decimal places.

You may use a single **PRINT USING** statement to print several numbers on the same line. For example, the statement

```
10 PRINT USING ##.##; A,B,C
```

will print the values of A, B, and C on the same line, all in the format ##.##. Only one space will be allowed between each of the numbers. Additional spaces may be added by using extra #s, If you wish to print numbers on one line in two different formats, then you must use two different **PRINT USING** statements, with the first ending in a ; to indicate a continuation on the same line.

If you try to display a number larger than the prototype, the number will be displayed preceded by %. For example, consider the statement:

```
10 PRINT USING ### ; A
```

If the value of A is 5000, then the display will look like:

%5000

Test Your Understanding 4.4

Write a program to calculate and display the numbers 2[J, J = 1, 2, 3, . . . , 15. The columns of the numbers should be properly aligned on the right.

You may have the computer insert a dollar sign on a displayed number. The following two statements illustrate the procedure:

```
10 PRINT USING $####.##; A
20 PRINT USING $$####.##;A
```

Suppose that the value of A is 34.78. Then the results of lines 10 and 20 will then be the display:

```
$  34.78
  $34.78
```

Note the difference between the displays produced by line 10 and 20. The single $ produces a dollar sign in the fifth position to the left of the decimal point. That is, just to the left of the four digits specified in the prototype ####.##. However, the $$ in line 20 indicates a "floating dollar sign." The dollar sign is printed in the first position to the left of the number without leaving any space.

Example 1. Here is a list of checks written by a certain family during the month of March.

$15.32, $387.00, $57.98, $3.47, $15.88

Print the list of checks on the screen with the columns properly aligned and the total displayed below the list of check amounts, in the form of an addition problem.

Solution. We first read the check amounts into an array A(J), J = 1, 2, 3, 4, 5. While we read the amounts, we accumulate the total in the variable B. We use a second loop to print the display in the desired format.

```
10 DATA 15.32, 387.00, 57.98, 3.47, 15.88
20 FOR J=1 TO 5
30 READ A(J)
40 B=B+A(J)
50 PRINT USING $###.##; A(J)
60 NEXT J
70 PRINT "_______"
80 PRINT USING $###.##; B
90 END
```

Here is what the output will look like:

```
$ 15.32
$387.00
$ 57.98
$   3.47
$ 15.88
-------
$479.65
```

Note that line 70 is used to print the line under the column of figures.

The **PRINT USING** statement has several other variations. To print commas in large numbers, insert a comma anywhere to the left of the decimal point. For example, consider the,statement:

10 PRINT USING ###,###; A

If the value of A is 123456, it will be displayed as:

123,456

The **PRINT USING** statement may also be used to position + and − signs in connection with displayed numbers. A + sign at the beginning or the end of a prototype will cause the appropriate sign to be printed in the position indicated. For example, consider the statement:

10 PRINT USING +####.###; A

Suppose that the value of A is −458.73. It will be displayed as:

4 spaces 3 spaces

− **458.730**

Similarly, consider the statement:

10 PRINT USING +###.##; A

Suppose that A has the value .05873. Then A will be displayed as

3 spaces 2 spaces

+ **.06**

Important Note. In the section, we have only mentioned output on the screen. However, all of the features mentioned may be used on a printer, if you have one. The appropriate instructions are **LPRINT** and **LPRINT USING**. Note, however, that the wider line of the printer allows display of more data than on the screen. In particular, there are more 16-character print fields (just how many depends on which printer you own), and you may TAB to a higher numbered column than on the screen.

Oversized Characters

The Model III has two character sizes: 64 characters per line and 32 characters per line. When the computer is first turned on, the display is initialized for 64 characters per line. To switch to 32 characters per line, type simultaneously **SHIFT** and [→]. From then on, the display will operate with 32 characters per line. The characters used are twice as wide as the usual characters, but of the same height.

To return to 64 characters per line, hit the **CLEAR** key while the computer is in the immediate mode (READY message displayed).

Note that it is not possible to simultaneously display characters of both sizes.

Some Other Variants of PRINT USING (Optional)

Here are several other things you can do with the **PRINT USING** statement. They are especially useful to accountants and those who are especially concerned with preparation of financial documents.

If you precede the prototype with **, it will cause all unused digit positions in a number to be filled with asterisks. For example, consider the statement:

```
10 PRINT USING **####.#;A
```

If A has the value 34.86, the value will be displayed as:

```
**34.9
```

Note that two asterisks are displayed since four digits to the left of the decimal point are specified in the prototype, but the value of A uses only two. The remaining two are filled with asterisks.

You may combine the action of ** and $. You should experiment with this combination. It is especially useful for printing dollar amounts of the form:

$*****387.98**

Such a format is especially useful in printing amounts on checks so as to prevent modification.

By using a − sign immediately after a prototype, you will print the appropriate number with a trailing minus sign if it is negative and with no sign if it is positive. Thus, for example, the statement

10 PRINT USING ####.##−; A

and A equal to −57.88 will result in the display:

57.88−

On the other hand, if A is equal to 57.88, the display will be:

57.88

This format for numbers is often used in preparing accounting reports.

EXERCISES (answers on 278)

Write programs which generate the following displays. The lines of dots are not meant to be displayed, but are furnished for you to judge spacing.

```
1. THE VALUE OF X IS 5.378
   . . . . . . . . . . . . . . . . .

2. THE VALUE OF X IS         5.378
   . . . . . . . . . . . .   . . . . .

3. DATE   QTY    @    COST    DISCOUNT     NET COST
   . . . .  . . .  .    . . . .    . . . . . . . .   . . . . . . .

4.   6.753
    15.111
   111.850
     6.702
   -------
             Calculate
             Sum
```

5.
```
$  12.82
$117.58
$   5.87
$     .99
$     .99
-------
         Calculate
         Sum
```

6. Date 3/18/81

   Pay to the Order of   Wildcatters, Inc.

   The sum of   *********$89,385.00

7.
```
  5,787
    387
127,486
 38,531
-------
         Calculate
         Sum
```

8.
```
 $385.41
-$17.85
-------
         Calculate
         Difference
```

9. Write a program which rounds a number to the nearest integer. For example, if the input is 11.7, the output is 12. If the input is 158.2, the output is 158. Your program should accept the number to be rounded via an INPUT statement.

10. Write a program which allows your computer to function as a cash register. Let the program accept purchase amounts via INPUT statements. Let the user tell the program when the list of INPUTs is complete. The program should then print out the purchase amounts, with dollar signs and columns aligned, compute the total purchase, add 5% sales tax, compute the total amount due, ask for the amount paid, and compute the change due.

11. Prepare the display of Exercise 6 using 32 characters per line.

Answers to Test Your Understanding

4.1:
```
10 INPUT A,B
20 PRINT A;"+";B;"=";A+B
30 END
```

4.2: 10 PRINT TAB(25) A;TAB(32) B

4.3: 10 PRINT USING ###.##; 456.7387

4.4:
```
10 FOR J=1 TO 15
20 PRINT USING ######; 2[J
30 NEXT J
40 END
```

3.5 GAMBLING WITH YOUR COMPUTER (ELEMENTARY LEVEL)

One of the most interesting features of your computer is its ability to generate events whose outcomes are "random." For example, you may instruct the computer to "throw a pair of dice" and produce a random pair of integers between 1 and 6. You may instruct the computer to "pick a card at random from a deck of 52 cards." You may program the computer to choose a two digit number "at random." And so forth. The source of all such random choices is the **random number generator** which is a part of BASIC. Let us begin by explaining what the random number generator is and how to access it. Then we will give a number of interesting applications involving computer-assisted instruction and games of chance.

You may generate random numbers using the BASIC function RND(X), where X is one of the numbers 0, 1, 2, 3, 4, ... (Later, we'll explain what the various choices of X mean.) To explain how this function works, let us consider the following program:

```
10 FOR J=1 TO 500
20 PRINT RND(0)
30 NEXT J
40 END
```

This program consists of a loop which prints the value of RND(0) 500 times. RND(0) is a number between 0.000000 (inclusive) and 1.000000 (exclusive). Each time RND(0) is called (that is, in line 20), the computer makes a "random" choice from among the numbers in the indicated range. This is the number that is printed.

To obtain a better idea of what we are talking about, you should generate some random numbers using a program like the one above. Unless you have a printer, 500 numbers will be too many for you to look at in one viewing. So you should print four random numbers on one line (one per print zone) and limit yourself to 16 displayed lines at one time. Here is a partial printout of such a program.

```
.245121    .305003    .311866    .515163
.984546    .901159    .727313    6.83401E–03
.896609    .660212    .554489    .818675
.583931    .448163    .86774     .0331043
.137119    .226544    .215274    .876763
```

What makes these numbers "random" is that the procedure the computer uses to select them is "unbiased," with all numbers having an equal likelihood of selection. Moreover, if you generate a large collection of random numbers, then numbers between 0 and .1 will comprise approximately 10% of those chosen, those between .5 and 1.0 will comprise 50% of those chosen, and so forth. In some sense, the random number generator provides a uniform sample of the numbers between 0 and 1. (Actually the numbers are only "pseudo-random numbers," but you need not concern yourself with this distinction.)

Test Your Understanding 5.1

Assume that RND(0) is used to generate 1,000 numbers. Approximately how many of these numbers do you expect would lie between .6 and .9?

The function RND(0) generates random numbers lying in the between 0 to 1. However, in many applications, we will require randomly chosen **integers** lying in a certain range. Model III BASIC has a built-in capability for producing such integers. For example, suppose that we wish to generate random integers chosen from among 1, 2, 3, 4, 5, 6. We could use the function RND(6). Similarly, to generate random integers lying between 1 and 100 inclusive, we use the function RND(100). The next example shows how to generate a game of chance using your computer.

Test Your Understanding 5.2

Generate random numbers from 0 to 1. (This is the computer analogue of flipping a coin: 0 = heads, 1 = tails.) Run this program to generate 50 coin tosses. How many heads and how many tails occur?

Example 1. Write a program which turns the computer into a pair of dice. Your program should report the number rolled on each as well as the total.

Solution. We will hold the value of die #1 in the variable X and the value of die #2 in variable Y. The program will compute values for X and Y, print out the values and the total X + Y.

```
5 RANDOM
10 CLS
20 LET X=RND(6)
30 LET Y=RND(6)
40 PRINT "LADIES AND GENTLEMEN, BETS PLEASE!"
50 INPUT "ARE ALL BETS DOWN(Y/N)"; A$
60 IF A$="Y" THEN 100 ELSE 40
100 PRINT "THE ROLL IS",X,Y
110 "PRINT "THE WINNING TOTAL IS " ; X+Y
120 INPUT "PLAY AGAIN(Y/N)"; B$
130 IF BS="Y" THEN 10 ELSE 200
200 PRINT "THE CASINO IS CLOSING. SORRY"
210 END
```

Note the use of computer-generated conversation on the screen. Note also, how the program uses lines 120–130 to allow the player to control how many times the game will be played. Finally, note the use of the command **RANDOM** in line 5. This requires some explanation.

The random number generator is controlled by a so-called "seed number" which determines which sequence of random numbers will be generated. When the random number generator is first accessed by a program, a standard seed number is used. This has the implication that the computer will always generate the same string of random numbers. Thus, for example, every dice game would begin in the same way! To prevent this, we use the command **RANDOM** to choose a random seed number. This, in effect, starts the random number generator at a random place, so that the output is completely unpredictable. You need use the command **RANDOM** only once in any given program.

You may enhance the realism of a gambling program by letting the computer keep track of bets, as in the following example.

Test Your Understanding 5.3

Write a program which flips a "biased" coin. Let it report "heads" one-third of the time and tails two-thirds of the time.

Example 2. Write a program which turns the computer into a roulette wheel. Let the computer keep track of bets and winnings for up to five players. For simplicity, assume that the only bets are on single numbers. (In the next section, we will let you remove this restriction!)

Solution. A roulette wheel has 34 positions: 1–32, 0 and 00. In our program, we will represent these as the numbers 1–34, with 33 corresponding to 0 and 34 corresponding to 00. A spin of the wheel will consist of choosing a random integer between 1 and 34. The program will start by asking the number of players. For a typical spin of the wheel, the program will ask for bets by each player. A bet will consist of a number (1–32, 0, 00) and an amount bet. The wheel will then spin. The program will determine the winners and losers. A payoff for a win is 32 times the amount bet. Each player has an account, stored in an array A(J), J = 1, 2, 3, 4. At the end of each spin, the accounts are adjusted and displayed. Just as in Example 1, the program asks if another play is desired. Here is the program.

```
2 CLEAR 200
5 RANDOM
10 INPUT "NUMBER OF PLAYERS";N
20 DIM A(5),B(5),C(5): "AT MOST 5 PLAYERS ALLOWED
25 LINES 30–60 ALLOW PLAYERS TO PURCHASE CHIPS
30 FOR J=1 TO N:   ' FOR EACH OF THE PLAYERS
40 PRINT "PLAYER "; J
50 INPUT "HOW MANY CHIPS"; A(J)
60 NEXT J
100 PRINT "LADIES AND GENTLEMEN! PLACE YOUR BETS PLEASE!"
110 FOR J=1 TO N :   ' FOR EACH OF THE PLAYERS
120 PRINT "PLAYER "; J
130 INPUT "NUMBER,AMOUNT"; B(J),C(J):"INPUT BET
140 IF B(J)=0 THEN 160
150 IF B(J)=00 THEN 170
155 GOTO 180
160 B(J)=33
165 GOTO 180
170 B(J)=34
180 NEXT J
200 X=RND(34):   'SPIN THE WHEEL
210 REM LINES 210-300DISPLAY THE WINNING NUMBER
220 PRINT "THE WINNER IS NUMBER"; X
230 IF X<=32 THEN 260
240 IF X=33 THEN 280
250 IF X=34 THEN 300
```

```
260 PRINT X
270 GO TO 310
280 PRINT 0
290 GO TO 310
300 PRINT 00
305 'DETERMINE WINNINGS AND LOSSES
310 FOR J=1 TO N :  'FOR EACH PLAYER
320 IF X=B(J) THEN 400 ELSE 330
330 A(J)=A(J)-C(J):  'PLAYER J LOSES. DEDUCT BET
340 PRINT "PLAYER ";J;"LOSES"
360 GO TO 420
400 A(J)=A(J)+32*C(J):  'PLAYER J WINS. ADD WINNINGS
410 PRINT "PLAYER ";J;"WINS "; 32*C(J); "DOLLARS"
420 NEXT J
430 PRINT "PLAYER BANKROLLS"
440 PRINT
450 PRINT "PLAYER", "CHIPS"
460 FOR J=1 TO N
470 PRINT J,A(J)
480 NEXT J
500 INPUT "DO YOU WTSH TO PLAY ANOTHER ROLL(Y/N)";R$
510 CLS
520 IF R$="Y" THEN 100
530 PRINT "THE CASINO IS CLOSED. SORRY!"
600 END
```

You should try a few spins of the wheel. The program is fun as well as instructive. Note that the program allows you to bet more chips than you have. We will leave it to the exercises to add in a test that there are enough chips to cover the bet. Alternatively, you could build lines of credit into the game!

You may treat the output of the random number generator as you would any other number. In particular, you may perform arithmetic operations on the random numbers generated. For example, 5*RND(0) multiplies the output of the random number generator by 5 and RND(0) + 2 adds 2 to the output of the random number generator. Such arithmetic operations are useful in producing random numbers from intervals other than 0 to 1. For example, suppose that you wish to select numbers randomly from the interval 0 to 5. Such numbers may be generated as 5*RND(0). Indeed, since RND(0) lies between 0 and 1, 5 times RND(0) lies between 0 and 5. Similarly, to generate random numbers between 2 and 3, we may use RND(0) + 2.

Example 3. Write a program which generates 10 random numbers lying in the interval from 5 to 8.

Solution. Let us build up the desired function in two steps. We start from the function RND(0), which generates numbers from 0 to 1. First, we adjust for the length of the desired interval. From 5 to 8 is 3 units, so we multiply RND(0) by 3. The function 3*RND(0) generates numbers from 0 to 3. Now we adjust for the starting point of the desired interval, namely 5. By adding 5 to 3*RND(0), we obtain numbers lying between 0 + 5 and 3 + 5, that is between 5 and 8. Thus, 3*RND(0) + 5 generates random numbers between 5 and 8. Here is the program required.

```
10 FOR J=I TO 10
20 PRINT 3*RND(0)+5
30 NEXT J
40 END
```

Example 4. Write a function to generate random integers from among 5, 6, 7, 8, . . . , 12

Solution. There are 8 consecutive integers possible. So let us start with the function RND(8), which generates the 8 consecutive integers 1, 2, . . . , 8. To adjust the starting integer 1 to the desired starting integer 5, we must add 4. So the desired function is RND(8) + 4.

EXERCISES (answers on 280)

Write BASIC functions which generate random numbers of the following sorts.

1. Numbers from 0 to 100
2. Numbers from 100 to 101
3. Integers from 1 to 50
4. Integers from 4 to 80
5. Even integers from 2 to 50
6. Numbers from 50 to 100
7. Integers divisible by 3 from 3 to 27
8. Integers from among 4,7,10,13,16,19,22

9. Modify the dice program so that it keeps track of payoffs and bankrolls, as in the roulette program of Example 2. Here are the payoffs on a bet of $1 for the various bets:

outcome	payoff
2	35
3	17
4	11
5	8
6	6.20
7	5
8	6.20
9	8
10	11
11	17
12	35

10. Modify the roulette program of Example 2 to check that a player has enough chips to cover the bet.

11. Modify the roulette program of Example 2 to allow for a 100 dollar line of credit for each player.

12. Construct a program which tests one digit arithmetic facts, with the problems randomly chosen by the computer.

13. Construct a program which tests multiplication facts, with the problems randomly chosen by the computer. Use the real-time clock to allow three levels of difficulty corresponding to 10, 5, and 3 second response times.

14. Make up a list of 10 names. Write a program which will pick four of the names at random. (This is a way of impartially assigning a nasty task!)

Answers to Test Your Understanding

5.1: 30%

5.2:
```
10 PRINT RND(2)-1
20 END
```

5.3:
```
10 LET X=RND(3)
20 IF X=1 THEN PRINT "HEADS" ELSE PRINT "TAILS"
30 END
```

3.6 SUBROUTINES

In writing programs, it is often necessary to use the same sequence of instructions more than once. It may not be convenient (or even feasible) to retype the set of instructions each time it is needed. Fortunately, BASIC offers a convenient alternative, namely the subroutine.

A **subroutine** is a program which is incorporated within another, larger program. The subroutine may be used any number of times by the larger program. Often, the lines corresponding to a subroutine are isolated toward the end of the larger program. This arrangement is illustrated in Figure 3-1. The arrows to the subroutine indicate the points in the larger program at which the subroutine is used. The arrows pointing away from the subroutine indicate that, after completion of the subroutine, execution of the main program resumes at the point at which it was interrupted.

Subroutines are handled with the pair of instructions **GOSUB** and **RETURN**. The statement

100 GOSUB 1000

sends the computer to the subroutine which begins at line 1000. The com-

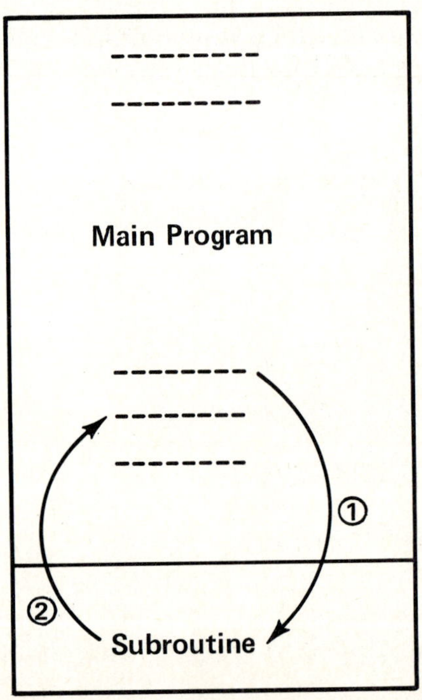

Figure 3-1. A subroutine.

puter starts at line 1000 and carries out statements in order. When a **RETURN** statement is reached, the computer goes back to the main program, starting at the first line after 100.

The next example illustrates the use of subroutines.

Example 1. Modify the roulette program of Example 5.2, so that it allows bets on EVEN and ODD. A one dollar bet on either of these pays one dollar in winnings.

Solution. Our program will now allow three different bets–on a number and on EVEN or ODD. Let us design subroutines, corresponding to each of these bets, which determine whether player J wins or loses. For each subroutine, let X be the number (1–34) which results from spinning the wheel. In the preceding program, a bet by player J was described by two numbers: B(J) = the number bet and C(J) = the amount bet. Now let us add a third number to describe a bet. Let D(J) = 1 if J bets on a number, 2 if J bets on EVEN, and 3 if J bets on ODD. In case D(J) is 2 or 3, we will again let C(J) equal the amount bet, but B(J) will be 0. The subroutine for determining the winners of bets on numbers can be obtained by making small modifications to the corresponding portion of our previous program, as follows:

```
1000 IF B(J)=X THEN 1100 ELSE 1010
1010 PRINT "PLAYER";J;"LOSES"
1020 A(J)=A(J)-C(J)
1030 RETURN
1100 PRINT "PLAYER";J;"WINS"; 32*C(J);"DOLLARS"
1110 A(J)=A(J)+32*(J)
1120 RETURN
```

Here is the subroutine corresponding to the bet EVEN.

```
2000 FOR K=0 TO 16
2010 IF X=2*K THEN 2100 ELSE 2020
2020 NEXT K
2030 PRINT "PLAYER";J;"LOSES"
2040 A(J)=A(J)-C(J)
2050 RETURN
2100 PRINT "PLAYER";J;"WINS";C(J);"DOLLARS"
2110 A(J)=A(J)+C(J)
2120 RETURN
```

Finally, here is the subroutine corresponding to the bet ODD.

```
3000 FOR K=0 TO 16
3010 IF X<>2*K THEN 3100 ELSE 3020
3020 NEXT K
3030 PRINT "PLAYER";J;"LOSES"
3040 A(J)=A(J)-C(J)
3050 RETURN
3100 PRINT "PLAYER";J;"WINS";C(J);"DOLLARS"
3110 A(J)=A(J)+C(J)
3120 RETURN
```

Now we are ready to assemble the subroutines together with the main portion of the program, which is almost the same as before. The only essential alteration is that we must now determine, for each player, which bet was placed.

```
2 CLEAR 200
5 RANDOM
10 INPUT "NUMBER OF PLAYERS";N
20 DIM A(5),B(5)C(5):   'AT MOST 5 PLAYERS ALLOWED
25 LINES 30–60 ALLOW PLAYERS TO PURCHASE CHIPS
30 FOR J=1 TO N:   'FOR EACH OF THE PLAYERS
40 PRINT "PLAYER"; J
50 INPUT "HOW MANY CHIPS"; A(J)
60 NEXT J
100 PRINT "LADIES AND GENTLEMEN! PLACE YOUR BETS PLEASE!"
110 FOR J=1 TO N:   'FOR EACH OF THE PLAYERS
120 PRINT "PLAYER"; J
121 PRINT "BET TYPE:1=NUMBER BET, 2=EVEN, 3=ODD"
122 INPUT "BET TYPE (1,2,OR 3)"; D(J)
123 IF D(J)=1 THEN 130 ELSE 124
124 INPUT "AMOUNT"; C(J)
125 GOTO 180
130 INPUT "NUMBER,AMOUNT"; B(J),C(J):   'INPUT BET
140 IF B(J)=0 THEN 160
150 IF B(J)=00 THEN 170
155 GOTO 180
160 B(J)=33
165 GOTO 180
170 B(J)=34
180 NEXT J
200 X=RND(34):   'SPIN THE WHEEL
210 LINES 210–300 DISPLAY THE WINNING NUMBER
220 PRINT "THE WINNER IS NUMBER";
```

```
230 IF X<=32 THEN 260
240 IF X=33 THEN 280
250 IF X=34 THEN 300
260 PRINT X
270 GOTO 310
280 PRINT 0
290 GOTO 310
300 PRINT 00
305 LINES 310–330:  'DETERMINE WINNINGS AND LOSSES
310 FOR J=1 TO N:  'FOR EACH PLAYER
320 IF D(J)=1 THEN GOSUB 1000
330 IF D(J)=2 THEN GOSUB 2000
335 IF D(J)=3 THEN GOSUB 3000
340 NEXT J
430 PRINT "PLAYER BANKROLLS"
440 PRINT
450 PRINT "PLAYER", "CHIPS"
460 FOR J=1 TO N
470 PRINT J,A(J)
480 NEXT J
500 INPUT "DO YOU WISH TO PLAY ANOTHER ROLL(Y/N)";R$
510 CLS
520 IF R$="Y" THEN 100
530 PRINT "THE CASINO IS CLOSED. SORRY!"
600 END
1000 IF B(J)=X THEN 1100 ELSE 1010
1010 PRINT "PLAYER";J;"LOSES"
1020 A(J)=A(J)-C(J)
1030 RETURN
1100 PRINT "PLAYER";J;"WINS"; 32*C(J);"DOLLARS"
1110 A(J)=A(J)+32*(J)
1120 RETURN
2000 FOR K=0 TO 16
2010 IF X=2*K THEN 2100 ELSE 2020
2020 NEXT K
2030 PRINT "PLAYER";J;"LOSES"
2040 A(J)=A(J)-C(J)
2050 RETURN
2100 PRINT "PLAYER";J;"WINS";C(J);"DOLLARS"
2110 A(J)=A(J)+C(J)
2120 RETURN
3000 FOR K=0 TO 16
3010 IF X<>2*K THEN 2100 ELSE 2020
3020 NEXT K
```

```
3030 PRINT "PLAYER";J;"LOSES"
3040 A(J)=A(J)-C(J)
3050 RETURN
3100 PRINT "PLAYER";J;"WINS";C(J);"DOLLARS"
3110 A(J)=A(J)+C(J)
3120 RETURN
```

Note how the subroutines helped to organize our programming. Each subroutine is easy to write since it is a small task and you have less to think about than when considering the entire program. If is always advisable to break a long program into a number of subroutines. Not only is it easier to write in terms of subroutines, but it is much easier to check the program and locate errors since the subroutines may be tested individually.

Test Your Understanding 6.1

Consider the following program.

```
10 GOSUB 500
20 A=5
500 B=7
510 GOSUB 600
600 C=9
700 RETURN
800 END
```

What is the line executed after line 700?

Example 2. Here are the production figures for the six assembly lines of a certain factory for January 1980 and January 1981. Calculate the percentage increase (decrease) for each assembly line and determine the assembly line with the largest percentage increase:

Assembly Line	January 1980	January 1981
1	235,485	239,671
2	298,478	301,485
3	328,946	322,356
4	315,495	318,458
5	198,487	207,109
6	204,586	221,853

Solution. Let us plan this program in terms of subroutines. Let us store the January 1980 data in the array A(J) and the January 1981 data in the array

B(J), J = 1, 2, 3, 4, 5, 6. Our first step will be to read the data into the arrays from **DATA** statements. The second step will be to calculate the percentage increase (decrease) for each assembly line. This will be done by using a subroutine which we will put beginning at line 1000. We will store the percentage increases in the array C(J), J = 1, 2, 3, 4, 5, 6. Finally, we will determine which of the numbers C(J) is the largest. Let this calculation be carried out in a subroutine beginning in line 2000. We will let K be the number of the assembly line with largest percentage increase. Then we can write our program as follows:

```
10 DIM A(6),B(6),C(6)
20 DATA 235485, 239671, 298478, 301485
30 DATA 328946, 322356, 315495, 318458
40 DATA 198487, 207109, 204586, 221853
50 FOR J=1 TO 6:   'READ ARRAYS
60 READ A(J), B(J)
70 NEXT J
80 FOR J=1 TO 6:   'COMPUTE PERCENT INCREASES
90 GOSUB 1000
100 NEXT J
200 PRINT "ASSEMBLY LINE","PERCENT INCREASE"
210 FOR J=1 TO 6:   'DISPLAY PERCENT INCREASES
220 PRINT J, C(J)
230 NEXT J
300 GOSUB 2000:   'DETERMINE LARGEST PERCENT INCREASE
310 PRINT "ASSEMBLY LINE",K,"IS THE WINNER"
400 END
```

The above program is not complete. It is still necessary to complete the subroutines in lines 1000 and 2000. The point we wish to make, however, is that the use of subroutines allowed us to organize the program and to plan it so that programming may be done in small steps. It is now possible to write the subroutines without worrying about the program in its entirety. In order for you to obtain some practice, we will leave construction of the two subroutines for the exercises. (If you are impatient, you may look at the answers!)

Here is a useful variation of the **GOSUB** statement. Suppose that you wish to use the subroutine beginning at line 100 if the value of J is 1, the subroutine beginning at line 500 if the value of J is 2, and the subroutine beginning at line 1000 if the value of J is 3. This complex set of decisions can be requested by a simple statement of the form:

```
10 ON J GOSUB 100,500,1000
```

If the value of J is 1, then the program goes to line 100; if the value of J is 2, then the program goes to line 500; if the value of J is 3, then the program goes to line 1000. If J is not an integer, then any fractional part will be ignored. For example, if the value of J is 5.5, then the value 5 will be used. After dropping the fractional part, the value must be between 0 and 255 or an error will occur. If the value of J does not correspond to a given subroutine (for example, if J is 0 or more than 3 in the above example), then the instruction will be ignored. Instead of J, we could use any valid expression, such as J[2 + 3 or 3*J − 2. The expression will be evaluated and all of the above rules apply.

EXERCISES (answers on 281)

1. Write a subroutine which computes the value of 5*J[2 − 3*J. Incorporate it in a program to evaluate the given expression at J = .1, .2, .3, .4, .5.
2. Write the subroutine of Example 2 which computes the percentage rates of change for each assembly line. You may use the formula:

   <% rate of change>

   = 100 × (<Jan.1981 Prod.>−<Jan.1980 Prod.>)/<Jan.1980 Prod.>
3. Write the subroutine of Example 2 which determines the largest percentage increase. Hint: Let the variable M hold the largest number among C(1), . . . , C(6). Initially set M to C(1). Successively compare M (that is C(1)) to C(2), C(3), . . . , C(6)). After each comparison, replace M by the larger of M and what it is compared to. At the end of 5 comparisons, M will contain the largest among C(1), C(2), . . . , C(6). You may then determine which assembly line that value of M belongs to. That is, is the final value of M equal to C(1), C(2), C(3), C(4), C(5), or C(6)? For example, if M equals C(5), then assembly line 5 has the largest percentage increase.
4. Run the program of Example 2 with the subroutines in place.
5. Modify the roulette program of Example 1 to allow the following bets: first 12 (1–12), second 12 (13–24), and third 12 (25–36). A winning one dollar bet of this type pays two dollars. In adding these bets, you may find the ON . . . GOSUB instruction convenient.

Answer to Test Your Understanding

6.1: 600

4

Easing the Frustrations of Programming

As you have probably discovered by now, programming can be a tricky and frustrating business. First, you must figure out the instructions to give the computer. Next, you must type the instructions into RAM. Finally, you must run the program and, usually on the first run, figure out why your program will not work. This process can be tedious and frustrating, especially in dealing with long or complex programs. Fortunately, however, your computer has a number of features which are designed to ease some of the burdens of programming and help you in tracking down errors and correcting them. In this chapter, we will describe these features. In addition, we will present some further tips which should help you develop your programs more quickly and with fewer errors.

4.1 USING THE LINE EDITOR

Suppose that you discover a program line with an error in it. How can you correct it? Up to this point, the only way was to retype the line. However, there is a much better way. The Model III has a powerful *line editor* which allows you to add, delete, or change text in existing program lines. This section is designed to make you proficient in the use of the editor.

Entering Edit Mode. The line editor may be used to make changes only to the program currently in RAM. Moreover, as its name indicates, the line editor, allows you to make changes on any specified line, where a line is designated by its line number. To initiate the line editor type **EDIT** followed by the line number to be corrected and **ENTER.** For example, to correct line

50, you would type:

EDIT 50

followed by **ENTER.** Note that this command is a system command and therefore does not use a line number. The computer will respond to this command by displaying the line number followed by a space and the cursor:

50 ▮

The computer is now in *edit mode*. While in this special mode, many of the keys take on special roles and the video display operation is slightly altered. During the current session with the editor, you may make changes only in line 50. To edit some other line, you must first exit from the edit mode and re-enter it using the other line number.

Operation of the Editor

The editor can perform three sorts of operations:

A. *Editing Operations*. These operations add, delete, or change characters.

B. *Cursor Positioning*. The position of the cursor indicates the character position at which an editing operation is to be performed.

C. *Control Operations*. These operations can be used to record or cancel changes already made.

A Typical Session With the Editor. Suppose that the current version of line 100 reads as follows:

100 PRIMT X

The word PRIMT must be corrected to read PRINT. To make the correction, we first call the editor by typing:

EDIT 100

The computer displays:

100 ▮

The next step is to position the cursor on the M. We can do this by typing

1SM

The letter S indicates that the editor should Search; the 1 and M indicate that the search should be for the first occurrence of the letter M. Note that the command itself will not be displayed. Rather, the cursor will move over to the first occurrence of the letter M and the display will look like this:

100 PRI█

We are now prepared to make the correction. We wish to change 1 letter, beginning at the cursor position. The command for this is 1C. We wish to change the letter to N. So we type the command:

1CN

Again, the command does not show on the display. Instead, the display is altered to:

100 PRIN█

To terminate the edit mode, type **ENTER.** The entire line (with the change) will now be displayed:

100 PRINT X

Moreover, the changed line has been inserted into the program. As you can see, the editor is quite easy to use. With a little practice, you will become quite adept at using it to fashion program lines to your specifications.

Cursor Positioning Instructions

SPACEBAR. This key moves the cursor one character to the right and uncovers any character which was under the cursor. For example, consider the line 100 from above. Suppose that the display reads:

100 █

Hitting the **SPACEBAR** will result in the display:

100 P█

To move the cursor 2 spaces to the right, we may hit the keys:

2 SPACEBAR

In the above example, this will result in the display:

100 PRI▮

[←] The backspace key moves the cursor to the left. For example, let's continue with the last display. Hitting the backspace key will result in the following display:

100 PR▮

The letter I is no longer displayed. Note, however, that this letter has not been erased. *In the edit mode the backspace key does not erase*. We may backspace any number of spaces. For example, to backspace 2 spaces, we type:

2 [←]

The last display will be altered as follows:

100 ▮

nSc. This instruction moves the cursor to the nth occurrence of the character c. Searching begins from the current cursor position and goes to the end of the line. If you do not specify a value for n, then the first occurrence is assumed. Thus, for example, 2S, searches for the second occurrence of a comma, whereas Sa searches for the first occurrence of a. Suppose, for example, that we are editing line 200 which reads:

200 IF X>5.5 THEN 450 ELSE END

The initial display will read:

200 ▮

The command S5 will change the display to:

200 IF X>▮

The further command 2S5 will change the display to:

200 IF X>5.5 THEN 4▮

The further command SX will change the display to:

200 IF X>5.5 THEN 450 ELSE END▮

(There were no characters X to the right of the cursor.)

Editing Commands

Here are the commands which may be used to insert, delete, and change text. All these commands refer to text positioned beginning at the current cursor position.

Delete (**nD**). This command deletes the n characters beginning with the current cursor position. For example, consider the line 200 from our discussion above. Suppose that the cursor has been positioned so that the display reads:

200 IF X>5.5 ▮

The command 3D will change the display to read:

200 IF X>5.5 !THE!▮

Note that the three letters THE are enclosed between exclamation points. This indicates that these three letters are to be deleted. It is mildly confusing to see the deleted letters still on the screen. However, seeing them allows you to approve of the change before committing yourself to it. (For changing your mind, see below.)

Change (**nC**). This command changes n characters beginning with the current character position. For example, let's go back to the original version of line 200. Suppose that we moved the cursor to create the display:

200 IF X>▮

Suppose we wish to change the next three characters (5.5) to read 100. We first type the command 3C to indicate that we wish to change the next three characters. Then we type the desired characters (100). The new display will read:

200 IF X>100█

Insert (**I**). This command allows you to insert characters beginning at the current cursor position. For example, consider the display we have just created. Suppose that we wish to change the number 100 to 100500. That is, we wish to add the characters 500 beginning at the current cursor position. Type the command **I** and then type the characters to be inserted. The display will read as follows:

200 IF X>100500█

At this point, you have two choices. First, you may terminate the edit mode by typing **ENTER.** Second, you may end the **I** command by typing **SHIFT** and [↑] simultaneously. Using the latter command sequence you will remain in edit mode, with the cursor positioned as in the current display.

Extend Line (**E**). It is often necessary to add characters at the end of a line. This might occur, for example, if you wish to add : followed by another instruction (whose omission you discovered in trying to run your program). For example, suppose you wish to add to the most current version of line 200 the characters : PRINT M , S . Type the command **E.** The cursor will automatically move to the end of the line and the display will read:

100 IF X>100500 THEN 450 ELSE END█

We now type the characters to be appended to the line. Here is the new display:

100 IF X>100500 THEN 450 ELSE END: PRINT M, S█

We may now either terminate the edit mode (by typing **ENTER**) or remain in the edit mode by typing **SHIFT** [↑]. In the latter case, we could perform further editing on the current line.

Hack (**H**). This command enables you to hack off the portion of the line beginning at the current cursor position. For example, consider the most recent version of line 200. Suppose we now wish to delete all material beginning with the word THEN. Position the cursor at the T and type the command **H.** The display will not change, but the computer will delete the characters:

THEN 450 ELSE 800: PRINT M, S

You may now insert any characters after the portion of the line remaining. For example, if we now type THEN 100: READ A,B, the display will read:

200 IF X>100500 THEN 100: READ A,B█

You may exit from the Hack command by typing either **ENTER** (in which case you will exit from the edit mode) or **SHIFT** ↑ (in which case you will remain in the edit mode and can perform further editing on the current line.)

Kill (**nKc**). This command is similar to the delete command. It instructs the computer to delete all characters from the current cursor position to the nth occurrence of the character c. For example, consider the latest version of line 200. Suppose that the display currently reads:

200 IF X>█

Suppose that we wish to delete the number 100500. Since there are 4 zeros between the current cursor position and the end of the text to be deleted, we use the command 4K0. This display will now read:

200 IF X>!100500!█

Note that the deleted characters are enclosed in exclamation marks. If we now terminate the editing session by typing **ENTER,** line 200 will read:

200 IF X> THEN 100: READ A,B

Instead, however, let us add the number 750 at the current cursor position via the **I** command. The display will now read:

200 IF X>750█

Moreover, line 200 actually reads:

200 IF X>750 THEN 100: READ A,B

Edit Control Commands. These line editor commands do not do editing functions, but rather perform useful management functions while in edit mode.

ENTER. This command terminates the edit mode. All changes in the current line are recorded in the current program.

Cancel and Start Again (**A**). This command cancels all changes since the start of the editing session and positions the cursor as at the start of the session. Note that this may not be given while you are in the middle of an editing operation such as **I**, **H** or **X**. You must terminate any such operations using **SHIFT** [↑] before giving the command **A**.

Exit (**E**). End editing and save all changes made. This command may not be given in the middle of an editing operation. (See comment under command **A.**)

Quit (**Q**). End editing and cancel all changes since the start of the editing session.

List Line (**L**). List the line being edited. This command may be used in the edit mode when you are not in the middle of an editing operation. (See comment under command **A.**) It displays the current version of the line being edited and positions the cursor as at the beginning of an editing session.

EXERCISES

What is an editing instruction(s) to do to the following?

1. Move the cursor to the 4th letter q.
2. Delete the 4th letter q to the right of the cursor.
3. Insert the characters 538 at the current cursor position.
4. Delete the portion of the line to the right of the cursor position.
5. Move the cursor to the left 8 spaces.
6. Move the cursor to the right 3 spaces.
7. List the current version of the line.
8. Change the 4th 0 to a 1.
9. Delete the 8th letter a.
10. Cancel all changes and exit edit mode.

Use the line editor to make the indicated changes in the following program line. The exercises are to be done consecutively.

300 FOR M=11 TO 99, SETP .5 : X=M[2−5

11. Delete the , .
12. Correct the misspelling of the word STEP.
13. Change M[2 − 5 to M[3 − 2.
14. Change .5 to −1.5
15. Add the following characters to the end of the line. : Y = M + 1

4.2 FLOW CHARTING

In the last two chapters, our programs, for the most part, were fairly elementary, although by the end of Chapter 3 we saw them becoming more involved. However, there are many programs which are much more lengthy and complex. You might be wondering how it is possible to plan and execute such programs. Well, the key idea is to reduce large programs to a sequence of smaller programs which can be written and tested separately.

The old saying "A picture is worth a thousand words." is equally applicable to programming. In designing a program, especially a long program, it is helpful to draw a picture which depicts the instructions of the program and their interrelationships. Such a picture is called a *flowchart*.

A flowchart is a series of boxes connected by arrows. Within each box is a series of one or more computer instructions. The arrows indicate the logical flow of the instructions. For example, consider the following flowchart, which depicts a program for calculating the sum 1 + 2 + 3 + . . . + 100. The arrows indicate the sequence of operations. Note that the third box contains the notation J = 1, 2, . . . , 100. This notation indicates a loop on the variable J. That is, the operation in the box is to be repeated 100 times for J = 1, 2, . . . , 100. Note how easy it is to proceed from the above flowchart to the corresponding BASIC program:

10 LET S=0 (box 2)
20 FOR J=1 TO 100
30 LET S=S+J (box 3)
40 NEXT J
50 PRINT S (box 4)
60 END (box 5)

There are many flowcharting conventions regarding, for example, the shapes of boxes representing particular operations. However, we will adopt

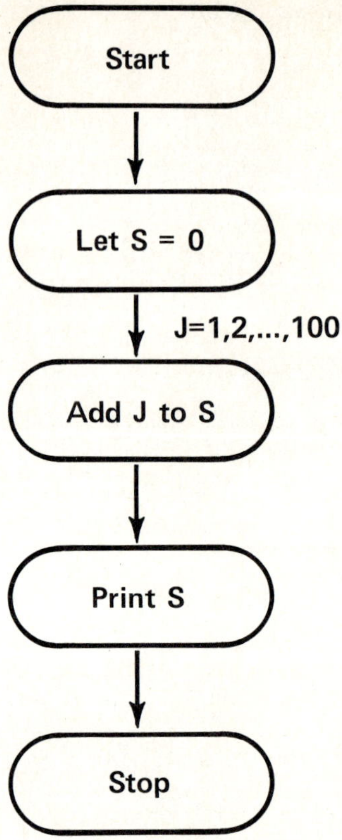

Figure 4-1.

a very simple rule that all boxes are rectangular, except for decision boxes, which are diamond-shaped. The following flowchart depicts a program which decides whether a credit limit has been exceeded.

Note that the diamond-shaped block contains the decision "Is D > L"? Corresponding to the two possible answers to the question, there are two arrows leading from the decision box. Note also how we used the various boxes to help assign letters to the program variables. Once the flowchart is written, it is easy to transform it into the following program:

```
10 INPUT C
20 INPUT#-1 D,L
30 LET D=D+C
40 IF D>L THEN 100 ELSE 200
100 PRINT "CREDIT DENIED"
110 LET D=D-C
120 GOTO 300
200 PRINT "CREDIT OK"
300 END
```

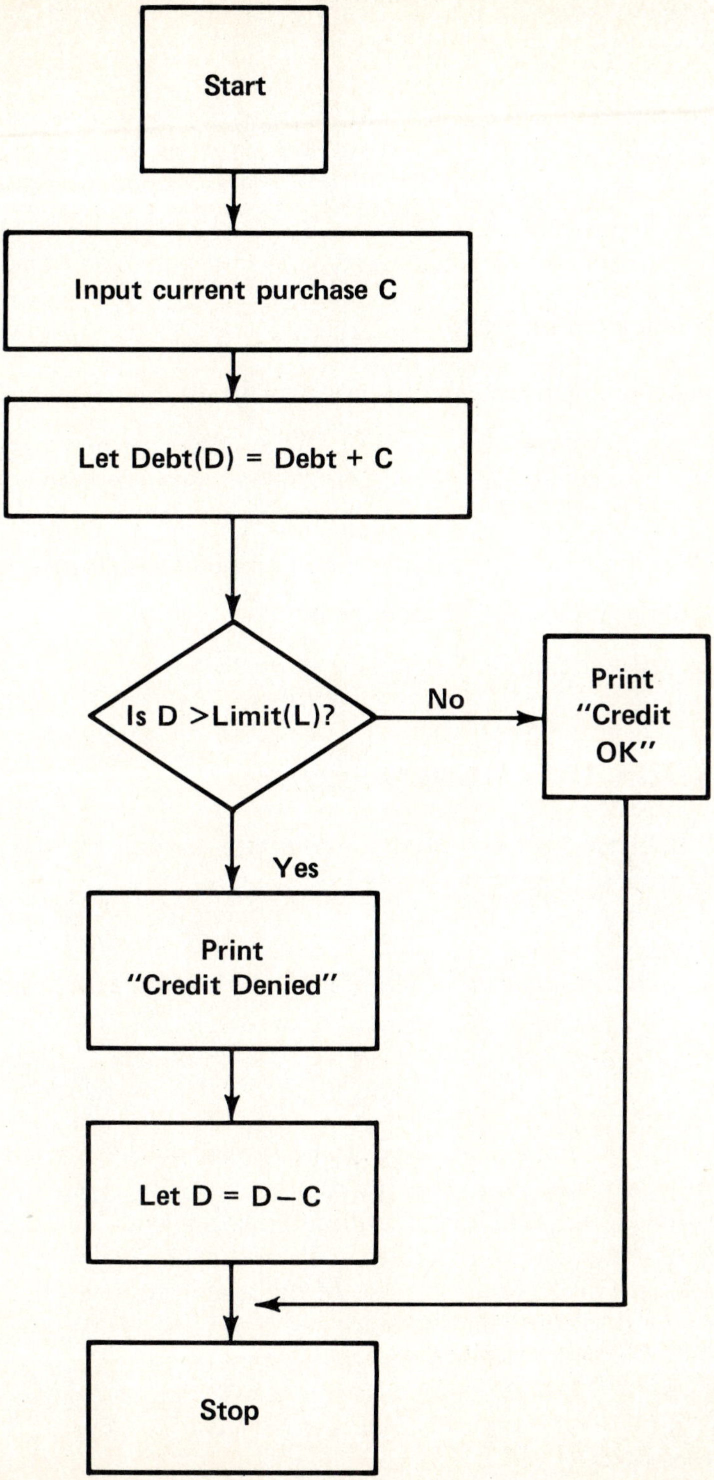
Start
Input current purchase C
Let Debt(D) = Debt + C
Is D >Limit(L)?
No
Print "Credit OK"
Yes
Print "Credit Denied"
Let D = D – C
Stop

Figure 4-2.

(Line 20 reads the values of L and C from a cassette file. More about that in Chapter 5.)

You will find flowcharting helpful in thinking out the necessary steps of a program. As you do more of it, you will develop your own style and conventions. That's fine. I support all personalized touches, provided they are comfortable and helpful *to you*.

EXERCISES (answers on 283)

Draw a flowchart to plan computer programs to do the following.

1. Calculate the sum $1^2 + 2^2 + . . . + 100^2$, print the result, and determine whether the result is larger than, smaller than, or equal to 487^3.
2. Calculate the time elapsed since the computer was turned on.
3. The roulette program of Section 3.6.
4. The payroll program in Example 2 of Section 3.2.

4.3 ERRORS AND DEBUGGING

An error is sometimes called a "bug" in computer jargon, and the process of finding the errors in a program is called *debugging*. This can sometimes be a ticklish task. Witness the fact that even manufacturers of commercial software must regularly repair bugs they discover in their programs. Your Model III is equipped with a number of features to assist in detecting bugs.

The Trace

Often your first try at running a program results in failure, but gives no indication as to why the program is not running correctly. For example, your program might just run indefinitely, without giving you a clue as to what it is actually doing. How can you analyze such mishaps? One method is to use the *trace* feature. To illustrate the use of the trace, consider the following program designed to calculate the sum 1 + 2 + . . . + 100.

```
10 LET S=0
20 LET J=0
30 LET S=S+J
```

```
40 IF J=100 THEN 100 ELSE 200
100 LET J=J+1
110 GOTO 20
200 PRINT S
300 END
```

This program has two errors in it. (Can you spot them right off?) However, all you know initially is that the program is not functioning normally. The program runs, but prints out the answer 0, which we recognize as nonsense. How can we locate the errors? Let's turn on the trace function by typing TRON (TRace ON). The computer will respond by typing READY. Now type RUN. The computer will run our program and print out the line numbers of all executed instructions. Here is what our display looks like:

```
TRON
READY

RUN
<10> <20> <30> <40> <200> 0
<300>
```

The numbers in brackets indicate the line numbers executed. That is, the computer executes, in order, lines 10, 20, 30, 40, 200, and 300. The 0 not in brackets is the output of the program resulting from execution of line 200. The list of line numbers is not what we were expecting. Our program was designed (or so we thought) to execute line 100 after line 40. There is no looping going on. But how did we get to line 200 after line 40? This suggests that we examine line 40. Lo and behold! There is an error. The line numbers 100 and 200 appearing in line 40 have been interchanged (an easy enough mistake to make). Let's correct this error by retyping the line.

```
40 IF J=100 THEN 200 ELSE 100
```

In triumph, we run our program again. Here is the output:

```
<10> <20> <30> <40> <100> <110> <20> <30>
<40> <100> <110> <20> <30> <40> <100> <110>
<20> <30> <40> <100>
BREAK IN 110
```

Actually, the above output goes whizzing by us as the computer races madly on executing the instructions. After about 30 seconds, we sense that something is indeed wrong since it is unlikely that our program could take that long. So we stop execution by means of the Break key. The last line indicates that we interrupted the computer while it was executing line 110. Actually your screen will be filled with output resembling the above. You notice that the computer is in a loop. Each time it reaches line 110, it goes back to line 20. Why doesn't the loop ever end? In order for the loop to terminate, J must equal 100. Well, can J ever equal 100? Of course not! Every time the computer executes line 20, the value of J is reset to 0. Thus, J is never equal to 100 and line 40 always sends us back to line 20. We clearly do not want to always reset J to 0. After increasing J by 1 (line 100), we wish to add the new J to S. That is, we want to go to 30, not 20. So we correct line 110 to read:

```
110 GOTO 30
```

Now we **RUN** our program yet another time. There will be a rush of line numbers on the screen followed by the output 5050, which appears to be correct. Our program is now running properly. We now turn off the trace by typing **TROFF** (TRace OFF). Finally, we run our program once more for good measure. The above sequence of operations is summarized in the following display:

```
<40> <200> 5050
<300>
READY

TROFF
READY

RUN
5050
READY
```

Error Messages

In the example above, the program actually ran. A more likely occurrence is that execution is prematurely terminated by the computer due to one of the many errors it is trained to recognize. In this case, the computer will print an error message indicating the error type and the line number in which it occurred. You should immediately **LIST** the indicated line and attempt to determine the source of the error. For example, suppose that the error reads:

```
SYNTAX ERROR IN LINE 530
```

To analyze the error, you type

LIST 530

resulting in the display:

530 LET Y=(X+2(X[2−2)

We note that there is an open parenthesis (without a corresponding close parenthesis). This is enough to trigger an error. So we modify line 530 to read:

530 LET Y=X+2(X[2−2)

We **RUN** the program again and find that there is still a syntax error in line 530! This is the frustrating part, since not all errors are easy to spot. However, if you look closely at the expression on the right, you will note that we have omitted the * to indicate the product of 2 and (X[2−2). This is an extremely common mistake, especially for those facile in algebra. (In algebra the product is usually indicated without any operation sign.) We correct line 530 again. (You may either retype the line or use the line editor.)

530 LET Y=X+2*(X[2−2)

Now we find that there is no longer a syntax error in line 530!

The appendix to this chapter contains a list of the Model III error messages.

EXERCISES (answers on 285)

1. Use the Model III error messages to debug the following program to calculate $(1^2 + 2^2 + \ldots + 50^2)(1^3 + 2^3 + \ldots + 20^3)$.

```
10 LET S="0"
20 FOR J=1 TO 100
30 S=S+J(2
40 NEXT K
50 LET T=0
60 FOR J=1 TO 30
70 LET T=T+J[3
80 NXT T
90 NEXT T
100 LET A=ST
110 PRINT THE ANSWER IS, A
120 END
```

2. Use the trace function to debug the following program to determine the smallest integer N for which N^2 is larger than 175263.

```
10 LET N=0
20 IF N[2>175263 THEN 100
30 PRINT "THE FIRST N EQUALS"
100 N=N+1
110 GOTO 10
200 END
```

4.4 APPENDIX—MODEL III ERROR MESSAGES

Each error recognized by the Model III has a numerical code and a two letter abbreviation. Let us briefly describe each of the errors and some possible conditions which can cause them. After the name of each error, we list, in parentheses, the numerical code and abbreviation.

Syntax Error (2; SN)

Unrecognizable instruction (misspelled?), mismatched parentheses, incorrect punctuation, illegal character, illegal variable name.

Undefined Line (7; UL)

The program uses a line number which does not correspond to an instruction. This can easily occur as a result of deleting lines which are mentioned elsewhere. It can also occur when testing a portion of a program which refers to a line not yet written.

Overflow (5;OV)

Number too large for the computer.

Division by Zero (11; /0)

Attempt to divide by 0. This may be hard to spot. The computer will round to 0 any number smaller than the minimum allowed. Use of such a number in subsequent calculations could result in division by 0.

Illegal Function Call (5;FC)

Attempt to evaluate a function outside of its mathematically defined range. For example, the square root function is defined only for non-negative arguments, the logarithm function only for positive arguments and the arctangent only for arguments between −1 and 1. Any attempt to evaluate a function at a value outside these respective ranges will result in an FC error.

Missing Operand (21; MO)

Attempt to execute an instruction missing required data.

Subscript Out of Range (9; BS)

Attempt to use an array element with one or more subscripts outside the range allowed by the appropriate DIM statement.

String Too Long (15; LS)

Attempt to specify a string containing more than 255 characters.

Out of Memory (6;OM)

Your program will not fit in memory. Could result from large arrays or too many programs, steps or a combination.

Out of String Space (14;OS)

Attempt to use more string space than was allocated by CLEAR. (If no CLEAR instruction is used, string space is limited to 50 characters.)

String Formula Too Complex (16;ST)

Due to the internal processing of your formula, your string formula resulted in too complex or too long a string expression. This error can be rectified by breaking the string expression into a series of simpler expressions.

Type Mismatch (13; TM)

Attempt to assign a string constant as the value of a numeric variable or a numeric constant to a string variable.

Redimensioned Array (9;DD)

Attempt to DIMension an array which has already been dimensioned. Note that once you refer to an array within a program, even if you do not specify the dimensions, the computer will regard it as dimensioned at 10.

NEXT without FOR (1;NF)

A NEXT statement which does not correspond to a FOR statement.

RETURN without GOSUB (3;RG)

A RETURN statement encountered while not in a subroutine.

Out of Data (4;OD)

Attempt to read data which is not there. This can occur in reading data from DATA statements, cassettes, or diskettes.

Bad File Data (22;FD)

File data from a cassette or disk does not match the program. (For example, a string constant is read when a numerical constant is expected.)

Disk BASIC Only (L3;23)

Attempt to use a disk BASIC command when running Model III BASIC.

Can't Continue (17;CN)

Attempt to give a CONT command after the program has ENDed or before the program has been RUN (such as after an EDIT session).

5

Your Computer as a File Cabinet

In the preceding chapters, we learned the fundamentals of programming the Model III. However we avoided any substantive discussion of the two devices available for mass storage: the cassette and the disk file. In this chapter, we will discuss the operation of these two devices and their application to writing and reading program and data files. In Section 5.1, we will discuss the difference between program files and data files. Section 5.2 is devoted to cassette operations. Sections 5.3, 5.4, and 5.5 provide an introduction to disk operations.

5.1 WHAT ARE DATA FILES?

Computer programs used in business and industry usually refer to files of information which are stored within the computer. For example, a personnel department would keep a file of personal data on each employee containing name, age, address, social security number, date employed, position, salary, and so forth. A warehouse would maintain an inventory. For each product, the following information might be maintained: name of product, supplier, current inventory, units sold in the last reporting period, date of last shipment, size of last shipment, and units sold in last 12 months. Files of the sort just described are called *data files*. In actual applications, they could contain hundreds, thousands, or even hundreds of thousands of entries.

Data files are usually stored in one of the mass storage devices available: in the case of the Model III, either cassette or diskette. Such files are to be distinguished from *program files*, which result from saving programs. Program files and data files exist side by side in mass storage.

To obtain a better idea of how a file is organized within mass storage, let's consider the following example. Suppose that a teacher stores his grades in a data file. For each student in his class, there are four exam grades. Then a typical entry in the data file would contain the following data items:

student name, exam grade #1, exam grade #2,

exam grade #3, exam grade #4

In a data file, the data items are organized in sequence. So, for example, the beginning of the above data file might look like this:

"John Smith", 98, 87, 93, 76, "Mary Young",

99, 78, 87, 91, "Sally Ronson", 48, 63, 72,

80, . . .

That is, the data file consists of a sequence of either string constants (the names) or numeric constants (the grades), with the various data items arranged in a particular pattern (name followed by four grades). The particular arrangement is designed so that the file may be read and understood. For instance, in the above example, if we read the data items, we know in advance that the data items are in groups of five with the first one a name and the next four the corresponding grades. In order to be able to know where one data item ends and another begins, consecutive data items must be separated by characters called *delimiters*. Our files recognize as delimiters spaces, commas, form feed, and ENTER. (More about inserting delimiters later in this chapter.)

Your Model III has facilities for reading data from a data file during program execution, so that the information in the data file may be utilized within the program. For example, a personnel department might have a program which (1) enters changes in the personnel data file and (2) displays requested information about a given employee. To perform task (1), the program would read the personnel data file, alter the relevant items and rewrite the file into mass storage. To perform task (2), the program would read the data file, search for the requested information and display it on the screen or printer. In effect, your computer is serving as a convenient file cabinet for the storage of data. Moreover, the programming capability of the computer allows you to easily "shuffle through" the data for a specific piece of information.

In this chapter, we will discuss the mechanics of setting up, writing, and reading data files. We will also take this opportunity to introduce the operation and use of disk files and the features of Disk BASIC.

5.2 DATA FILES—FOR CASSETTE USERS

Let us now describe the process of creating a data file on a cassette. For general information on operation of the cassette recorder, you should refer back to the Appendix to Chapter 2.

To send output to the cassette recorder, we use the instruction **PRINT #–1.** This instruction is very similar to the **PRINT** and **LPRINT** instructions, which send output to the display and printer, respectively. For example, suppose that you wish to output the string constants "Employee", "Soc. Sec. Number", and "Hourly Rate". This could be done via the instruction:

```
10 PRINT #-1 "EMPLOYEE","SOC. SEC. NUMBER","HOURLY RATE"
```

Similarly, to output the values of the variables A1, A2, and B$ to the cassette, we use the instruction:

```
20 PRINT #-1 A1, A2, B$
```

The **PRINT #–1** instruction automatically inserts the necessary delimiter between the data items. For cassette data files, you do not need to worry at all about delimiters.

Example 1. Create a data file which consists of names, addresses, and telephone numbers drawn from your personal telephone directory. Assume that you will type the addresses into the computer and will tell the computer when the last address has been typed.

Solution. We use **INPUT** statements to enter the various data. Let A$ denote the name of the current person, B$ the street address, C$ the city , D$ the state, E$ the zip code, and F$ the telephone number. For each entry, there is an **INPUT** statement corresponding to each of these variables. The program then writes the data to the cassette. Here is the program:

```
5 CLEAR 5000
10 INPUT "NAME"; A$
20 INPUT "STREET ADDRESS"; B$
30 INPUT "CITY"; C$
40 INPUT "STATE"; D$
50 INPUT "ZIP CODE"; E$
60 INPUT "TELEPHONE"; F$
70 PRINT #-1 A$, B$, C$, D$, E$, F$
80 INPUT "ANOTHER ENTRY (Y/N)"; G$
90 IF G$="Y" THEN 10 ELSE END
100 END
```

You should set up such a computerized telephone directory of your own. It is instructive and it will be useful when coupled with the search program given below, which will allow you to look up addresses and phone numbers using your computer and the data file you have created.

Test Your Understanding 2.1

Use the above program to enter the following address into the file.

John Jones
1 South Main St., Apt. 308
Phila. Pa. 19107
527-1211

In setting up a data file, you should always note the reading of the tape counter at the beginning of the file. This is to allow you to subsequently find the file to read it. You should set up the cassette recorder according to the instructions already given. To write on the cassette, you press both the PLAY and RECORD buttons on the recorder. Whenever the computer encounters a **PRINT #–1** instruction, it will turn on the motor of the recorder and write the desired data on the tape. When the motor is running, the red light on the top of the recorder will be on.

Note that you need not create a data file in a single operation. For example, suppose that you wish to add entries to the address file created above. Just position the tape to a counter number which is one digit more than the counter reading at the end of the previous write operation. Then run the program in Example 1 to add as many entries to the file as you wish.

Test Your Understanding 2.2

Add to the telephone file you began in Test Your Understanding 2.1 the following entry:

Mary Bell
2510 9th St.
Phila. Pa. 19138
937-4836

Let us now describe the process of reading data files. To do so, we use the instruction **INPUT #–1.** It is important to realize that data items may be read from cassette files **only** in the order in which they were written into the file. Therefore, in order to read a file, it is necessary to know the contents of the file and the format in which the file was written. Moreover, in order to retrieve a given piece of data, it may be necessary to read much (or even all) of the file. For example, consider the telephone directory file created in Example 1 above. To read the first entry in the file, we first position the tape to the beginning of the file, push the play button, and then execute the instruction:

```
10 INPUT #-1 A$, B$, C$, D$, E$, F$
```

Note that in order to read the 10th entry in the file, it is necessary to read the first 9 entries, even if you merely discard them after they are read.

Example 2. Write a program which searches for a particular entry of the telephone directory file created in Example 1.

Solution. We will **INPUT** the name corresponding to the desired entry. The program will then read the file entries until a match of names occurs. Here is the program:

```
10 INPUT "NAME TO SEARCH FOR"; Z$
20 INPUT #-1 A$,B$,C$,D$,E$,F$
30 IF A$=Z$ THEN 100 ELSE 40
40 GOTO 20
100 CLS
110 PRINT A$
120 PRINT B$
130 PRINT C$,D$,E$
140 PRINT F$
150 END
```

This program will read each entry on the tape until it encounters a match in names. The test for matching names occurs in line 30. Note that we may compare two string constants and ask if they are equal, just as if they were numbers.

Test Your Understanding 2.3

Use the above program to locate the number of Mary Bell in the telephone file created in Test Your Understanding 2.1 and 2.2.

There is a potential difficulty with the above program. If the end of the file is reached without a match, the program will attempt to read a nonexistent file entry and thereby create an error. For this reason, it is a good idea to let the last entry of a file be a string constant like "END" and have the program test for the end of the file. We will leave to the exercises the necessary modifications of the programs of examples 1 and 2.

Note the following important facts.

1. The program which reads a file need not be the same as the program which created the file. For example, the file created in Test Your Understanding 2.1 and 2.2 is read in Test Your Understanding 2.3 by the program of Example 3 which is not the program which created the file.
2. Reading a file does not destroy it. A file may be read any nunber of times without erasing it. (Of course, for each reading, you must position the cassette tape properly.)

EXERCISES (answers on 285)

1. Write a program which creates a cassette data file containing the numbers 5.7, −11.4, 123, 485, and 49.
2. Write a program which reads the data file created in Exercise 1 and displays the data items on the screen.
3. Write a program which adds to the data file of Exercise 1 the data items 5, 78, 4.79, and −1.27.
4. Write a program which reads the expanded file of Exercise 3 and displays all the data items on the screen.
5. Write a program which records the contents of checkbook stubs in a data file. The data items of the file should be as follows:

   check #, date, payee, amount, and explanation.

   Use this program to create a data file corresponding to your previous month's checks.
6. Write a program which reads the data file of Exercise 5 and totals the amounts of all the checks listed in the file.
7. Modify the programs of Examples 1 and 2 so that the computer will know when the end of the data file has been reached.

5.3 USING A MODEL III DISK FILE

So far, we have ignored the use of any disk files which you may have installed on your Model III. In this section, we provide an introduction to the use of disk files and their associated language Disk BASIC, which is an extension of Model III BASIC.

On Disks and Disk Files

The Model III has provision for installing one or two (internal) disk files in the same cabinet as the computer. When installed, they are situated to the right of the video display. In addition, the Model III is capable of utilizing one or two additional (external) drives, which are outside the main computer cabinet. In this section, we cannot hope to completely discuss all topics relevant to the operation and use of the disk drives. For this purpose, we refer you to the **TRS-80 Model III Disk System Owner's Manual.** However, we will present sufficient information for you to start using your disk system in connection with BASIC programs.

The bottom internal drive is numbered 0, the top internal drive 1, and the two external drives 2 and 3. To store information, the disk drives utilize 5 1/4-inch floppy diskettes. Each diskette can accommodate approximately 179,000 characters (about 50 double-spaced typed pages).

Figure 5-1 illustrates the essential parts of a diskette. The jacket is designed to protect the diskette. The interior of the jacket contains a lubricant which helps the diskette to rotate freely within the jacket. The diskette is sealed inside the jacket. You should never attempt to open the protective jacket.

The disk file reads and writes on the diskette through the **read-write** window. Never, under any circumstances, touch the surface of the diskette. Diskettes are very fragile. Even a small piece of dust or oil from a fingerprint could damage the diskette and render all the information on it totally useless.

The **write protect notch** allows you to prohibit changes to information on the diskette. (When this notch is uncovered, the computer may read the diskette, but will not write or change any information on the disk. To prevent writing on a diskette, you must cover the write protect notch with one of the metallic labels provided with the diskettes.

To insert a diskette in a disk drive, open the door of the drive. Turn the diskette so that the label side is facing up and the read-write notch is away from you. Push the diskette into the drive until you hear a click. Close the drive door.

Diskettes are extremely fragile. Here are some tips in using them.

1. Always keep a diskette in its paper envelope when not in use.

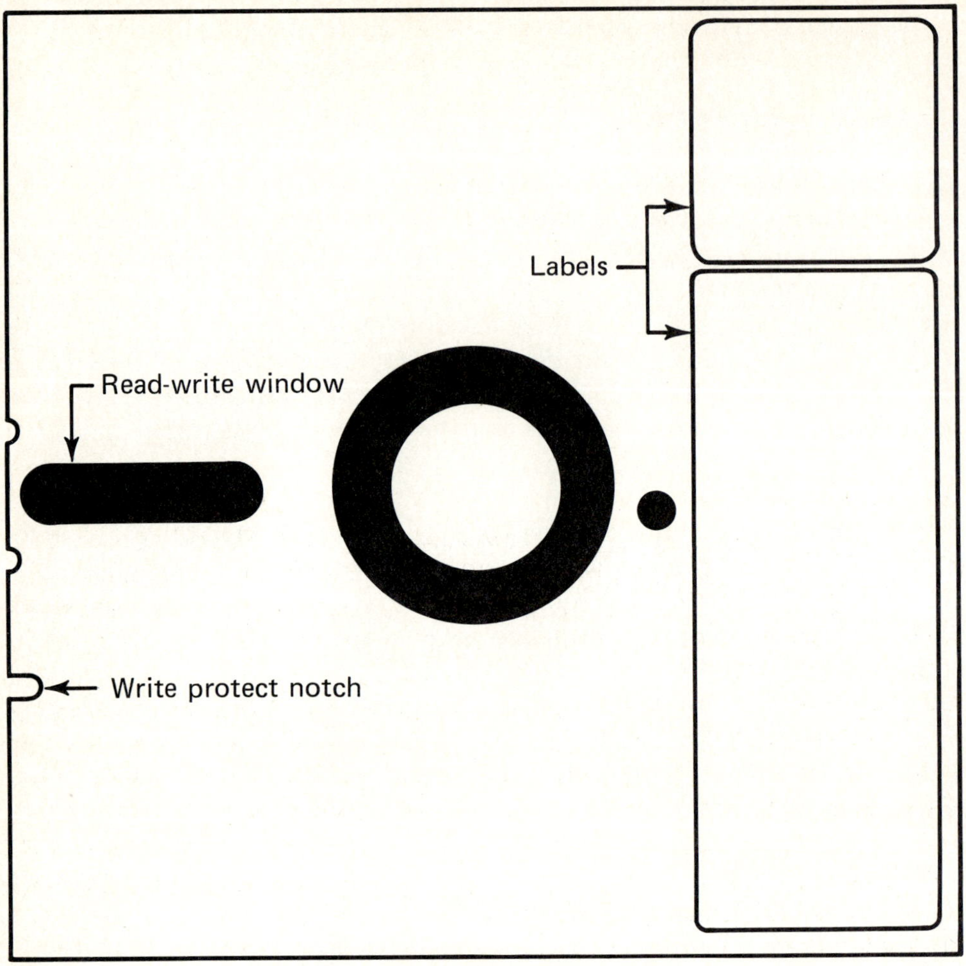

Figure 5-1. A diskette.

2. Store diskettes in a vertical position just like you would a phonograph record.
3. Never touch the surface of a diskette. Never try to wipe the surface of a diskette with a rag, handkerchief, or other item.
4. Keep diskettes away from extreme heat, such as that produced by radiators, direct sun, and other sources.
5. Never bend a diskette.
6. When writing on a diskette label, use only a felt-tipped pen. Under no circumstances should you use any sort of instrument with a sharp point.

7. Never insert a diskette into a disk drive until the computer has been turned on. Always remove diskettes from a disk drive before turning the computer off. Turning the computer on or off with a diskette in a drive may damage the diskette.
8 Keep diskettes away from magnetic fields, such as those generated by electrical motors, radios, televisions, tape recorders, and other sources. A strong magnetic field may erase data on a diskette.

The above list of precautions may seem overwhelming to a beginner, but once you set up a suitable set of procedures for handling and storing diskettes, you will find that they are a reliable, long-lasting storage medium.

Initialization

The version of BASIC contained in ROM is not sufficiently powerful to control the flow of information to and from the disk drives. For this purpose, we need a program called an **operating system.** Such a program acts as a manager for all the activities which go on in the computer, coordinates the flow of information between the keyboard, video display, RAM, ROM, disk files, and any other peripheral devices which you may have added to your computer system. Radio Shack provides you with an operating system called TRSDOS (TRS Disk Operating System—pronounced Triss-Doss). This program is contained on a **system diskette** which is provided when you purchase your disk files.

In order to make use of your disk files, it is necessary to read TRSDOS into the computer. (After all, TRSDOS is going to manage the entire show!) To do so, follow this procedure:

1. Turn the computer on. Wait until all disk drive motors stop. (When a disk drive motor is running, the red light on the door of the disk drive will be on.)
2. Insert a system diskette into drive 0.
3. Press the RESET button. (The orange button on the right side of the keyboard.)
4. Disk drive 0 will turn on and you will hear the whirring action of the disk drive. The screen will display the TRSDOS version number, the date of creation, the amount of RAM and the number of drives in the system.
5. TRSDOS will ask for the date. Input it in the form 12/03/81 (for Dec. 3, 1981) and hit **ENTER**.

5. If you have more than one disk drive, TRSDOS will prompt you to insert a blank diskette into drive 1. The contents of the diskette in drive 0 will be copied verbatim onto the disk in drive 1.

   If you have only one disk drive, TRSDOS will prompt you to take the system diskette out of drive 0 and replace it with a blank diskette. It will be necessary to swap the two diskettes several times to complete the **BACKUP** operation.

6. After the copy operation is complete, TRSDOS will display:

   Insert SYSTEM Diskette <ENTER>

   Insert the freshly copied system diskette and press **ENTER.**

Test Your Understanding 3.2

Make a copy of the TRSDOS system diskette supplied with your disk operating system.

A Word to the Wise

The **BACKUP** procedure just described may be used to copy the contents of any diskette onto any other. Because of the fragile nature of diskettes, it is strongly urged that you maintain duplicate copies of all your diskettes. A good procedure is to update your copies at the end of each session with the computer. This may seem like a tremendous bother, but it will avert untold grief if, by some mishap, a diskette with critical programs or data is erased or damaged.

File Specification

A diskette will generally contain many different files. Some files may be BASIC programs while others may be data files. Each file is identified by a file name. Moreover, a file may have a password to prevent unauthorized disclosure. Finally, you may refer to a file on a particular disk drive. A complete description of a file takes the form:

filename/ext.password:d

Here 'filename' can contain at most 8 letters or numbers, and must begin with a letter; 'ext' is an optional extension consisting of at most 3 letters or numbers; 'password' is the password of the file and consists of at most 8 letters or numbers and also must begin with a letter; d is the number of the disk drive on which the file is located. All items are optional except for the file name. Here are some examples of file specifications.

PAYROLL/81.INFLATE:1

refers to a file whose name is PAYROLL/81. The password is INFLATE and the file is on drive 1.

INVENT/NY

refers to a file whose name is INVENT/NY.

Test Your Understanding 3.3

What is wrong with the following file specification?

9AARDVARK/8007.4WHITEGHOST;5

A password is assigned when a file is created (see below). If a file is given a password, then the password must be used whenever you desire access to the file. If a drive number is used in specifying a file, then the computer will look for the file only on the drive indicated. If no drive is specified, then the computer looks for the file on all the drives, in numerical order, beginning with drive 0.

EXERCISES (answers on 287)

1. Write a file specification for a program named "OTTO" with password "SKUNK" on drive 0.
2. Write a file specification for a program named "SHIRLEY.BAS" on drive 1.

Which of the following are valid program names in Disk BASIC?

3. PROTOTYPE
4. 12345678
5. 1ASDFGHG
6. A1234567
7. ADD.CIA
8. FIX/045

9. ACCOUNT/000.PAYROLL
10. ORDERS/1812.1COMP
11. A/1.ACCESSIBILITY
12. EXAMPLE/TXT.OPEN

Answer to Test Your Understanding

3.3: 9AARDVARK has 9 characters (only 8 are allowed) and begins with a number. The extension 8007 has four digits (only 3 are allowed). 4WHITEGHOST begins with a number and exceeds the 8 characters allowed. Finally the drive should be indicated :5 rather than ;5.

5.4 AN INTRODUCTION TO DISK BASIC

TRSDOS uses the version of BASIC stored in the Model III ROM. However, TRSDOS also provides a number of additional features which make BASIC more flexible and easy to use. It is beyond the scope of this book to cover all of these extra features. For a complete description, we refer you to the **TRS-80 Model III Disk System Owner's Manual.** However, here are a few of the features available in Model III Disk BASIC.

Saving and Loading Programs

To save a program, use the **SAVE** command. For example, to save a program named **BUDGET,** we use the command

SAVE "BUDGET"

The resulting file does not require a password to read it. Since no drive is specified, the file will be **SAVE**ed on drive 0. Here is another example. To save a program named ROULETTE/011 on drive 1 with password SECRET, we use the command:

SAVE "ROULETTE/011.SECRET:1"

Suppose that, at some later time, the disk containing this program is moved to drive 0. Then the program may be loaded into RAM via the command:

LOAD "ROULETTE/011.SECRET:0"

Note that specification of the drive is optional if there is only one program with the given specifications on any of the disk drives. However, since the file was created with a password, the password becomes an essential part of the file specification.

Test Your Understanding 4.1

(a) Save the program

```
10 PRINT 5+7
20 END
```

under the name A.BUTTER.

(b) Attempt to load the program without giving the password.

(c) Load the program from diskette.

TRSDOS is the traffic manager of your computer system. In order to manage certain "traffic" or "housekeeping" operations, it is necessary to talk directly to TRSDOS, rather than go through BASIC. When talking to TRSDOS, we say that we are at the **system level.** For example, we are at the system level when TRSDOS displays the **TRSDOS Ready** prompt. At that time, you may give any one of a number of TRSDOS commands, such as the **BACKUP** command used to make a copy of the contents of a diskette.

Directory

Another TRSDOS command is **DIR** which allows you to ask for the directory listing the names of all files on a given disk. For example, to display the directory of disk 0, just type:

DIR :0

followed by **ENTER.**

Erasing Files

You may erase files from a diskette. For example, to erase the file ROULETE/011, type:

KILL "ROULETTE/011.SECRET"

Note that if a file was created with a password, then the password must be used to erase the file.

Renaming A File

You may rename a file by using the **RENAME** command. For example, to change the name of ROULETTE/011.SECRET to ROULETTE/011, we use the command:

RENAME ROULETTE/011.SECRET TO ROULETTE/011

Note that in this example, the protection afforded by the password (SECRET) will be removed by the change of name. Similarly, we may use the **RENAME** command to add a password to protect a file. The disk drives are searched in increasing numerical order for the file to be changed. The first file with the designated name will have its name changed. However, if you use a drive number in the file specification, then the **RENAME** operation applies only to the indicated drive.

Return to TRSDOS

If you are in BASIC and wish to return to the system level, type:

CMD "S"

followed by **ENTER.** You may then execute TRSDOS commands. You may return to BASIC from TRSDOS by typing:

BASIC

Note, however, that if you leave BASIC to go to TRSDOS, then any program currently in RAM will be lost. If you wish to retain that program, do a **SAVE** before leaving BASIC. Another method is to reenter BASIC by typing:

BASIC*

Merging Programs

Disk BASIC has the ability to merge the program currently in RAM with any other program on a diskette. This is especially useful in inserting standard subroutines into a program and is accomplished via the **MERGE** command.

For example, to merge the current program with the program INTEGRAL/001, we use the command:

MERGE INTEGRAL/001

For instance, suppose that the program currently in RAM contained lines 10, 20, 30, and 100, and INTEGRAL/001 contained lines 40, 50, 60, 70, 80, 90, and 100. The merged program would contain the lines 10, 20, 30, 40, 50, 60, 70, 80, 90, and 100. The line 100 would be taken from INTEGRAL/001. (The lines from the program on disk will replace those of the current program in case of duplicate line numbers.) In order to use the merge feature, the program from diskette must have been **SAVE**d in a particular format called ASCII-format. In the case of the above example, the command which **SAVE**d INTEGRAL/001 must have been of the form:

SAVE "INTEGRAL/001", A

The comma and A at the end of the command indicate the desired format. In case INTEGRAL/001 was not **SAVE**d using such a command, it is first necessary to **LOAD** "INTEGRAL/001" and resave it using the above command. (Watch out! If you type in a program, say OX, to merge with INTEGRAL/001, remember to save it before giving the **MERGE** command. Otherwise you will lose OX.)

Test Your Understanding 4.2

(a) Save the following program in ASCII format.

```
10 PRINT 5+7
100 END
```

under the name GHOST.

(b) Type in the program:

```
30 PRINT 7+9
40 PRINT 7-9
```

(c) **MERGE** the programs of (a) and (b).

Non-System Diskettes

Drive 0 must always contain a system disk when operating under TRSDOS. However, the copy of the TRSDOS programs occupy a significant portion of the space on the disk. If you have only a single disk drive, there is nothing you can do about this loss of disk space. Every disk you use must contain a copy of TRSDOS (produced by the **BACKUP** procedure). However, the diskettes in disk drives 1, 2, and 3 need not contain the TRSDOS program and therefore can contain more programs and data than the diskette in drive 0.

All diskettes must be **formatted.** That is, they must have electronic boundaries written onto them which show where information is to be recorded. When you create a system disk via a **BACKUP** procedure, the formatting is done automatically. However, if you wish to use non-system disks in drives 1, 2, and 3, you must specifically format the disks you are going to use. Here is the procedure:

1. Obtain the **TRSDOS Ready** display (either by initializing the computer or by giving the **CMD "S"** command from BASIC).
2. Put the disk to be formatted in drive 1.
3. Give the command

   FORMAT

   followed by **ENTER.**
4. TRSDOS will ask:

   Which Drive is to be Used?

   type a **1** followed by ENTER. TRSDOS will then format the disk. It will tell you when the operation is complete. At that time, remove the disk from drive 1. This disk may now be used in any drive except drive 0. Since it does not contain a copy of TRSDOS, all of its space is available for programs and data.

Note that the **FORMAT** command erases the disk to be formatted. If the disk contains any data, TRSDOS will warn you of this and give you a chance to cancel the command.

EXERCISES (answers on 288)

1. (a) Write a program which computes $1^2 + 2^2 + \ldots + 50^2$.

   (b) **SAVE** the program under the name SQUARES. Use the **SAVE, A** command.

2. (a) Write a program which computes $1^3 + 2^3 + \ldots + 30^3$. Write it in such a way that the line numbers do not overlap with those of the program in 1(a).
   (b) **MERGE** the program of 1(a) with the program of 2(a).
   (c) **LIST** the **MERGE**d program.
   (d) **RUN** the **MERGE**d program.
   (e) **SAVE** the **MERGE**d program under the COMBINED.
3. Recover the program of 2(a) without retyping it.
4. Erase the program SQUARES of 1(a).
5. Make a copy of the diskette you are using.
6. Create a non-system disk.

Answers to Test Your Understanding

4.2: (a) Type in the program and then give the command: SAVE "GHOST",A
(b) Type NEW followed by the given program.
(c) Type MERGE "GHOST"

5.5 DATA FILES FOR DISK USERS

In this section, we discuss the procedures for reading and writing data files on diskettes. In order to allow for easy comparison, we will work out the same examples as we did for cassette data files.

In order to either read or write a data file on diskette, it is necessary to **OPEN** the file. When opening a file, you give it a reference number by which you will refer to it in the program. For example, to write a file with name INVOICE/034, we would use an instruction of the form

100 OPEN "O",1,"INVOICE/034"

The "O" indicates that the file is to be opened for output (to the file: that is, for writing the file). The number 1 is the identification number assigned to the file. Note that this instruction does not actually write any data into the file. It merely prepares the file for output. Suppose now that we wish to enter the following data into the file:

DJ SALES $358.79 4/5/81

We would use the following instruction:

200 PRINT #1, "DJ SALES"; ","; "$358.79"; ","; "4/5/81"

The #1 portion of the instruction refers to the identification number given to the file, namely 1. We could print further data items to the file using similar instructions, and in this way build up the desired data file. Note that a data file can consist of any keyboard characters, including, for example, **ENTER,** space, SHIFT, and so forth.

The commas and semicolons in the above instruction take some explanation. The PRINT #1 statement works like any other print statement. The semicolons indicate that no spaces are to be left between consecutive items in the print statement. The commas are placed in quotation marks so that they are actually written as part of the file. They enable us to tell where one data item ends and the next begins. (As we mentioned in section 1, the commas serve as delimiters.) In the disk file, the above data items are stored as follows:

DJ SALES,$358.79,4/5/81

It is necessary to go through the tortuous typing to insert the commas only to separate strings from one another. For numerical data, a space between data items suffices as a delimiter.

When you are finished writing a file, you must close it with a **CLOSE** instruction. For example, to close the file we have just been considering, we use the instruction:

300 CLOSE 1

Example 1. Create a data file which consists of names, addresses, and telephone numbers drawn from your personal telephone directory. Assume that you will type the addresses into the computer and will tell the computer when the last address has been typed.

Solution. We use **INPUT** statements to enter the various data. Let A$ denote the name of the current person, B$ the street address, C$ the city, D$ the state, E$ the zip code, and F$ the telephone number. For each entry, there is an **INPUT** statement corresponding to each of these variables. The program then writes the data to the diskette. Here is the program:

```
5 OPEN "O",1,"TELEPHON"
10 INPUT "NAME"; A$
20 INPUT "STREET ADDRESS"; B$
30 INPUT "CITY"; C$
40 INPUT "STATE"; D$
50 INPUT "ZIP CODE"; E$
60 INPUT "TELEPHONE"; F$
70 PRINT #1, A$; ","; B$; ","; C$; ","; D$; ","; E$; ","; F$
80 INPUT "ANOTHER ENTRY (Y/N)"; G$
90 IF G$="Y" THEN 10 ELSE 100
100 PRINT #1, "END"; ","; ","; ","; ","; ",";
110 CLOSE 1
120 END
```

You should set up such a computerized telephone directory of your own. It is very instructive. Moreover, when coupled with the search program given below, it will allow you to look up addresses and phone numbers using your computer.

Test Your Understanding 5.1

Use the above program to enter the following address into the file.

John Jones
1 South Main St., Apt. 308
Phila. Pa. 19107
527-1211

Test Your Understanding 5.2

Add to the telephone file begun in Test Your Understanding 5.1 the following entry.

Mary Bell
2510 9th St.
Phila. Pa. 19138
937-4896

Let us now discuss the procedure for reading data files from a diskette. As is the case with writing files, it is first necessary to open the file. For example, consider the telephone file from example 1. To open it for input, we could use the instruction:

300 OPEN "I",2,"TELEPHON"

The "I" stands for "Input" (to the program). The number 2 identifies the file in the program. Once the file is open, it may read via an instruction of the form:

400 INPUT #2, A$,B$,C$,D$,E$,F$

Note that this instruction will read one of the telephone-address entries from the file. In order to read a file, it is necessary to know the precise format of the data in the file. For example, the form of the above **INPUT** statement was dictated by the fact that each telephone-address entry was entered into the file as 6 consecutive string constants, separated by commas. The input statement works like any other input statement: Faced with a list of items separated by commas, it assigns values to the indicated variables, in the order in which the data items are presented. Note here that the commas in the data file are essential. In order for an INPUT statement to assign values to several variables at once, the values must be separated by commas!

Example 2. Write a program which searches for a particular entry of the telephone directory file created in example 1.

Solution. We will **INPUT** the name corresponding to the desired entry. The program will then read the file entries until a match of names occurs. Here is the program:

```
5 OPEN "I",2,"TELEPHON"
10 INPUT "NAME TO SEARCH FOR"; Z$
20 INPUT #2, A$,B$,C$,D$,E$,F$
30 IF A$=Z$ THEN 100 ELSE 40
40 IF A$="END" THEN 200
50 GOTO 20
100 CLS
110 PRINT A$
120 PRINT B$
130 PRINT C$,D$,E$
140 PRINT F$
150 GOTO 1000
200 CLS
210 PRINT "THE NAME IS NOT ON FILE"
1000 CLOSE 2
1010 END
```

Test Your Understanding 5.3

Use the above program to locate the number of Mary Bell in the telephone file created in Test Your Understanding 5.1 and 5.2.

Here is an important fact about writing data files: writing a file destroys any previous contents of the file. (In contrast, however, you may read a file any number of times without destroying its contents.) For example, consider the file "TELEPHON" created in example 1 above. Suppose we write a program which opens the file for output and writes what we suppose are additional entries in our telephone directory. After this write operation, the file "TELEPHON" will contain *only* the added entries. All of the original entries will have been lost! How, then, may we add items to a file which already exists? Easy. We temporarily stash the current contents of the file into some other file and create the entire file from scratch! The next example illustrates this procedure.

Example 3. Write a program which adds entries to the file TELEPHON. The additions should be typed via INPUT statements. The program may assume that the file is on the disk in drive 0.

Solution. To add items to the file, we first **OPEN** the file for *input*. We read the file into the temporary file with the name "T". Then we **CLOSE** both files TELEPHON and T. Next, we **OPEN** both files, TELEPHON for output and T for input. We read the contents of T and write them back into TELEPHON. We next close T. Finally, we ask for the new entry via an **INPUT** statement and write the new entry into TELEPHON. Here is the program.

```
10 OPEN "I",1,"TELEPHON"
20 OPEN "O",2,"T"
30 INPUT #1, A$,B$,C$,D$,E$,F$:   'INPUT ENTRY
40 PRINT #2, A$;",";B$;","; C$;",";D$;",";E$;",";F$
45 REM 40 WRITES ENTRY IN "T"
50 IF A$="END" THEN 100 ELSE 60:   'END OF FILE?
60 GOTO 30
100 CLOSE 1,2 :   ' CLOSE FILES "TELEPHON" AND "T"
110 OPEN "O",1,"TELEPHON" :   'OPEN "TELEPHON" TO OUTPUT
120 OPEN "I",2,"T":   'OPEN "T" TO INPUT
130 INPUT #2, A$,B$,C$,D$,E$,F$:   'INPUT ENTRY FROM "T"
135 IF A$="END" THEN 200 ELSE 160:   'END OF FILE?
140 PRINT #1, A$;",";B$;",";C$;",";D$;",";E$;",";F$
145 REM 140 WRITES ENTRY TO "TELE."
160 GOTO 130:   'GO TO NEXT ENTRY
200 CLOSE 2:   'CLOSE "T"
```

```
210 PRINT "TYPE ENTRY:NAME,STREET ADDRESS,CITY, STATE,"
220 PRINT "ZIP CODE, TELEPHONE NO."
230 INPUT A$,B$,C$,D$,E$,F$
240 PRINT #1,A$;",";B$;",";C$;",";D$;",";E$;",";F$;","
250 INPUT "ANOTHER ENTRY (Y/N)"; Z$
260 IF Z$="Y" THEN 300 ELSE 500
300 CLS
310 GOTO 210
500 CLOSE 1
510 END
```

It may seem that we are doing unnecessary work in writing and then reading the file "T". If "TELEPHON" is a short file, then we could temporarily store all of its data in RAM as values of appropriate arrays A$(J), B$(J), etc. However, we have no way of knowing in advance how much memory this will require. This procedure might actually require more RAM than exists in the computer. Therefore, we have taken a more conservative approach via the file "T". Note that at any given moment, only a single address-telephone entry is in RAM. Thus the possible shortage of RAM is avoided.

In the above programs, we have indicated the end of a data file by writing "END" as the last data item. This allows us to read to the end of the file and no further, thereby avoiding an error. Another method of handling the end of file problem is to read the data items until an error actually does occur. We prepare for the expected error by placing an **ON ERROR GOTO** statement before the point at which the error will occur. The statement should send the computer to a line containing a **RESUME** statement which in turn sends the computer back to the next line after that in which the error occurred.

Recall that when Disk BASIC is initialized, it asks for the number of files. Until now, we have responded to this question by typing ENTER. This response allows for 3 data files to be open simultaneously. In order to have more open files, it is necessary to respond to this question with the number of open files you will need during the current session.

In the next example, I present a genuinely useful program for parents who wish to teach organizational skills to their children. Most children love to play with the computer. Here is a program which acts as an assignment book and monitors progress on homework. This program was designed for my son, a 9 year-old computer enthusiast.

Example 4. Write a program which sets up a data file for homework assignments. The child should enter the assignments, by subject, on returning from school. As assignments are completed, the child may check them off. The program should inform the child whether his homework is complete.

Solution. Our program will first ask if the assignment has been recorded previously. If so, it will be in a file. If not, the program will prompt the child to type in the assignments by subject, with prompts like:

What is your math assignment?

The only rule is that assignments cannot have commas in their statement. The child types in the assignment followed by ENTER and the computer responds with the next subject. If there is no assignment, type ENTER. (You may customize the program by entering your own subjects.) After all assignments are entered, the computer asks the child if he wishes the assignments displayed. If the answer is yes, then the computer produces a list of all subjects with their corresponding assignments, in the form:

```
SUBJECT        ASSIGNMENT

MATH           P45 1–20
READING        CHAP 3
SPELLING       P80 SENTENCES
.
.
.
```

Now the computer gives the child a chance to check off a completed assignment. The computer does not allow for any forgetfulness. It asks for the subject, then displays the assignment and asks if, in fact, that assignment has been completed. If so, the next time the list of assignments is displayed an X will appear beside completed assignments. Finally, the computer scans the list of assignments and decides whether all are complete. If so, it prints "HOMEWORK DONE"; if not, it prints "HOMEWORK NOT DONE." Here is the program.

```
10 CLEAR 10000
20 DIM B$(20),C$(20),D$(20)
30 CLS
40 PRINT "HAVE YOU ENTERED THIS ASSIGNMENT BEFORE?"
50 INPUT A$
60 IF A$="Y" THEN 70 ELSE 140
70 OPEN "I",1,"SCHED"
80 PRINT "SUBJECT";TAB(20) "ASSIGNMENT"
90 FOR J=1 TO 6
100 INPUT #1, B$(J),C$(J),D$(J)
```

```
120 NEXT J
130 CLOSE;GOTO 380
140 CLS
150 DATA "MATH", "SPELLING", "LANGUAGE", "SOCIAL STUDIES",
    "READING"
160 DATA "SCIENCE", "CURRENT EVENTS"
170 FOR J=1 TO 6
180 READ B$(J)
190 PRINT "DO YOU HAVE ANY ";B$(J);" HOMEWORK TONIGHT?"
200 INPUT A$
210 IF A$="Y" THEN 220 ELSE 260
220 PRINT "WHAT IS THE ";B$(J);" ASSIGNMENT?"
230 INPUT C$(J)
240 GOTO 260
260 NEXT J
270 PRINT "DO YOU WISH TO SEE YOUR ASSIGNMENTS?"
280 INPUT A$
290 IF A$="Y" THEN 300 ELSE GOTO 380
300 CLS
310 PRINT "SUBJECT";TAB(20) "ASSIGNMENT"
320 PRINT
330 FOR J=1 TO 6
340 PRINT B$(J); TAB(20) C$(J)
350 NEXT J
360 GOTO 380
380 PRINT "DO YOU WANT TO CHECK OFF AN ASSIGNMENT?"
390 INPUT A$
400 IF A$="Y" THEN 410 ELSE 520
410 INPUT "SUBJECT";B$
420 FOR J=1 TO 6
430 IF B$(J) THEN PRINT B$(J) ELSE NEXT J
440 PRINT "IS THIS ASSIGNMENT DONE?"
450 PRINT C$(J)
460 INPUT A$
470 IF A$="Y" THEN D$(J)="X"
480 CLS
490 FOR J=1 TO 6
500 PRINT B$(J),C$(J);TAB(60) D$(J)
510 NEXT J
520 FOR J=1 TO 6
530 IF D$(J)<>"X" AND C$(J)<>"" THEN E$="W"
540 NEXT J
```

```
550 IF E$="W" THEN PRINT "HOMEWORK IS NOT DONE" ELSE
    PRINT "HOMEWORK DONE"
560 INPUT "DO YOU WISH TO CHECK OFF ANOTHER
    ASSIGNMENT";A$
570 IF A$="Y" THEN GOTO 380 ELSE 390
580 OPEN "O",1,"SCHED"
590 FOR J=1 TO 6
600 PRINT #1,B$(J);",";C$(J);",";D$(J);","
610 NEXT J
620 CLOSE
700 END
```

The files we have been discussing are called *sequential files*. These files must be read in the exact order in which they were written. Disk BASIC also allows *random access* files. Such files allow you to read a given piece of data without reading all the data written ahead of it. A discussion of random access files is beyond the scope of this book. The interested reader may refer to the **TRS-80 Model III Disk System Owner's Manual.**

EXERCISES (answers on 288)

1. Write a program which creates a diskette data file containing the numbers 5.7, −11.4, 123, 485, 49.
2. Write a program which reads the data file created in Exercise 1 and displays the data items on the screen.
3. Write a program which adds to the data file of Exercise 1 the data items 5, 78, 4.79, and −1.27.
4. Write a program which reads the expanded file of Exercise 3 and displays all the data items on the screen.
5. Write a program which records the contents of checkbook stubs in a data file. The data items of the file should be as follows: check #, date, payee, amount, explanation. Use this program to create a data file corresponding to your previous month's checks.
6. Write a program which reads the data file of Exercise 5 and totals the amounts of all the checks listed in the file.
7. Write a program which keeps track of inventory in a retail store. The inventory should be described by a data file whose entries contain the

following information: item, current price, and units in stock. The program should allow three different operations: display the data file entry corresponding to a given item, record receipt of a shipment of a given item, and record the sale of a certain number of units of a given item.

8. Write a program which creates a recipe file to contain your favorite recipes.
9. (For Teachers) Write a program which maintains a student file containing your class roll, attendance, and grades.
10. Write a program which maintains a file of your credit card numbers and the party to notify in case of loss or theft.

6

An Introduction to Computer Graphics

In many applications, it is helpful to present data in pictorial form. Indeed, by displaying numerical information in graphical form, it is often possible to develop insights and to draw conclusions which are not immediately evident from the original data. In this chapter, we will discuss procedures for using your Model III to create various kinds of pictorial displays on the screen. Such procedures belong to the field of **computer graphics** and this chapter provides an introduction to that field.

6.1 ELEMENTARY GRAPHICS PRINCIPLES

Let us begin by discussing the geometry of the video display. As we have already noted, the video display of the Model III is capable of displaying 16 rows of 64 characters each. This gives us $16 \times 64 = 1024$ possible character positions. These various character positions divide the screen into small rectangles, with one rectangle corresponding to each character position. For graphics purposes, each of these rectangles is divided into six smaller rectangles, as shown in Figure 6-1. Thus, for graphics purposes, the screen is represented as a grid of rectangles, 128 rectangles across and 48 rectangles high. See Figure 6-2. Each rectangle is an independent spot of light which may be turned on or off. The basic idea of computer graphics is to develop programs which turn on appropriate rectangles to make bar charts, graphs, pie charts, designs, and so forth.

The rectangles into which we have divided the screen are arranged in rows and columns. We number the rows from 0 to 47, with row 0 being at the top

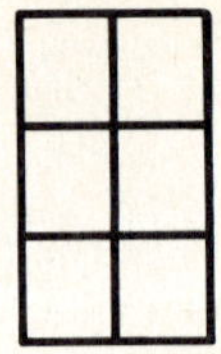

Figure 6-1.

of the screen and row 47 at the bottom. The columns are numbered from 0 to 127, with column 0 being at the extreme left and column 127 at the extreme right. Each rectangle on the screen is identified by a pair of numbers, indicating the row and column. For example the pair of numbers (16,12) represents the sixteenth column and twelfth row. (Note the order: the column number comes first!) This rectangle is indicated in Figure 6-2.

You may turn on the rectangle at position (x,y) by using the BASIC instruction:

SET (x,y)

To turn off the rectangle at position (x,y), you may use the instruction:

RESET (x,y)

Most graphics programs consist of appropriate sequences of these two instructions. The next examples illustrate procedures for drawing various straight lines.

Test Your Understanding 1.1

Write a program to turn on the graphics block at the 8th row, 35th column.

Example 1. Write a program which draws a horizontal line across row 10 of the screen.

Solution. The horizontal line across row 10 consists of the rectangles (0,10), (1,10), (2,10), . . . , (127,10). Our program should turn on all these rectangles. Moreover, just in case the screen contains some extraneous characters,

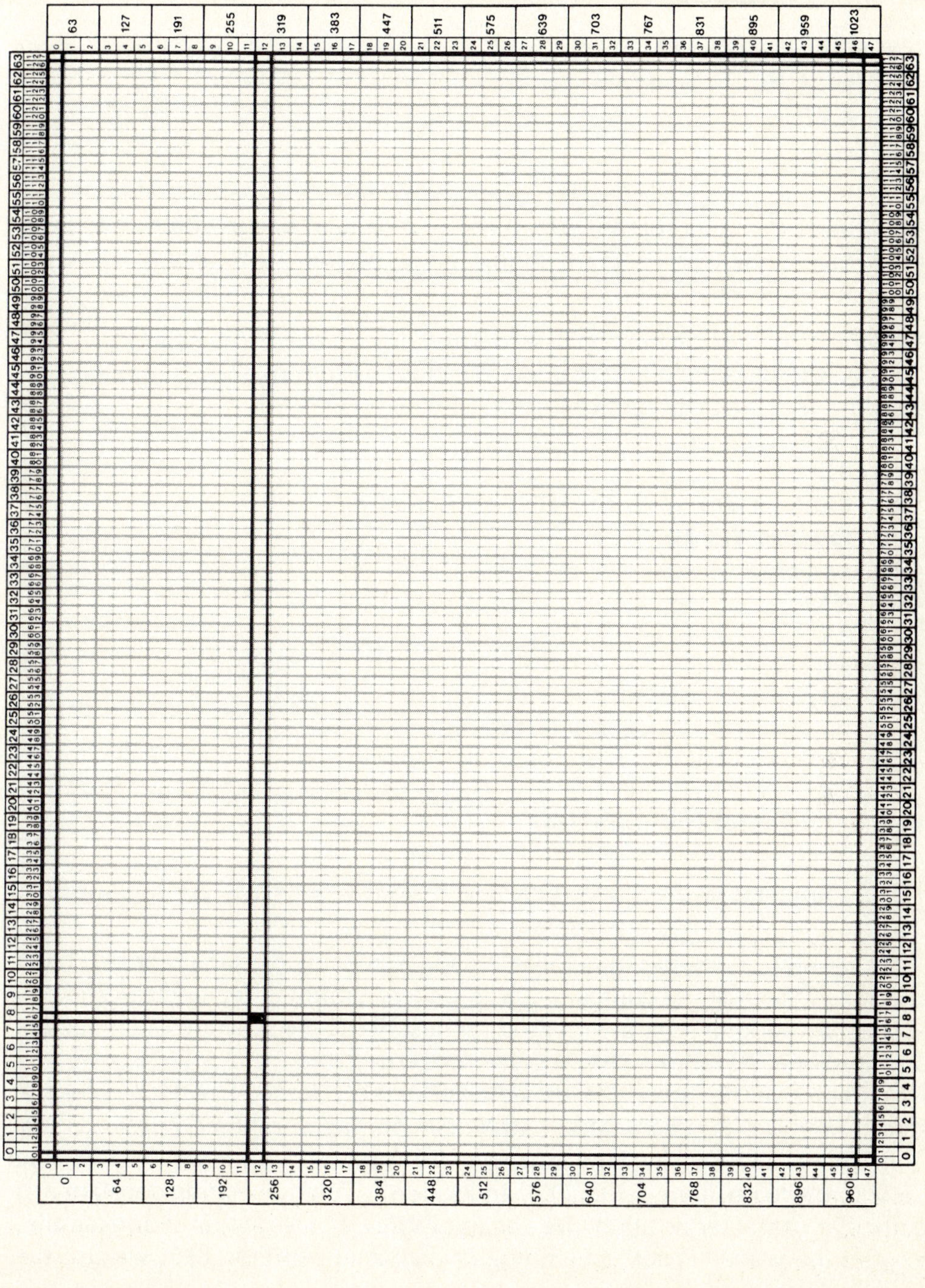

Figure 6-2.

let us begin by clearing the screen using the **CLS** instruction. Here is the program.

```
10 CLS
20 FOR J=0 TO 127
30 SET (J,10)
40 NEXT J
50 END
```

Example 2. Write a program which draws a vertical line in column 25 from row 5 to row 40. The program should blink the line 50 times.

Solution. The rectangles on the desired line are (25,5), (25,6), . . . , (25,40). The blinking effect may be achieved by turning these rectangles on and off. Here is our program.

```
10 CLS
20 FOR K=1 TO 50:'K CONTROLS BLINKING
30 FOR J=5 TO 40
40 SET (25,J)
50 NEXT J
60 CLS
70 NEXT K
80 END
```

Test Your Understanding 1.2

Write a program to draw a vertical line from row 2 to row 20 in column 8.

Let us now learn to add words on the screen with our graphics. Each keyboard character occupies a 2 x 3 grid of graphics rectangles. For this reason, we adopt a separate method for describing the position of characters on the screen. As far as characters are concerned, there are only 16 rows and 64 columns on the screen. This yields a total of 16 × 64 = 1024 possible screen positions for characters. These positions are numbered consecutively from 0 to 1023. The first row corresponds to position numbers 0 to 63, the second row to positions 64 to 127, and so forth. To print a string constant at a particular character position, we use the **PRINT @** instruction. For example, to print the word "Profit" beginning at character position 135, we use the instruction:

```
10 PRINT @135, "PROFIT"
```

To print characters and graphics together, we utilize a mix of **SET** and **PRINT @** statements.

It can be confusing to plan a display containing both characters and graphics because of the two different position numbering systems. To minimize confusion, you should use a video display work sheet, as shown in Figure 6-3. Note that the horizontal and vertical edges contain two different numbering systems. The inner numbers correspond to the numbering system for graphics blocks. The outer numbers on the left side of the sheet correspond to the character position number for the first character in a row. Pads of video display work sheets are available from Radio Shack.

Test Your Understanding 1.3

Write an instruction which places a character "A" directly under the graphics block (80,10).

Example 3. Draw a pair of x and y axes as shown in Figure 6-4. Label the vertical axis with the word "Profit" and the horizontal axis with the word "Month".

Solution. Our program must draw two lines and print two words. The only real problem is to determine the positioning. The word "Profit" has six letters. So let us start the vertical line in the position corresponding to the sixth character column, which corresponds to the 12th graphics block column. We will run the vertical line from the top of the screen (graphics row 0) to within two character rows from the bottom. (On the next-to-last row, we will place the word "month". We will not print in the last row, since this will cause some of what is printed above to scroll off the screen!) Therefore, our vertical line will occupy graphics blocks (12,0), (12,1), . . . , (12,41). (Remember that a character row is three graphics blocks tall. So the last character row corresponds to graphics rows 45, 46, and 47.) The word "Profit" will be printed at position 0. The horizontal line will extend from graphics column 12 across the entire screen and so will occupy graphics blocks (12,41), (13,41), . . . , (127,41). The word "Month" has 5 letters and so should be printed at position 954. (Note that we have not gone to the end of the line with the Word "Month". This is to prevent the display from

Figure 6-3. A video display worksheet. Reprinted with permission of the Tandy Corp.

Figure 6-4.

automatically scrolling.) In Figure 6-5, we have filled in a display worksheet corresponding to the above graph. Here is our program to generate that display.

```
10 CLS
20 PRINT @0, "Profit"
30 PRINT @954, "Month"
40 FOR J=0 TO 41
50 SET (12,J)
60 NEXT J
70 FOR J=12 TO 127
80 SET (J,41)
90 NEXT J
100 GOTO 110
110 GOTO 100
200 END
```

Note the infinite loop in lines 100–110. This loop will keep the display on the screen indefinitely while the computer spins its wheels. To stop the program, press the **BREAK** key. To see the reason for the infinite loop, try running the program after deleting lines 100 and 110. Note how the **READY** interferes with the graphics. The infinite loop prevents the READY message from appearing on the screen.

Another important point to observe: When intermingling **SET** and **PRINT** @ statements, you should always put the **PRINT** @ statements first and these should print from the top of the screen down and from left to right in each line. If you do not observe this rule, then your computer may do some funny things due to the operation of various automatic features of the video display.

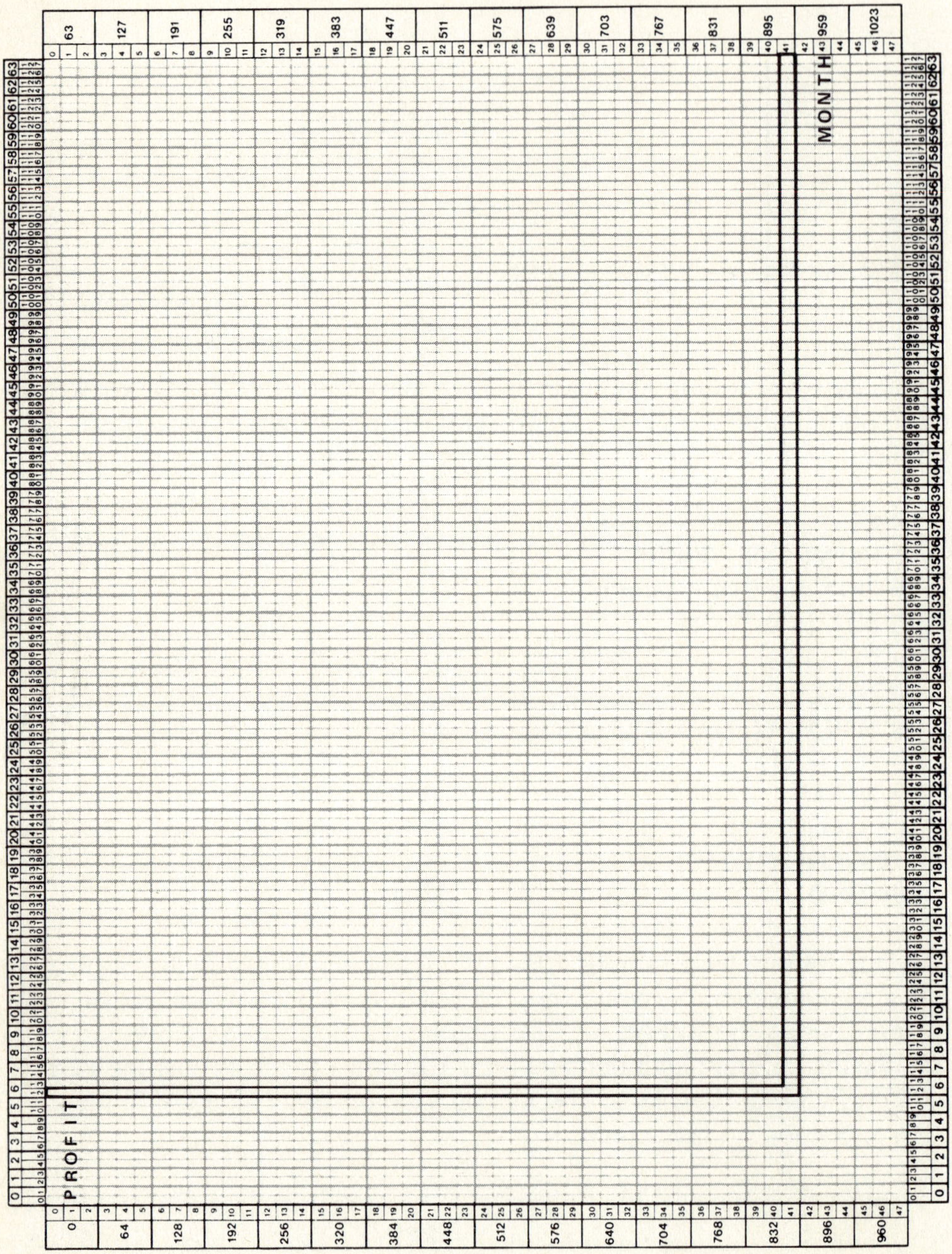

Figure 6-5. Display layout for chart in Figure 6-4.

128 129 130 131 132 133 134 135
136 137 138 139 140 141 142 143
144 145 146 147 148 149 150 151
152 153 154 155 156 157 158 159
160 161 162 163 164 165 166 167
168 169 170 171 172 173 174 175
176 177 178 179 180 181 182 183
184 185 186 187 188 189 190 191

You may illuminate any of the graphics squares using the **SET** instruction. However, to speed up the process of creating graphics, the Model III is equipped with a number of graphics characters. These characters are the same size as the regular keyboard characters and therefore occupy a 3 × 2 set of graphics blocks. The graphics characters are identified by the numbers 128–191. Figure 6-6 shows the graphics characters and their identifying numbers.

You position graphics characters on the screen just as you would ordinary keyboard characters, using the position numbers 0–1023 as above. For example, to display graphics character 170 in screen position 540, we use the instruction:

```
10 PRINT @540, CHR$(170)
```

You may display all the graphics characters on the screen using the program:

```
10 FOR J=128 TO 191
20 PRINT @4*(J–128), CHR$(J)
30 NEXT J
40 END
```

Since J–128 runs from 0 to 63, 4*(J–128) runs through the numbers 0, 4, 8, 12, 16, . . . , 252. Thus, the above program displays the various graphics characters in every fourth character position.

EXERCISES (answers on 290)

Draw the following straight lines.

1. A horizontal line completely across the screen in row 38.
2. A vertical line completely up and down the screen in column 17.
3. A pair of straight lines which divide the screen into four equal squares.
4. Horizontal and vertical lines which convert the screen into a tic-tac-toe board.
5. A vertical line of double thickness from rows 0 to 24 in column 30.
6. A diagonal line consisting of the graphics blocks (0,0), (1,1), (2,2), . . . , (48,48).
7. A horizontal line with "tick marks" as follows:

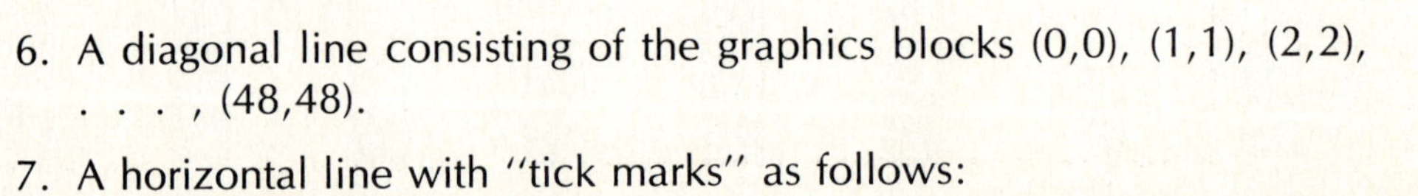

(Hint: Look for a graphics character out of which to form the "tick marks".)

8. A vertical line with "tick marks" as follows:

9. Display your name in a box formed from asterisks:

```
*****************
*   Your Name   *
*****************
```

10. Display a number axis as follows:

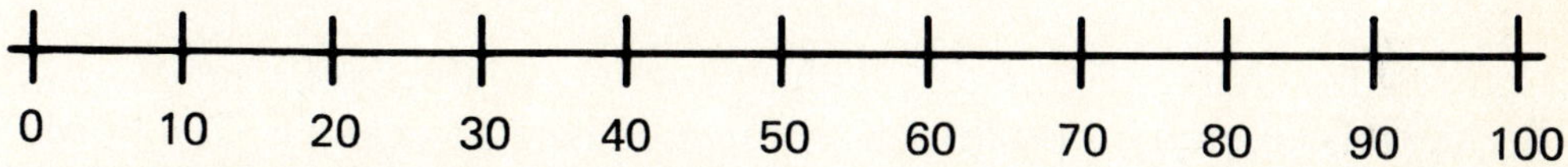

11. Write a program which displays a graphics character which you specify in an **INPUT** statement.

12. Create a display of the following form:

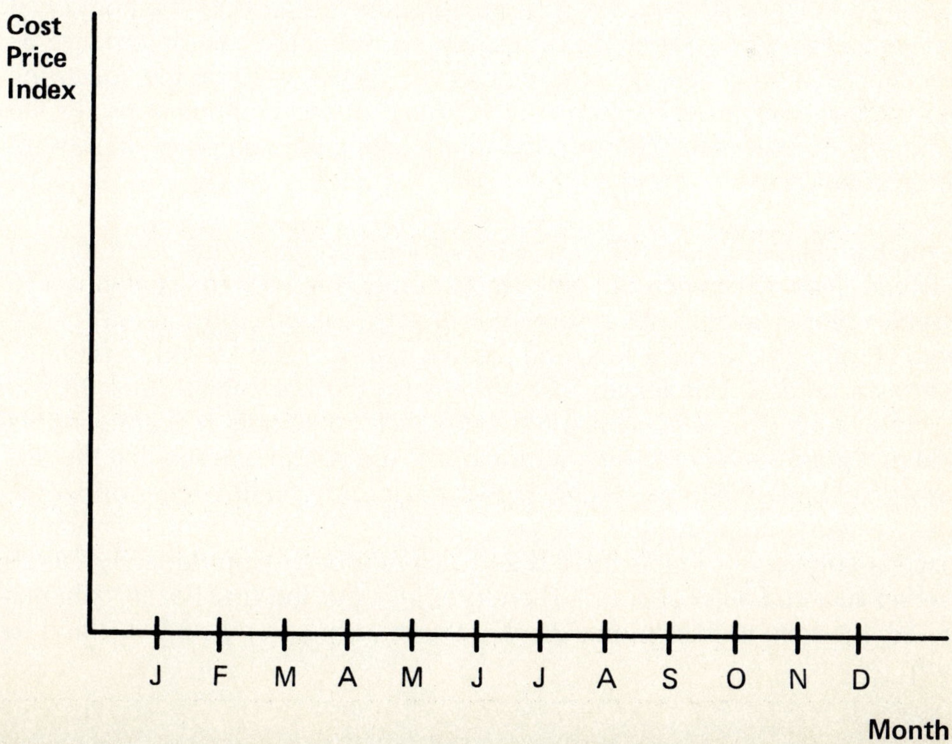

Answers to Test Your Understanding

1.1:
```
10 CLS
20 SET(35,8)
30 END
```

1.2:
```
10 CLS
20 FOR J=2 to 20
30 SET (8,J)
40 NEXT J
50 END
```

1.3:
```
10 PRINT @296,"A"
```

6.2 DRAWING BAR CHARTS VIA COMPUTER

Consider the chart of Figure 6-7. It illustrates the monthly profits of a certain business. Each month's profits are represented by a vertical bar. The height of the bar is determined by the amount of profit for the month. Such a chart is called a *bar chart.* It is common to construct bar charts in business reports in order to illustrate trends in various statistics. In this section, we will show how to use the Model III to construct bar charts from given data.

In the preceding section, we showed you how to construct the horizontal and vertical axes of a bar chart. Let us now construct the bars. In order to be specific, let's draw the bar chart given in Figure 6-7. In the following analysis, we will proceed manually for most of the computations. In the exercises, we will enhance our program by letting the computer do most of the calculations.

The bar chart of Figure 6-7 has 12 bars corresponding to the 12 months of the year. Let's make each bar two graphics blocks thick. The screen is 128 graphics blocks wide. Let's reserve the first 16 columns on the left for the word "Profit", the vertical axis, and the tick marks. Leave 16 columns on the right as a border. This leaves 96 columns for the bars. (Note that 96 is a multiple of 12. This is good planning!) So each bar should be centered in a field of 8 graphics blocks. After a moment's calculation, we see that the first bar should be in columns 19–20. However, in order to fit a letter under the bar, we must move the bar over one graphics block. (The first character space is columns 0–1, the second 2–3, and so forth. Unfortunately 19–20 overlap two character spaces.) Therefore, let's put the first bar in columns 18–19, the second in columns 26–27, the third in columns 34–35, and so forth.

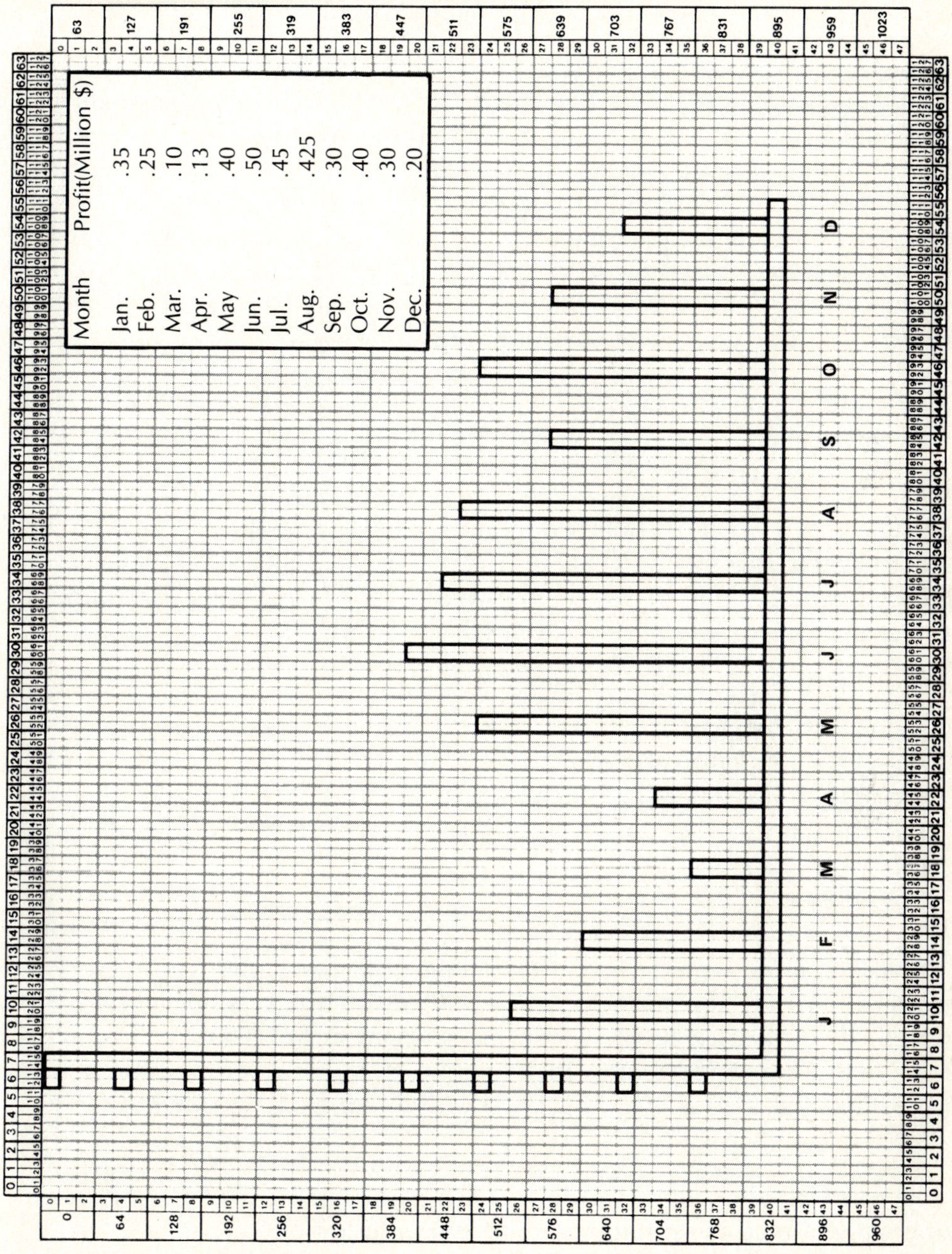
Month Profit(Million $)
Jan. .35
Feb. .25
Mar. .10
Apr. .13
May .40
Jun. .50
Jul. .45
Aug. .425
Sep. .30
Oct. .40
Nov. .30
Dec. .20
J F M A M J J A S O N D

Figure 6-7.

Test Your Understanding 2.1

Suppose that the bar chart above contained only 8 bars and that the axes are to be positioned as above. In what columns would the first bar appear?

Now for the vertical spacing. Let's place the horizontal axis in row 41. This leaves us some space for tick marks and month indicators. The bars will go immediately above the line, beginning in row 40. The chart in Figure 6-7 indicates profits from $100,000 to $1,000,000 on the scale of the vertical axis. There are 10 tick marks on the vertical axis, so let us divide the 40 tick marks by 10 and derive that one tick mark corresponds to 4 vertical graphics blocks. The tick marks will be placed in rows 36 (=$100,000), 32 (=$200,000), . . . , 0 (=$1,000,000). Our display design is indicated in the video display worksheet in Figure 6-8.

Let's now design a program to create the display. Our program will consist of three parts: draw the axes, display the text, and draw the bars. Let's first concentrate on drawing the bars.

To indicate a profit of J hundred thousand dollars, we draw a bar which is from row 40 to row 40 − 4*J. For example, a profit of $200,000 corresponds to J = 2 and to a bar from row 40 to row 40 − 4*2 = 32. Thus, for example, here is a program which draws the bar corresponding to January, which recorded a profit of $350,000.

```
100 LET P=350000
110 LET J=350000/1000000
120 FOR K=40 TO 40–4*J STEP −1
130 SET (18,K)
140 SET (19,K)
150 NEXT K
```

Note that if we were to use other values of P then J and K in the above computation may not turn out to be integers. This is perfectly all right. Indeed, if K is not an integer, then the instruction **SET(18,K)** will round K down to the largest integer less than or equal to K. Thus, for example, if K = 9.75, then the instruction **SET(18,K)** will illuminate the graphics block (18,9).

Let us store the monthly profits in a **DATA** statement. The first part of the program will read the monthly profits into an array A(K) (K = 1, 2, . . . , 12). Next, the program will draw the bar for each month, using a program like the one above. The only new point is that the bars for month M (M = 1, 2, . . . , 12) are located in columns 18 + (M−1)*8 and 19 + (M−1)*8.

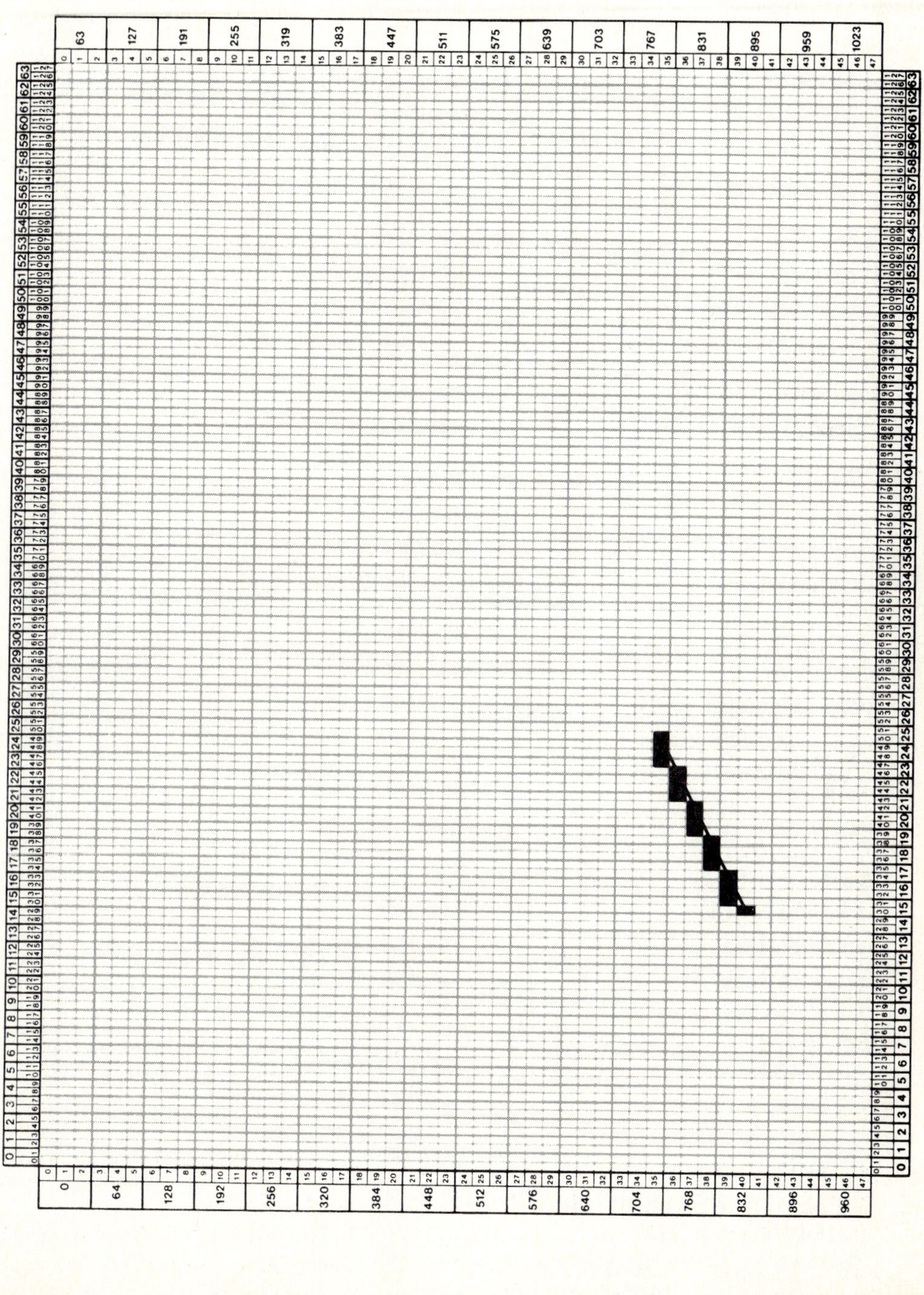

Figure 6-8. Video display design.

Indeed, this positioning is correct for M = 1 (columns 19 and 20) and as M is increased by 1, the columns increase by 8. Thus, the initial part of our program, up to and including drawing the bars is as follows:

```
10 DIM A(12)
20 DATA 350000, 250000, 100000, 130000, 400000, 500000
30 DATA 450000, 425000, 300000, 400000, 300000, 200000
40 FOR M=1 TO 12
50 READ A(M)
60 NEXT M
1000 FOR M=1 TO 12
1010 LET J=A(M)/100000
1020 FOR K=40 TO 40-4*J STEP -1
1030 SET (19+(M-1)*8,K):   'BARS
1040 SET (20+(M-1)*8,K)
1050 NEXT K
1060 NEXT M
```

Recall that we reserved the first 16 columns for the word "Profit", the vertical axis and the tick marks. Let's put the word "Profit" at position 0, the vertical axis in column 14 and the tick marks at graphics blocks (13,0), (13,4), (13,8), . . . , (13,36). The horizontal axis will consist of the graphics blocks (14,40), (15,40), . . . , (111,40). Finally, we will put letters under the bars. Referring to Figure 6-8, we see that the letters of the months go in character display positions 906, 910, 914, . . . , 950. Here is a program which creates this part of the display.

```
100 DIM B$(12)
110 DATA J,F,M,A,M,J,J,A,S,O
120 DATA N,D
130 FOR J=1 TO 12
140 READ B$(J)
150 NEXT J
160 FOR J=1 TO 12
170 PRINT @ 902+4*J, B$(J):'MONTH LABELS
180 NEXT J
190 PRINT @0, "Profit"
200 FOR J=0 TO 40
210 SET (14,J):'VERTICAL AXIS
220 NEXT J
230 FOR J=0 TO 36 STEP 4
240 SET (13,J) : ' TICK MARKS
250 NEXT J
```

```
260 FOR J=14 TO 111
270 SET (J,40): ' HORIZONTAL AXIS
280 NEXT J
```

We may now put together all the parts of the program together with an initial clearing of the screen and a loop to keep the display on the screen. We obtain our final result:

```
5 CLS
10 DIM A(12)
20 DATA 350000, 250000, 100000, 130000, 400000, 500000
30 DATA 450000, 425000, 300000, 400000, 300000, 200000
40 FOR M=1 TO 12
50 READ A(M)
60 NEXT M
100 DIM B$(12)
110 DATA J,F,M,A,M,J,J,A,S,O
120 DATA N,D
130 FOR J=1 TO 12
140 READ B$(J)
150 NEXT J
160 FOR J=1 TO 12
170 PRINT @ 902+4*J, B$(J):'MONTH LABELS
180 NEXT J
190 PRINT @0, "Profit"
200 FOR J=0 TO 40
210 SET (14,J):'VERTICAL AXIS
220 NEXT J
230 FOR J=0 TO 36 STEP 4
240 SET (13,J): ' TICK MARKS
250 NEXT J
260 FOR J=14 TO 111
270 SET (J,40): ' HORIZONTAL AXIS
280 NEXT J
1000 FOR M=1 TO 12
1010 LET J=A(M)/100000
1020 FOR K=40 TO 40-4*J STEP -1
1030 SET (19+(M-1)*8,K): ' BARS
1040 SET (20+(M-1)*8,K)
1050 NEXT K
1060 NEXT M
1100 GOTO 1110
1110 GOTO 1100
1200 END
```

It is possible to refine the above graphing procedure so that the computer does more of the work. We will guide you through some of the refinements in the exercises.

EXERCISES (answers on 292)

Exercises 1–6 refer to the bar chart program developed in the above example.

1. Type and RUN the bar chart program of the example.
2. Modify your program so that, instead of DATA statements, the program asks for the monthly profits via an INPUT statement.
3. Use the program of Exercise 2 to make a bar chart for the following set of data:

Jan.	$175,238	Jul.	$312,964
Feb.	$ 35,275	Aug.	$345,782
Mar.	$240,367	Sep.	$126,763
Apr.	$675,980	Oct.	$324,509
May	$390,612	Nov.	$561,420
Jun.	$609,876	Dec.	$798,154

4. Modify the program of Exercise 2 to include the label "Mil. $" on the left of vertical axis under the word "Profit." Moreover add calibrations .1, .2, .3, .4, . . . , 1.0 by the tick marks on the vertical axis.
5. Modify the program of Exercise 2 so that it asks for the labels to be placed on the vertical axis. This is a first step in developing a program to draw bar charts for any set of data. You should limit your labels to 2 lines of 6 characters or less, so that you may use the same position for the axes. Modify the program so that it asks you for the number to be placed beside the first vertical tick mark and the interval between consecutive tick mark labels. For example, you might wish to label the tick marks .3, .7, 1.1, . . . , 3.0. In this case, you would INPUT the numbers .3 as the first tick mark label and .4 as the interval between consecutive labels. Your program should generate the desired tick mark labels. Moreover, your program should ask for the "scale factor." This is the number corresponding to $100,000 in Example 1 and is the amount represented by the length of each interval on the vertical axis. To put it another way, the scale factor is the number you must divide each data item by to get the height of the appropriate bar in terms of intervals (tick marks) on the vertical axis.

6. Enhance the program of Exercise 5 so that it asks for the labels on the horizontal axis (the month labels in Example 1). Your program should allow for a variable number of bars, up to the 12 bars in Example 1. (Just omit the bars and labels on the right if you have fewer than 12 pieces of data.)

7. Use the program of Exercise 6 to produce a bar chart corresponding to the following data.

Income	Percentage of Population
Under $10,000	15.8
10,000–20,000	25.7
20,000–30,000	27.4
30,000-40,000	11.1
Over 40,000	20.0

Answers to Test Your Understanding

2.1: Columns 20 and 21.

6.3 GRAPHING FUNCTIONS VIA COMPUTER

In the previous section, we demonstrated the use of the Model III to prepare bar charts. However, bar charts are not the only type of graph used in making business decisions. Another very important type of graph is a broken-line graph formed by connecting given data points. An example of such a graph is given in Figure 6-9.

In this section, we will learn to use the Model III to produce such graphs.

Let us begin with the problem of drawing a straight line connecting two graphics blocks. For example, let us consider the graphics blocks (30,40) and (50,35) (See Figure 6-10). The line between them will extend over columns 30, 31, 32, . . . , 50, and will thus consist of graphics blocks of the form:

(30,40,), (31,?), (32,?), . . . , (49,?), (50,35)

We must figure out how to fill in the question marks. In going from column 30 to column 50 (a distance of 20 columns), our line falls from row 40 to row 35 (a distance of 5 rows). Since it does so at a uniform rate, the line must fall

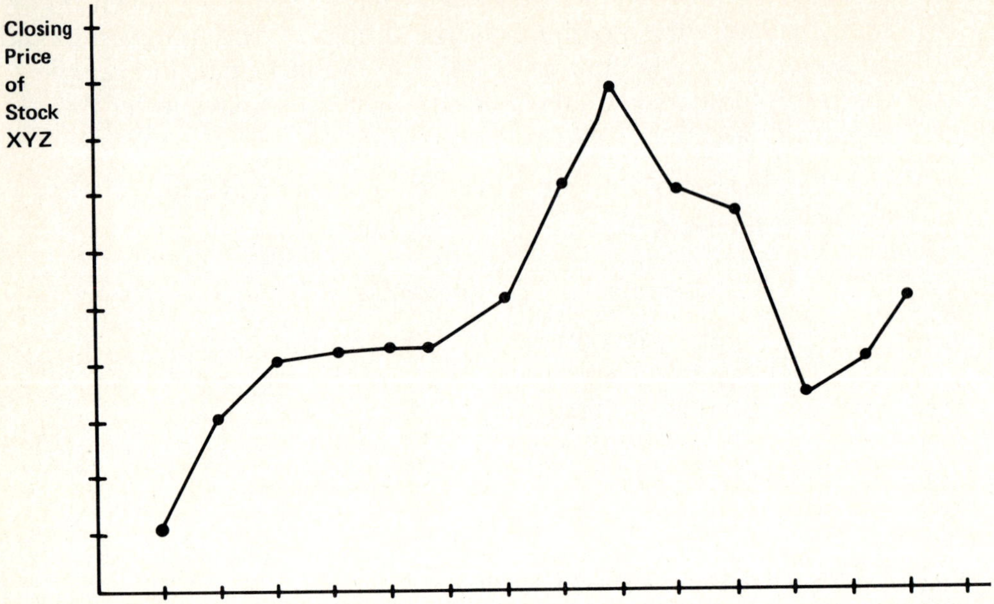

Figure 6-9.

5/20ths of a row for each column we move over. So in column 31, the line is at height 40 − 5/20, and the graphics block in column 31 is

(31, 40 − 5/20).

Similarly, to get to column 32, we must move over 2 columns from 30 and hence must fall 2 × (5/20) rows. Therefore, the graphics block in column 32 is

(32, 40 − 2 × (5/20))

Generally, the graphics block in column J is at

(32+J,40J*(5/20))

Note that some of these graphics blocks contain fractions. Of course, we can not locate such blocks exactly because of the limited resolution of the screen. However, the **SET** command will illuminate the nearest block. The set of blocks so illuminated will give an approximation to the desired line. Here is a program to draw the approximation.

```
10 FOR J=0 TO 20
20 SET (32+J,40-J*(5/20))
30 NEXT J
40 END
```

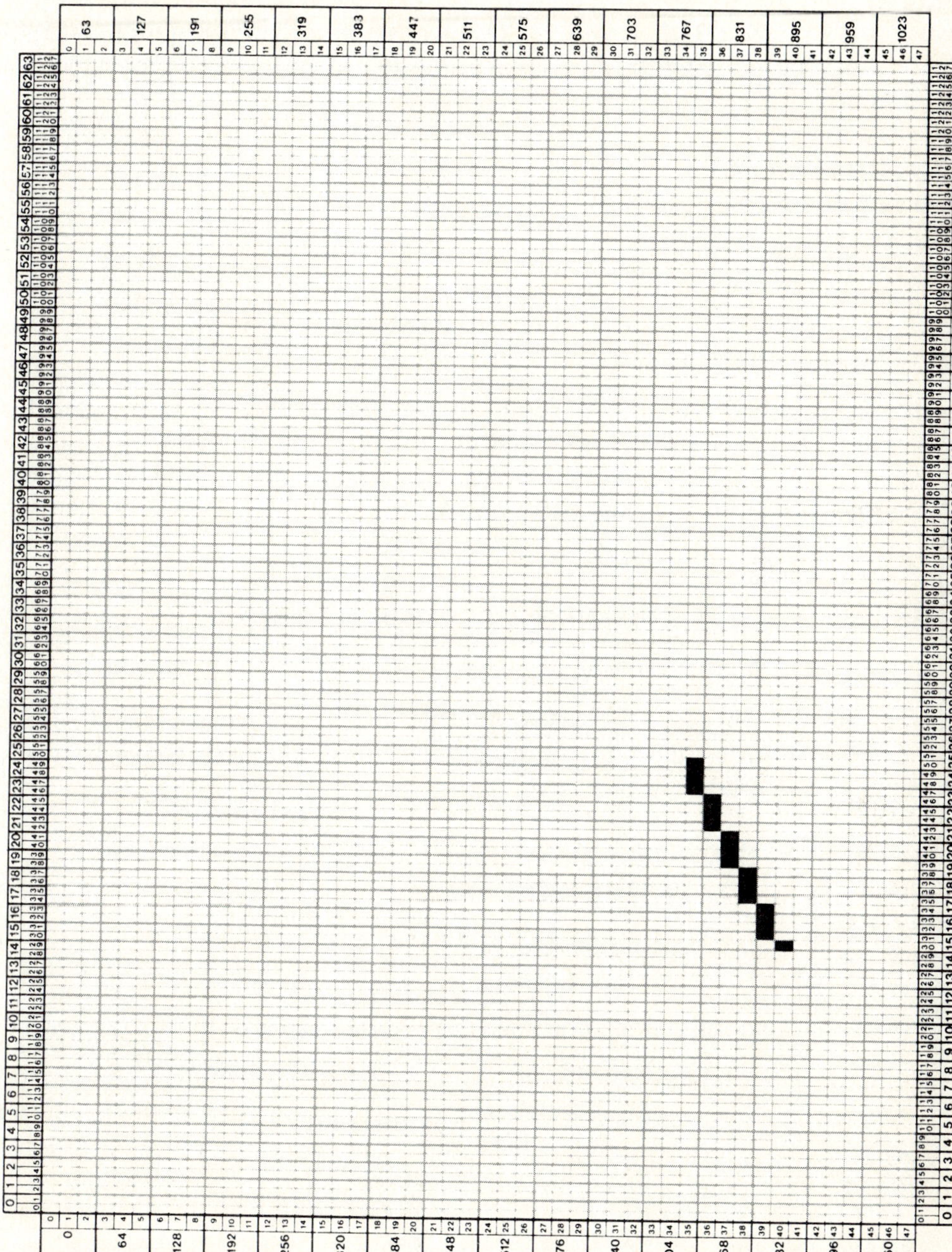

Figure 6-10. The line joining (30,40) and (50,35).

Example 1. Write a program which draws a line connecting graphics blocks (0,40) and (40,20).

Solution. In moving from column 0 to column 40 (40 columns), we must go from row 40 to row 20 (20 rows). So for every column, you must increase by 20/40ths of a row. Using the same reasoning as above, we write the following program:

```
10 FOR J=0 to 40
20 SET (0+J, 40+J*(20/40))
30 NEXT J
40 END
```

Example 2. Write a program to draw a line between graphics blocks (X1,Y1) and (X2,Y2).

Solution. We follow exactly the same reasoning as in the two cases considered above. We must move horizontally X2–X1 graphics blocks. Vertically, we must move Y2–Y1 graphics blocks. Thus, for each column we move over, we must move vertically by

(Y2−Y1)/(X2−X1)

blocks. Thus, in moving over J columns, we must be at row

Y1 + J*(Y2 − Y1)/(X2 − X1)

(This reasoning may seem a bit complicated. But to convince yourself, just go through it step-by-step in the two special cases worked out above.) Thus, we arrive at the following program.

```
10 FOR J=0 TO X2-X1
20 SET (X1+J, Y1+J*(Y2-Y1)/(X2-X1))
30 NEXT J
40 END
```

In many applications, it is necessary to produce a graph from experimentally observed data. For example, consider the following set of data

Year	Sales($100,000)
1975	2.55
1976	3.00
1977	2.00
1978	2.50
1979	3.80
1980	4.05

Let us draw a line graph as shown in Figure 6-11.

The procedure is just a combination of all the techniques we have already learned:

i) Draw axes and tick marks.

ii) Label the axes.

iii) Draw the line segments.

To draw the axes, we will use the same positioning and hence the same instruction as we used for the bar chart programs of the preceding section. We must have five tick marks on the horizontal axis, so let's use every second tick mark in our bar chart program. As for the scale on the vertical axis, we must go from 0 to 5.00. Let us use the same 10 tick marks as we

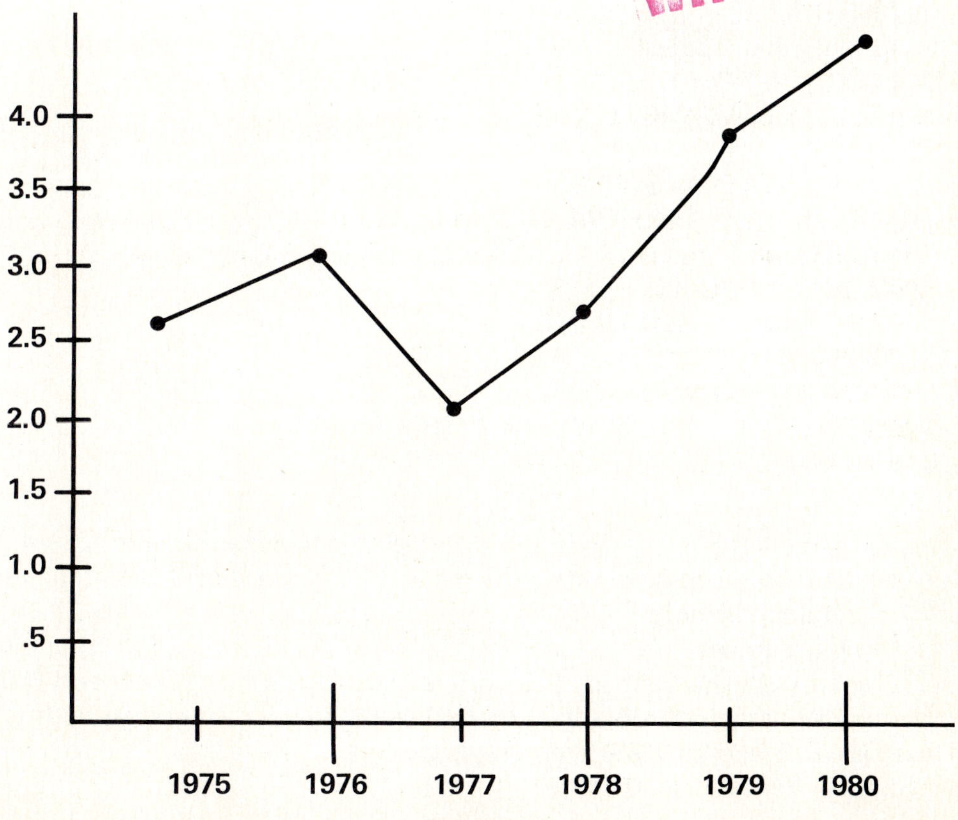

Figure 6-11.

used in the bar chart program and label them .5, 1.0, 1.5, ... , 5.0. Based on this analysis, here is a program which accomplishes i) and ii):

```
100 DIM B$(12), C(10)
110 DATA "1975", "1976", "1977", "1978", "1979", "1980"
120 DATA 4.5,4.0,3.5,3.0,2.5,2.0,1.5,1.0,0.5
130 FOR J=1 TO 12
140 READ B$(J)
150 NEXT J
160 FOR J=1 TO 9
170 READ C(J)
175 K=4*J*64-1
180 PRINT @K, C(J): 'VERT LABELS
190 NEXT J
200 FOR J=1 TO 12
205 K=900+4*J
210 PRINT @K, B$(J): 'YEAR LABELS
220 NEXT J
230 PRINT @0, "Sales"
240 FOR J=0 TO 40
250 SET (14,J):'VERTICAL AXIS
260 NEXT J
270 FOR J=0 TO 36 STEP 4
280 SET (13,J):   ' VERTICAL TICK MARKS
290 NEXT J
300 FOR J=14 TO 111
310 SET (J,40):   ' HORIZONTAL AXIS
320 NEXT J
330 FOR J=1 TO 5
340 SET (18+(J-1)*16,39):'HORIZ. TICK MARKS
350 NEXT J
```

We have already learned to draw a line connecting two graphics blocks. Our only problem now is to determine how the given data translates into graphics block numbers. The column for the Jth piece of data equals 18 + (J−1)*16. (The first piece of data corresponds to column 18 and consecutive columns are 16 apart.) On the vertical, 5.0 corresponds to graphics row 0 and 0.0 corresponds to graphics row 40. Therefore, each unit of data corresponds to 8 graphics rows and thus if A(J) represents the sales for year J, then the row for the J th data item is

40 − A(J)/8

So here is the remainder of our program.

```
500 DIM A(10),X(10),Y(10)
510 DATA 2.55, 3.00, 2.00, 2.50, 3.80, 4.05
520 FOR J=1 TO 6
525 REM COMPUTE GRAPHICS BLOCK X(J),Y(J)
530 READ A(J)
540 LET X(J)=18+(J-1)*16, Y(J)=40-A(J)/8
550 NEXT J
600 FOR J=1 TO 5
605 REM DRAW LINE BETW (X(J),Y(J)) AND (X(J+1),Y(J+1))
610 LET X1=X(J), Y1=Y(J), X2=X(J+1), Y2=Y(J+1)
630 GOSUB 1000
640 NEXT J
700 GOTO 710
710 GOTO 720
800 END
1000 FOR J=0 TO X2-X1
1010 SET (X1+J, Y1+J*(Y2-Y1)/(X2-X1))
1020 NEXT J
1030 RETURN
```

EXERCISES (answers on 293)

1. Type and RUN the program developed in the text.
2. Modify the program so that the sales data is requested in INPUT statements.
3. Use the modified program to prepare a line graph of the following data for a certain town.

Year	Births
1970	358
1971	330
1972	315
1973	302
1974	290
1975	282
1976	270
1977	285
1978	272
1979	300
1980	310

4. Write a program to create the following figure:

5. Write a program to create the following figure:

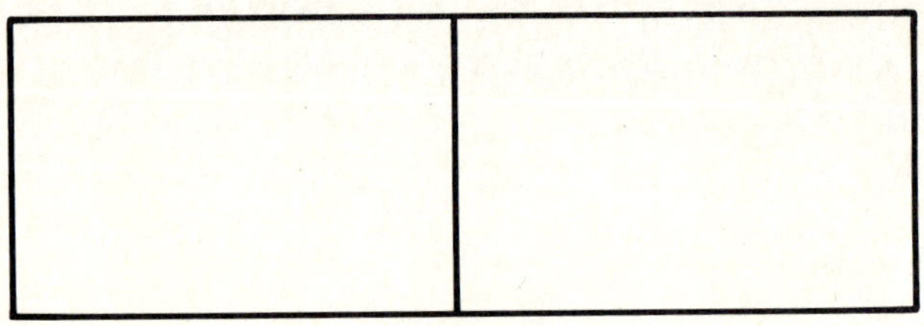

6. Write a program to create the following figure:

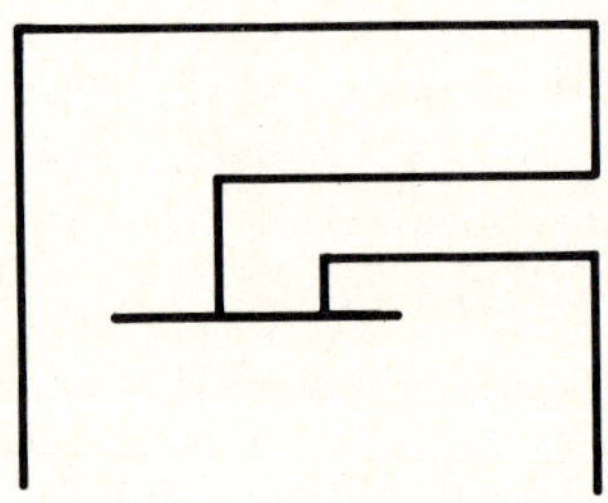

6.4 COMPUTER ART (FOR PRIMITIVES)

The computer may be used for creation of interesting pieces of graphics art. In this book, we will not dwell long on this application, but it is interesting and certainly deserves a mention.

We will discuss two forms of computer art. The first arises when we allow the computer free "artistic license" to create random patterns on the screen. Let us create a program which runs down the rows of graphics blocks and randomly illuminates some of them. We will control the number of blocks to be illuminated by a "density factor" which we input. This factor will be a number between 0 and 1 and will be denoted by the variable A (for density). Our program will consider each graphics block separately. It will use the output of RND(0) to make the decision on whether to illuminate the block or not. Namely, if RND(0) is less than A, the block will be illuminated; if RND(0) is at least A then the block will not be illuminated. Here is our program.

```
5 INPUT "DENSITY FACTOR"; A
6 CLS
7 RANDOM
10 FOR R=0 TO 47 : ' R=ROW NUMBER
20 FOR C=0 TO 127: ' C=COLUMN NUMBER
30 IF RND(0)<A THEN 40 ELSE 100
40 SET (C,R)
100 NEXT C
110 NEXT R
200 GOTO 210
210 GOTO 200
300 END
```

You should run this program for assorted values of A. Some suggested values are A = .1, .5, and .7, respectively. Note that because of the unpredictability of the random number generator, the same value of A will usually yield quite different pictures on successive runs.

A second method of generating art using the computer is to use a graphics pad to effectively "trace" a picture. For example, suppose that your picture is a photograph. Place a video display worksheet over the picture. Fill in all graphics blocks which touch the subject of the photograph. In this way, you will create an impression of the subject which you may then display on the screen.

To close our very brief discussion, we should mention some related equipment which has recently come within the range of the computer hobbyist. In our above description of tracing, we suggested a rather laborious procedure. However, there are special devices called digitizing pads which enable you to trace a shape with an electronic "pen" and have the same shape transferred to the screen. In addition, there are the so-called light pens which enable you to touch a point on the screen and have the computer read the location of the point. This sort of device can be useful in creating computer art as well as in playing computer games.

EXERCISES (answers on 294)

1. Run the above program three times for the value A = .4.
2. Run the above program for the values A = .1, .2, .3, . . . , 1.0. Can you predict the display for A = 1.0 in advance?
3. Create a computer impression of a member of your family using a large photograph. (5″ × 7″ or larger will work best.)

7

Word Processing

7.1 WHAT IS WORD PROCESSING?

Microcomputers are currently in the process of causing a revolution in the office. As microcomputers have become cheaper and easier to use, they have found their way into every nook and cranny of business. But nowhere does the revolutionary impact of microcomputers promise to be greater than in the area of word processing. In brief, a *word processor* is a device which is obtained by marrying the traditional typewriter with the capabilities of the computer for storing, editing, retrieving, displaying, and printing information. It is no exaggeration to say that the traditional typewriter is now as obsolete as a Model T and over the next decade or so will be completely replaced by increasingly sophisticated word processors.

The fundamental concept of a word processor is to use the microcomputer as a typewriter. However, instead of using paper to record the words, we use the computer memory. Initially, the words are stored in RAM. When you wish to make a permanent record of them, you store them on disk as a data file. As you type, the text can be viewed on the video display. This much is not revolutionary. The true power of a word processor does not come into play until you need to edit the data in a document. Using the power of the computer, you can perform the following tasks quickly and with little effort: move to any point in the document; add words, phrases, sentences, or even paragraphs; delete portions of the text; move a block of text from one part of the document to another; insert "boiler-plate" information from another data file (for example, you could add a name and address from a mailing list); selectively change all occurrences of one word (say, "John") to another (say, "Jim"); print the contents of a file according to a requested format.

All of the above operations are possible since the computer is able to manipulate strings in addition to numbers. Actually, your Model III is equipped with a wide variety of commands to manipulate string data In fact, you may turn your Model III into quite a respectable word processor.

In this chapter, we will discuss the Model III BASIC instructions for string manipulation. Moreover, we will discuss formatting output on a printer. Next, we will discuss the features available in commercially available word processing packages which you can purchase for your Model III. Finally, to give you a taste of word processing proper, we will build a rudimentary word processor which you can use to prepare letters, term papers, memos, and other material.

7.2 MANIPULATING STRINGS

ASCII Character Codes

Each keyboard character is assigned a number between 1 and 255. The code number thus assigned is called the *ASCII code* of the character. For example, the letter "A" corresponds to the number 65 whereas the number 97 corresponds to the letter "a". Also included in this correspondence are the punctuation marks and other keyboard characters. For example, 28 corresponds to the symbol "("and 62 to the symbol ">". Even the various control keys have corresponding numbers. For example, the space bar corresponds to the number 20, the Break key to the number 1, and the ENTER key to number 13. There also are corresponding numbers to various combinations of keys. For example, the combination of the SHIFT, ↓, and Z keys is assigned the number 26. This combination of keys is a control code which moves the cursor down one line. Table 1 lists all of the printable characters

Table 1. ASCII Character Codes for Printable Characters.

ASCII Code	*Character*	*ASCII Code*	*Character*
32	blank		
33	!	43	+
34	"	44	,
35	#	45	-
36	$	46	.
37	%	47	/
38	&	48	0
39	'	49	1
40	(	50	2
41	)	51	3
42	*	52	4

Table 1. ASCII Character Codes for Printable Characters. (Continued)

ASCII Code	*Character*	*ASCII Code*	*Character*
53	5	91*	[
54	6	92*	\
55	7	93*	]
56	8	94*	^
57	9	95*	—
58	:	96*	‘
59	;	97	a
60	<	98	b
61	=	99	c
62	>	100	d
63	?	101	e
64	@	102	f
65	A	103	g
66	B	104	h
67	C	105	i
68	D	106	j
69	E	107	k
70	F	108	l
71	G	109	m
72	H	110	n
73	I	111	o
74	J	112	p
75	K	113	q
76	L	114	r
77	M	115	s
78	N	116	t
79	O	117	u
80	P	118	v
81	Q	119	w
82	R	120	x
83	S	121	y
84	T	122	z
85	U	123*	{
86	V	124*	¦
87	W	125*	}
88	X	126*	~
89	Y	127*	±
90	Z		

*** These characters cannot be typed directly on the Model III keyboard, but can be printed on a printer having a full set of ASCII characters.**

and their corresponding ASCII codes. We will discuss the various control codes in Section 4.

The computer uses ASCII codes to refer to letters and control operations. Indeed, any file, whether program or data, may be reduced to a sequence of ASCII codes. For example, consider the following address.

John Jones
2 S. BROADWAY

As a sequence of ASCII codes, it would be stored:

74,111,104,110,32,74,111,110,101,115,13
50,32,83,46,32,65,114,111,,97,100,119,97,121,13

Note that the spaces are included (numbers 32) as are the carriage returns (ENTER) at the end of each line (number 13). ASCII codes allow us to describe any piece of text generated by the keyboard, including all formatting instructions (like spaces, carriage returns, upper and lower case, and so forth). Moreover, once a piece of text has been reduced to a sequence of ASCII codes, it may be faithfully reproduced on the screen or on a printer. This is the fundamental principle underlying the design of word processors.

Test Your Understanding 2.1

Write a sequence of ASCII codes which will reproduce this ad:

FOR SALE: Beagle puppies. Pedigreed.
8 weeks. $125.

You may refer to characters by their ASCII codes by using CHR$. For example, CHR$(74) is the character corresponding to ASCII code 74 (upper case J); CHR$(32) is the character corresponding to ASCII code 32 (space). The **PRINT** and **LPRINT** instructions may be used in connection with CHR$. For example, the instruction

```
10 PRINT CHR$(74)
```

will display an upper case J in the first position of the first print field.

Test Your Understanding 2.2

Write a program which will print the ad of TYU 7.1 from its ASCII codes.

To obtain the ASCII code of a character, use the instruction **ASC**. For example, the instruction

```
20 PRINT ASC("B")
```

will print the ASCII code of the character "B", namely 66. In place of "B", you may use any string. The computer will return the ASCII code of the first character of the string. For example, the instruction

```
30 PRINT ASC(A$)
```

will print the ASCII code of the first character of the string A$.

Test Your Understanding 2.3

Determine the ASCII codes of the characters $, g, X, + without looking at the chart.

You may compute the length of a string using the **LEN** instruction. For example, **LEN("BOUGHT")** is equal to 6 since the string "BOUGHT" has 6 letters. Similarly, if A$ is equal to the string "Family Income", then **LEN(A$)** is equal to 13. (The space between the words counts!) Here is an application of the **LEN** instruction.

Example 1. Write a program which inputs the string A$ and then centers it on a line of the display.

Solution. A line is 64 characters long, with the spaces numbered from 0 to 63. The string A$ takes up LEN(A$) of these spaces, so there are 64–LEN(A$) spaces to be distributed on either side of A$. That is, the line should begin with (64–LEN(A$))/2 spaces. But since the first space is numbered 0, we should tab to column (64-LEN(A$))/2 − 1. Here is our program.

```
10 INPUT A$
20 CLS
30 PRINT TAB((64–LEN(A$))/2–1) A$
40 END
```

Test Your Understanding 2.4

Use the program of Example 1 to center the string "THE TRS-80 MODEL III".

More About Strings

A string may consist of as many as 255 characters. Of course, you cannot type more than 64 characters on a line. However, you may type strings that long by continuing to type *without hitting the ENTER key*. When a line is filled, the computer will automatically place the next letter at the beginning of the next line. However, if you do not hit the ENTER key at the end of the line, then the next line will be a continuation of the first. It is necessary to have long strings if you wish to be able to print hard copy. Most line printers have at least 80 characters per line and some accommodate 132 character lines.

There are a number of operations which may be performed on strings. First, strings may be "added" (or, in computer jargon, "concatenated"). Suppose that we have strings A$ and B$, with A$ = "word" and B$ = "processor". Then the sum of A$ and B$, denoted A$ + B$ is the string obtained by adjoining A$ and B$, namely:

"wordprocessor"

Note that no space is left between the two strings. To include a space, suppose that C$ = " ". That is, C$ is the string which consists of a single space. Then A$ + C$ + B$ is the string:

"word processor"

Test Your Understanding 2.5

If A$ = "4" and B$ = "7", what is A$ + B$?

The computer handles relations among strings in much the same way that it handles relations among numbers. For example, we say that two strings A$ and B$ are equal, denoted A$ = B$, provided that they consist of exactly the same characters, in the same order. Otherwise the strings are unequal, denoted A$ <> B$ or A$ >< B$. The notation A$ < B$ means that A$ precedes B$ in alphabetical order. (This is fine for strings consisting only of letters. For numbers or other characters, the ASCII codes of the characters are used to determine precedence.) Similarly, A$ > B$ means that A$ succeeds B$ in alphabetical order. Thus, for example, the following are true relations among strings:

"bear" < "goat"

"girl" > "boy"

The notation A$ >= B$ means that either A$ > B$ or A$ = B$—that is, that A$ either succeeds B$ in alphabetical order or A$ and B$ are the same. The notation A$ <= B$ has an analogous meaning.

Example 2. Write a program which alphabetizes the following list of words: egg, celery, ball, bag, glove, coat, pants, suit, clover, weed, grass, cow, and chicken.

Solution. We set up a string array A$(J) which contains these 13 words. We set B$ equal to the first word. We successively compare B$ with each of the words in the array. If any compared word precedes B$, we replace B$ with that word. At the end of the comparisons, B$ contains the first word in alphabetical order. We place this as the first item in the array C$(J). We now repeat the process with the first word eliminated. This gives us the second word in alphabetical order, and so forth. Here is our program.

```
5 CLEAR 100
10 DIM A$(13),D$(13),C$(13)
20 DATA EGG,CELERY,BALL,BAG,GLOVE,COAT
30 DATA PANTS,SUIT,CLOVER,WEED,GRASS
40 DATA COW,CHICKEN
50 FOR J=1 TO 13
60 READ A$(J):' SET UP ARRAY A$
70 NEXT J
80 FOR K=1 TO 13:'FIND KTH WORD IN ORDER
85 REM 90-200 CREATE AN ARRAY D$ CONSISTING OF THE
87 REM WORDS YET TO BE ALPHABETIZED
90 L=1
100 FOR J=1 TO 13
110 E=0
120 FOR M=1 TO 13
130 IF A$(J)=C$(M) THEN E=1
140 NEXT M
150 IF E=0 THEN 160 ELSE 200
160 D$(L)=A$(J)
170 L=L+1
200 NEXT J
210 B$=D$(1)
220 FOR L=1 TO 13-K+1
230 IF D$(L)<B$ THEN 250 ELSE 300
250 B$=D$(L)
300 NEXT L
400 C$(K)=B$
```

```
410 NEXT K
500 FOR K=1 TO 13
510 PRINT C$(K)
520 NEXT K
600 END
```

This program can clearly be modified to a program for alphabetizing any collection of strings. We will leave the details to the exercises.

It is possible to dissect strings using the three instructions **LEFT$, RIGHT$,** and **MID$.** These instructions allow you to construct a string consisting of a specified number of characters taken from the left, right, or middle of a designated string. For example, consider the instruction:

```
10 LET A$=LEFT$("LOVE",2)
```

The string A$ consists of the 2 leftmost characters of the string "LOVE". That is, A$ = "LO". Similarly, the instructions

```
20 LET B$="tennis"
30 LET C$=RIGHT$(B$,3)
```

set C$ equal to the string consisting of the three rightmost letters of the string B$, namely C$ = "nis". Similarly, if A$ = "Republican", then the instruction

```
40 LET D$=MID$(A$,5,3)
```

sets D$ equal to the string which consists of 3 characters starting with the fifth character of A$. That is, D$ = "bli". These last three instructions are absolutely indispensable in the design of word processors. The next example shows how they may be used to "form lines", one part of a word processing program.

Test Your Understanding 2.6

Determine the string constant

RIGHT$(LEFT$("computer",4),3).

Example 3. Suppose that A$ is a string consisting of a sequence of words. You may recognize a word by the space following it. Divide A$ into lines consisting of at most 80 characters. Make each line contain as close to 80 characters as possible. Do not break any words at the end of a line.

Solution. A program such as this one is used by a word processor to prepare lines for a printer with an 80 character wide carriage. Our program will first determine the length of the string. Then it will peel off the first 80 characters of the string as a new string B$. The program will then check whether the next character is a space. (This would indicate that B$ ends at the end of a word.) If so, then the line will consist of B$ itself. If not, the program will "count backwards" from the end of B$, throwing away characters until it finds a space, indicating the end of a word. The space will become the last character of the line. The finished line will be stored in the string C$(1). Any characters thrown away will be added to A$. The entire procedure will be repeated again, starting from A$, until all the characters of A$ are formed into lines. Here is the program:

```
5 CLEAR 1000
10 INPUT A$ :' INPUT CHARACTER STRING
20 LET L=LEN(A$)
30 LET N=INT(L/80)+1: ' N=# LINES
40 FOR J=1 TO N : ' J=CURRENT LINE #
50 LET B$=LEFT$(A$,80)
60 LET A$=RIGHT$(A$,L-80) : ' A$ IS NOW WHAT'S LEFT
70 LET L=LEN(A$) : 'L=LENGTH OF NEW A$
80 IF LEFT$(A$,1)=" " THEN 100 ELSE 200
100 LET C$(J)=B$: ' C$(J)=JTH FINISHED LINE
110 LET A$=RIGHT$(A$,L-1): 'DELETE LEFT HAND SPACE
120 GO TO 1000
190 REM 200-430 LOOK FOR WORD AT END OF B$
200 LET K=80: 'START FROM RIGHT OF B$
210 IF RIGHT$(B$,1)=" " THEN 300 ELSE 400
300 LET C$(J)=B$
310 IF J=N THEN 1000
400 LET A$=RIGHT$(B$,1)+A$
410 LET B$=LEFT$(B$,K-1)
420 K=K-1
430 GOTO 210
1000 NEXT J
1100 FOR J=1 TO N
1200 PRINT C$(J)
1300 NEXT J
1400 END
```

In manipulating strings, it is important to recognize the difference between numerical data and string data. The number 14 is denoted by 14; the string consisting of the two characters 14 is denoted "14". The first is a numerical constant and the second a string constant. We can perform arithmetic using the numerical constants. However, we cannot perform any of the character manipulation afforded by the instructions **RIGHT$, MID$,** and **LEFT$.** Such manipulation may only be performed on strings. So how may we perform character manipulation on numerical constants? BASIC provides a simple method. We first convert the numerical constants to string constants via STR$. For example, the number 14 may be converted into the string "14" via the instruction:

```
10 LET A$=STR$(14)
```

As a result of this instruction, A$ has the value " 14". Note the blank in front of the 14. This occurs because BASIC automatically leaves space for the sign of a number. If the number is positive, then the sign prints as a space. If the number is negative, then the sign prints as −. As another example, suppose that the variable B has the value 1.457. Then **STR$(B)** is equal to the string "1.457".

To convert strings consisting of numbers into numerical constants, use **VAL.** For example, consider this instruction:

```
20 LET B=VAL("3.78")
```

It sets B equal to 3.78. You may even use **VAL** for strings consisting of a number followed by other characters. **VAL** will pick off the initial number portion and throw away the part of the string which begins with the first non-numerical character. For example, VAL(12.5 inches) is equal to 12.5.

Test Your Understanding 2.7

Suppose that A$ = "5 percent", B$ = "758.45 dollars". Write a program which starts from A$ and B$ and computes 5% of $758.45.

EXERCISES (answers on 294)

1. Use the program of Example 2 to alphabetize the following sequence of words: justify, center, proof, character, capitalize, search, replace, indent, store, and password.
2. Use the program of Example 3 to form the following string into lines:

Word processing will revolutionize the office. Already, millions of word processing systems are in use. By the end of the decade, the typewriter will be totally obsolete. Word processing systems will increase in sophistication.

3. Modify the program of Example 3 so that the lines will be 64 characters long. (This will correspond to the standard length of lines on the video display.)

4. Modify the program of Example 3 so that the program requests the desired line length and forms lines of that length.

5. Write a program which rewrites the addition problem 15 + 48 + 97 = 160 in the form

```
 15
 48
 97
---
160
```

6. Write a program which inputs the string constants "$6718.49" and "$4801.96" and calculates the sum of the given dollar amounts.

Answers To Test Your Understanding

2.1:
70,79,82,32,83,65,76,69,58,32,66,101,97,103,108,101,32,112,117,
112,112,105,101,115,46,32,13,10,56,32,119,101,101,107,115,46,32,
36,49,50,53,46,13,10

2.2:
```
10 DATA 70,79, . . . . . . . . . . (insert data from 7.1)
11 DATA . . . . . . . .
12 DATA . . . . . . . .
20 FOR J=1 TO 42
30 READ A(J)
40 PRINT CHR$(A(J))
50 NEXT J
60 END
```

2.3:
```
10 DATA $,g,X,+
20 FOR J=1 TO 4
30 READ A$(J)
40 B(J)=ASC(A$(J))
50 PRINT A$(J), B(J)
60 NEXT J
70 END
```

2.4: Type RUN followed by the given string.

2.5: 47

2.6: "omp"

2.7:
```
10 A$="5 percent":B$="758.45 dollars"
20 A=VAL(A$):B=VAL(B$)
30 PRINT A$, "OF", B$, "IS"
40 PRINT A*B
50 END
```

7.3 PRINTER CONTROLS AND FORM LETTERS

Up to this point, we have mostly ignored the use of the printer. We have discussed the **LPRINT** and **LLIST** statements, but we have not discussed the fine points of printer use, such as controlling page format. However, for word processing applications, it is absolutely essential to the final appearance of your documents that you be able to control margins, number of lines per page, and so forth. In this section, we will discuss such printer controls and their use in producing form letters from a mailing list. Since most such applications utilize disk files, we will assume throughout this section that you are using disk BASIC.

Printer Operation

To use the printer, you must connect it properly to your computer. The simplest printers to connect are the ones sold by Radio Shack since the electronics necessary for the computer and printer to communicate with one another are already worked out. If you decide to buy a non-Radio Shack printer, make sure that your seller will assist you in interfacing the two pieces of equipment. (This can be a tricky job.) We will assume that your printer has been connected and is operational.

The printer accepts a stream of ASCII character codes. Some of these correspond to letters and symbols to be printed and some correspond to control characters which make the printer perform various non-print functions (such as carriage return, line feed, space to the top of the next page, and so forth). To the printer, a line consists of a sequence of printable characters followed by an ENTER. The ENTER actually tells the printer two things. First, it causes a carriage return; second, it causes the paper to advance one line (a so-called *line feed*).

Note that the printer will not respond to the graphics symbols of Model III BASIC. (For a discussion of graphics symbols, see the next chapter.) Certain printers allow the printing of graphics symbols, but the symbols are not likely to correspond to those of Model III BASIC. (For further information, see your printer manual.)

Setting Line Length

Printers have varied line lengths. In any case, paper comes in various widths so it is necessary to set the line length for your particular application. This is done via the **POKE** instruction. Line lengths are specified in terms of the number of characters per line. For technical reasons, the computer requires not the actual number of characters, but 2 less. So for 64 characters per line, you would specify the number 62; for 132 characters per line, you would specify 130; and so forth. This quantity is stored in memory location 16427. So to set the line length to 132 characters, use the instruction:

POKE 16427, 130

This instruction may be given when you first turn on the computer or within a BASIC program. In the latter case, you would not use a line number and the line length would be set for the entire programming session. The effect of **POKE**ing a line length into memory is to limit the number of characters which are allowed in a string variable. If you do not specify a line length, then the computer will automatically assume the default value of 255 characters per line.

Note that the line length is specified in number of characters and *not* in terms of inches. Some printers allow for either 10 or 12 characters per inch (10 or 12 pitch). In planning your line length, it is necessary to take into account both the pitch and the paper width.

Setting Page Length

The number of lines per page is also set via the **POKE** instruction. Memory location 16424 is used to control the number of lines per page. Actually, this location contains the number of lines plus 1. Most printers print 6 lines to the inch, so standard 11-inch long paper would accommodate 66 lines. This is the default (initial) value used by the computer. To change this value to 50 lines per page, for example, we would use the instruction:

POKE 16424, 51

This instruction may be given at the start of a programming session (without a line number) or within a BASIC program.

Top of Form

The computer keeps count of the number of lines on the page being currently sent to the printer. After the last line on the page, the computer sends the control character for a *form feed*. This causes the printer to space vertically to the beginning of the next page (as defined by the number of lines you specified). At the beginning of a program session, this line count is set equal to 1, corresponding to setting the paper to the beginning of a page. You may adjust the line count by **POKE**ing the desired line number into memory location 16425.

To advance to the top of the next page, give a BASIC instruction of the form:

10 LPRINT CHR$(12)

The character CHR$(12) is the ASCII code for "Form Feed". This command will cause the paper to advance by the number of lines remaining in the page.

To enter a form feed from the keyboard, strike the following keys simultaneously: **SHIFT** [↑] **L.** This sequence of keystrokes allows you to enter a form feed into a document you are preparing.

Margins

The line length and number of lines per page parameters do not take into account margins. Top and bottom margins are controlled by printing blank lines. The left margin is controlled by the position of the paper in the printer. The right margin is controlled by the line length.

Test Your Understanding 3.1

Suppose you are using 10 pitch type (10 characters to the inch) and are using vertical spacing of 3 lines to the inch. Write instructions which will set up your printer so as to leave one inch margins on both sides of standard 8 1/2" × 11" paper.

FORM LETTERS

You may use the string manipulating capability of your computer to prepare form letters that look like genuine correspondence. Let us illustrate the technique by preparing the following form letter to go to a mailing list of 100 customers.

April 1, 1981

Dear

All of us at Neighborhood building Supplies, Inc. have appreciated your patronage in the past. We are writing to let you know that we will move our store to 110 S. Main St., effective July 1. You will find the new store larger and more convenient than the old. In addition, we will now stock a more extensive line of energy-efficient doors and windows. We look forward to you continued patronage. Please let us know if we may be of assistance in your building plans.

Cordially yours,

Samuel Gordon,
President
Neighborhood Building Supplies, Inc.

Suppose that this letter is to go out to a mailing list of 100 customers. Suppose, further, that the mailing list is maintained in a data file on disk. Let us suppose that each address is stored as 4 strings, corresponding to the name of the individual, company name, street address, and city-state-zipcode. Finally, suppose that the name of the file is CUSTOMER. Let us write a program to produce the desired stack of 100 letters.

Our program will consist of two parts. The first will allow us to type in the body of the letter. The various lines of the letter will be typed exactly as if we were typing on a typewriter. The computer will use a string array A$(J) to store the body of the letter, with A$(1) holding the first line, A$(2) the second, and so forth. We will indicate to the computer that the body of the text is complete by typing **SHIFT,** [↑] and **A** simultaneously, followed by **ENTER.** This combination of keys generates a control character, namely ASCII code 2, but will not appear on the screen. The program will test each string input for this control character.

As soon as the control character is recognized, the program goes into its second phase, namely the actual generation of the letters. The program opens the address file for output. One by one it reads the address entries. After reading a given entry, it prints the date at the top of the letter, followed by the address. Next, the program determines the last name of the addressee from the first line of the address and inserts it after the "Dear". Finally, the body of the letter is printed. Here is the program which accomplishes all of this.

```
10 DIM A$(100)
20 CLEAR 10000
30 PRINT "AFTER EACH ? TYPE ONE LINE OF THE LETTER,"
40 PRINT "FOLLOWED BY ENTER"
45 PRINT " TO END LETTER, GENERATE CHR$(2)"
50 J=1 : ' J IS THE NUMBER OF LINES
60 INPUT A$(J)
70 IF A$(J)="CHR$(2)" THEN 100 ELSE 80
80 J=J+1: ' NEXT LINE
90 GOTO 60
100 OPEN "I",1,"CUSTOMER"
110 FOR N=1 TO 100:'N=CUSTOMER #
120 READ B$(1), B$(2), B$(3), B$(4)
130 LPRINT A$(1): ' PRINT DATE
140 LPRINT: ' PRINT BLANK LINE
145 REM 150-180 PRINT ADDRESS
150 LPRINT B$(1)
160 LPRINT B$(2)
170 LPRINT B$(3)
180 LPRINT B$(4)
190 REM FIND LAST NAME OF ADDRESSEE
200 LET L=LEN(B$(1))
210 FOR K=0 TO L-1
220 LET C$=MID$(B$(1),1,L-K)
230 IF C$=" " THEN 300 ELSE 240: 'TEST FOR SPACE BETWEEN
    WORDS
240 NEXT K
300 LET D$=RIGHT$(B$(1),K): 'D$=LAST NAME
310 LPRINT "Dear Mr. "; D$; ","
320 FOR M=2 TO J :' PRINT BODY OF LETTER
330 LPRINT A$(M)
340 NEXT M
350 NEXT N : ' GO TO NEXT CUSTOMER
360 CLOSE:' CLOSE CUSTOMER FILE
400 END
```

Note that for the above program to work properly, you should type the date in as the first line of the letter. However, you should not type in the line which begins "Dear". The program generates this line for you. Note also that this program always addresses the customer as "Mr.". This will insult a certain number of your customers. Suppose that your customer entries in the address list are labelled with "Mr.", "Mrs." or "Ms." preceding the name. Can you modify the above program to insert the correct title in the salutation of the letter?

The above program was used in the context of a specific letter. However, please note that the program is perfectly general and may be used to generate any set of form letters from an address list. In the exercises, we will suggest some modifications which you can use to generate invoices or other correspondence with variable text in the body of the letter.

EXERCISES

1. Add to the form letter of the text a second page. At the top of the page should be the date and the page number. The title should be "OPENING SPECIAL". The text should consist of the following message:

    This letter is being sent only to our most
    valued customers! Bring this coupon with
    you for a 10% discount on any order placed
    in the month of JULY, 1981.

2. Change the form letter of the text so that in the third and fourth sentences, the name of the addressee is used. (for example, "Ms. Thomas, you will find ...")
3. Write a program which prints invoices. Assume that the invoices are stored in a file called "INVOICE", where a particular invoice contains for each item shipped: quantity, price, item description (limited to 15 characters), and total cost. Assume that the invoice entry starts with a 4 string entry giving the customer name, address, and date. The file entry for a given invoice ends with the control character CHR$(2). You may assume that the first entry in the file is the number of invoices contained in the file. Your program should print out invoices corresponding to all entries in the file.
4. Suppose that the file INVOICE of Exercise 3 contains only a customer identification number rather than a customer name and address. Suppose that the list of customer addresses contains customer identifica-

tion numbers. Modify the program of Exercise 3 so that it locates the customer name and address automatically.

5. Suppose that a change in local ordinances now allows you not to charge local sales tax to any customer who lives outside the city limits. Suppose that city consists of ZIP CODE 91723. Modify the program of the text so that it checks the ZIP CODE of the customer. For customers not in ZIP CODE 91723, insert the following paragraph in the letter:

    Good news! You will no longer be charged
    local sales tax, in accordance with the
    change in local ordinances. This will
    yield even further savings from our
    already low prices.

Answer To Test Your Understanding

3.1: POKE 16427,63
POKE 16424,34
Position paper so that 1"of paper is to the left of column 1 on the printer.

7.4 CONTROL CHARACTERS

In performing word processing, it is necessary to use all the components of your computer system. The keyboard is used to type in documents; the memory (usually diskettes) is used to store copies of documents; and the video display allows you to inspect the current version of a document. In this section, we will discuss the control characters, which allow you to control the display.

General Information

The control characters correspond to ASCII codes 1 through 31. Codes 1-26 may be entered via the keyboard by hitting simultaneously SHIFT, [↓], and one of the letters A-Z. Not all of the codes 1-31 are recognized by the Model III, however. We will describe the most significant control codes below.

The control characters may be used in BASIC programs by means of the **PRINT CHR$** instruction. For example, ASCII code 24 moves the cursor one space backward without erasing. To execute this cursor motion from a BASIC program, use the instruction:

10 PRINT CHR$(24)

Since a control character does not correspond to a printable character, the above instruction will move the cursor but will not cause any other change in the display.

Control characters are also recognized by the printer. For example the control character with ASCII code 10 is a line feed, which causes the paper to advance one line. To send a control character to the printer use the **LPRINT CHR$** instruction. For example, the following instruction will cause the printer to advance the paper one line:

20 LPRINT CHR$(10)

Note that the same control character can mean one thing to the display and another to the printer. For example, consider the control character CHR$(10). This character causes the video display to advance the cursor to the start of the next line and erase that line.

Cursor Motion Controls

In a word processing system, the cursor indicates your current position in a document. Therefore, in order to move from place to place within a document, it is important to be able to move the cursor at will. There are four fundamental cursor motions: left, right, up, and down. Here are the corresponding ASCII codes and the method of ordering the indicated motions from the keyboard:

cursor motion	keyboard	ASCII code
left (no erase)	SHIFT [↓] or SHIFT [↓] X	24
right	SHIFT [↓] Y	25
down	SHIFT [↓] Z	26
up	SHIFT [↑]	27

We can determine the column in which the cursor is currently located by using the BASIC function **POS(0).** For example, if the cursor is currently located in column 37, then **POS(0)** is equal to 37. Unfortunately, Model III BASIC does not have a function giving the row in which the cursor is currently located. If you wish to utilize this quantity in a program, then it will be necessary for you to keep track of the vertical position of the cursor.

Test Your Understanding 4.1

(a) Using the keyboard, move the cursor two spaces to the right and two spaces down.

(b) Write BASIC instructions to perform the operations of (a) from a program.

Other Control Characters

Here are some other controls on the cursor. In some applications (especially some computer games), you may wish to turn the cursor off. This may be done via control character 15. To turn the cursor back on, use control character 14. To move the cursor to the upper left corner ("home" the cursor), use control code 28.

The ENTER key generates control character 13. Note that the ENTER key moves the cursor to the start of the next line and erases that line. However, when used as a printer control character, ASCII code 13 will generate a carriage return *without a line feed.* That is, code 13 will cause the printer to move to the beginning of the line. However, the paper will not advance.

The BREAK key corresponds to code 1. The CLEAR key corresponds to code 31.

The Model III recognizes several other control characters, but they are not very important for beginners. For a complete list of control characters and their keyboard equivalents, consult Appendix C of **TRS-80 Model III Operation and BASIC Language Reference Manual.**

EXERCISES (answers on 295)

1. Practice moving the cursor to various positions on the screen.
2. Write a program to move the cursor to the bottom of the column in which it currently resides.

3. Write a program which moves the cursor to the left of the screen in the row in which it now resides.

Answer To Test Your Understanding

4.1 (a) Hit SHIFT [↑] Y two times and SHIFT [↑] Z two times.

(b)
```
10 PRINT CHR$(25)
20 PRINT CHR$(25)
30 PRINT CHR$(26)
40 PRINT CHR$(26)
50 END
```

7.5 USING YOUR COMPUTER AS A WORD PROCESSOR

So far in this chapter, we have attempted to introduce you to the various text manipulation features of the TRS-80 Model III. We have mentioned "word processing" quite often and have attempted to give a smattering of word processing you can accomplish using homegrown programs. However, your computer is capable of quite a bit more. More, in fact, than we can possibly describe in this introductory book and more than a novice programmer can expect to accomplish on his or her own. Although we cannot go into great detail, we will close this chapter with a description of some of the word processing you can expect your computer to accomplish using commercially available software.

Let's begin by describing some of the typical features of a word processing system you can run on your Model III. A word processing system is a computer program for creating, storing, and editing text.

At its most basic level, you use a word processing system like you would a typewriter. Suppose, for example, that you wish to prepare a proposal. You would turn on the computer, and run the word processing program. The program first asks for the type of work you would like to perform. Possibilities include: type in a new document, edit an old document, save a document on diskette, or print a document. We would select the first option. We next describe various format parameters to the word processor: line width, number of characters per inch, number of lines per page, spacing between lines, and so forth.

Now we type the proposal exactly as we would on a typewriter. With several huge exceptions, however! First of all, we do not worry about carriage returns. The word processor takes care of the task of forming lines. It accepts the text we type, decides how much can go on a line, forms the line, and displays it. Any leftover text is automatically saved for the next line. The only function of the carriage return is to indicate a place where you definitely want a new line, such as at the end of a paragraph.

A second advantage of a word processor occurs in correcting errors. To correct an error, we move the cursor to the site of the mistake, give a command to erase the erroneous letter(s) or word(s), and type the replacement(s). Of course, such action will generally destroy the structure of the lines. (Some lines may now be too long and others too short.) However, by using a simple command, it is possible to "reform" the lines according to the requested format.

Typically, a word processor has commands which enable you to scroll through the text of a document, looking for a particular paragraph. Some word processors even allow you to mark certain points so that you may turn to them without a visual search.

When the proposal is finally typed to your satisfaction, you give an instruction which saves a copy of it on diskette. At a future time, you may recall the document and add to it at any point (even within the bodies of paragraphs!). Typically, word processors allow certain "block operations" which allow you to "mark" a block and then either delete it, copy it, or move it to another part of the document. You may also insert other documents into the current document. This is convenient, for example, in adding boiler plate, such as resumes, to your proposal. You may even use the block operations to alter boiler plate to fit the special needs of the current proposal.

You may construct your proposal in as many sessions as you wish. When your diskette finally contains the proposal as you want it, you finally give the instruction to print. Your printer will now produce a finished, error-free copy of the proposal.

As if the above were not enough of an improvement over the conventional typewriter, the typical word processor or can do even more. The features available depend, of course, on the word processor selected. However, here are some of the goodies to look for:

Global Search and Replace. Suppose that you wish to resubmit your proposal to another company, Acme Energetics. In your original proposal, you included numerous references to the original company, Jet Energetics. A global search and replace feature allows you to instruct the computer to replace every occurrence of a particular phrase with another phrase. For example, we could replace every occurrence of "Acme Energetics" with "Jet Energetics". Global search and replace can be even more sophisticated. In some systems, the word processor can be instructed to ask you whether or not to make each individual change. Another variation is to instruct the word processor to match any capitalization in the phrases replaced.

Centering. After typing a line you may center it using a simple command.

Boldface. You may print certain words in darker type.

Underscore. You may indicate underscoring portions of the text.

Subscripts and Superscripts. You may indicate printing of subscripts (as in a_1) and superscripts (as in a^2). This is extremely useful for scientific typing.

Justification. You may instruct the word processor to "justify" the right hand margins of your text, so that the text always ends exactly at the end of a line. (This is possible only if you have a printer which is capable of spacing in increments smaller than the width of a single letter.)

Spelling Correction. There now exist a number of spelling correction programs which compare words of your document against a dictionary (sizes range from 20,000 to 70,000 words). If the program does not find a match, it asks you if the word is spelled correctly and gives you an opportunity to add the word to the dictionary. In this way the output of a word processor can be proofread by computer.

The most natural and least expensive word processor for the owner of a Model III is the SCRIPSIT* program available from Radio Shack. It is not as powerful as some of the others available, but it is quite adequate for all but the most heavyduty document preparation. You should consider adding word processing capability to your computer at the earliest possible date.

7.6 A DO-IT-YOURSELF WORD PROCESSOR

It is really quite impractical for you to build your own word processor. For one thing, such a program is quite long and complicated. Moreover, if you write in BASIC, the operation of the program will tend of be rather slow. An

---

* Registered trademark of the Tandy Corporation.

efficient word processor will almost always be written in machine language. Nevertheless, in order to acquaint you with a few of the virtues of word processing, let's ignore what I just said and build a word processor anyway!

Our word processor will be line oriented. That is, you will type in each line just as if you are typing it on a typewriter. At the end of each line, you will give a carriage return by typing ENTER. The Jth line will be stored in the string variable A$(J). Let's assume you have a 16K version of the Model III. This will allow us to store and edit a document of about 5 double-spaced, typed pages. Our word processor will have 5 modes. In the first mode, we input the text of our document. This operation will proceed exactly as if you were typing on a typewriter. At the beginning of each line, the word processor will display a ?. You type your line after the question mark. Terminate the line with ENTER. In order to indicate that you do not wish to type any more lines, type SHIFT [↑] B (CHR$(2)). This generates a control character that is not otherwise used by the Model III.

A second mode allows us to save our document. For purposes of this word processor, let's assume that you have a disk file. The program then saves your document as a data file under a file name requested by the program. The first item in a document file will always by the number of lines in the document. This quantity will be denoted by the variable L. Next come the lines of the document: A$(1), A$(2), . . . , A$(L) .

A third mode allows you to produce a draft version of the document. In this mode, the document is printed with each line preceded by its line number. The line numbers allow you to easily identify lines having errors. Note that in order to print a document, you must save it on the disk first.

A fourth mode allows editing of the document. To correct errors, you identify the line by number and retype the line. To end the edit session type SHIFT [↑] B (CHR$(2)). This will bring you back to the beginning of the program, but you will still be working on the same document. After ending an edit session, your customary next action should be to save the document.

The fifth and final mode allows printing of a final draft of a document.

When the word processor is run, you will see the following prompt:

WORD PROCESSING PROGRAM
CHOOSE ONE OF THE FOLLOWING MODES
INPUT TEXT(I)
PRINT DRAFT (PD)
PRINT FINAL DRAFT (PF)

SAVE FILE (S)
EDIT (E)
QUIT (Q)

In response, you type one of I, PD, PF, S, E or Q, followed by ENTER. If you choose I, the screen will be cleared and you may begin typing your document. For the other modes, there are prompts to tell you what to do. Here is a listing of the program.

```
5 DIM A$(150)
10 PRINT "WORD PROCESSING PROGRAM"
20 PRINT "CHOOSE ONE OF THE FOLLOWING MODES"
30 PRINT , "INPUT TEXT(I)"
40 PRINT, "PRINT DRAFT(PD)"
50 PRINT , "PRINT FINAL DRAFT(PF)"
60 PRINT , "SAVE FILE(S)"
70 PRINT , "EDIT(E)"
80 PRINT , "QUIT(Q)"
90 INPUT X$
100 IF X$="I" THEN 1000
110 IF X$="PD" THEN 2000
120 IF X$="PF" THEN 3000
130 IF X$="S" THEN 4000
140 IF X$="E" THEN 5000
150 IF X$="Q" THEN 6000
160 GOTO 90: 'IF X$ DOES NOT MATCH ANY OF THE PROMPTS
1000 L=1
1010 LINE INPUT A$(L)
1020 IF A$(L)=CHR$(2) THEN 10
1030 L=L+1
1040 IF L>150 PRINT "DOCUMENT TOO LARGE" ELSE 1010
1050 GOTO 10
2000 INPUT "DOCUMENT NAME";Y$
2010 OPEN "I",1,Y$
2020 INPUT #1, L
2030 FOR K=1 TO L
2040 LINE INPUT #1,A$(K)
2050 LPRINT K;">";A$(K)
2060 NEXT K
2070 CLOSE 1
2090 GOTO 10
3000 INPUT "DOCUMENT NAME";Y$
3010 OPEN "I",1,Y$
3020 INPUT #1, L
3030 FOR K=1 TO L
```

```
3040 LINE INPUT #1,A$(K)
3050 LPRINT A$(K)
3060 NEXT K
3070 CLOSE 1
3090 GOTO 10
4000 INPUT "DOCUMENT NAME";Y$
4010 OPEN "O",1,Y$
4020 PRINT #1, L
4030 FOR K=1 TO L
4040 LINE PRINT #1, A$(K)
4050 NEXT K
4060 CLOSE 1
4070 GOTO 10
5000 INPUT "DOCUMENT NAME"; Y$
5010 OPEN "I",1,Y$
5020 INPUT #1, L
5030 FOR K=1 TO L
5040 LINE INPUT #1, A$(K)
5050 NEXT K
5060 INPUT "NUMBER OF LINE TO EDIT";Z
5070 CLS
5080 PRINT A$(Z)
5090 INPUT "TYPE CORRECTED LINE";A$(Z)
5100 IF A$(Z) <> "%" THEN 5060
5110 GOTO 10
6000 END
```

You should attempt to use this program to type a few letters. You will find it a big improvement over a conventional typewriter. Moreover, it will probably whet your appetite for the more advanced word processing features we have described in the preceding section.

EXERCISES

1. Modify the word processor to allow input of line width. (You will not be able to display lines longer than 64 characters on a single line. However, string variables may contain up to 255 characters.)
2. Modify the word processor so that you may extend a line. This modification should allow your corrected line to spill over into the next line of text. The program should then correct all of the subsequent lines to reflect the addition.
3. Modify the word processor to allow deletions from lines. Subsequent lines should be modified to reflect the deletion.

8

Computer Games

In the last few years computer games have captured the imaginations of millions of people. In this chapter, we will build several computer games which utilize both the random number generator and the graphics capabilities of the Model III.

8.1 BLIND TARGET SHOOT

The object of this game is shoot down a target on the screen by moving your cursor to hit the target. The catch is that you only have a two second look at your target! The program begins by asking if your are ready. If so, you type READY. The computer then randomly chooses a spot to place the target. It lights up the spot for two seconds. The cursor is then moved to the upper left position of the screen (the so-called "home" position). You must then move the cursor to the target, based on your brief glimpse of it. You have 10 seconds to hit the target. (See Figure 8-1.)

Your score is based on your distance from the target, as measured in terms of moves it would take to get to the target from your final position. Here is the list of possible scores:

Distance From Target	Score
0	100
1 or 2	90
3 to 5	70
6 to 10	50
11 to 15	30
16 to 20	10
over 20	0

Figure 8-1. Blind target shoot.

You move the cursor using the keys S, D, E, and X. The cursor moves the way these keys are arranged on the keyboard, namely:

S = move one unit to the left

D = move one to the right

E = move one unit up

X = one unit down

To input the above letters while the program is run, we need to use the **INKEY$** instruction. This instruction reads the keyboard and returns the last key depressed on the keyboard. That is, if the last key depressed was an A then **INKEY$** will equal the string constant "A".

Test Your Understanding 1.1

Assume that the program inputs the letter S via the **INKEY$** instruction. What should be the computer's next instruction?

Here is a sample session with the game. The underlined lines are those you type.

<u>RUN</u>

BLIND TARGET SHOOT
TO BEGIN GAME, TYPE "READY"
<u>READY</u>

Screen Clears. Target is displayed. See Figure 8-2.

The screen is cleared. The cursor is moved to the home position. See Figure 8-3A. The cursor is then moved to the remembered position of the target. See Figure 8-3B. Time runs out. See Figure 8-3C.

The score is calculated. See Figure 8-4.

Figure 8-2.

Figure 8-3A.

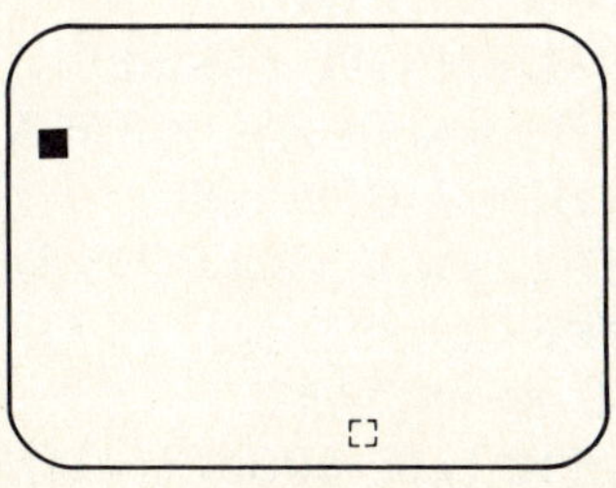

Figure 8-3B.

Figure 8-3C.

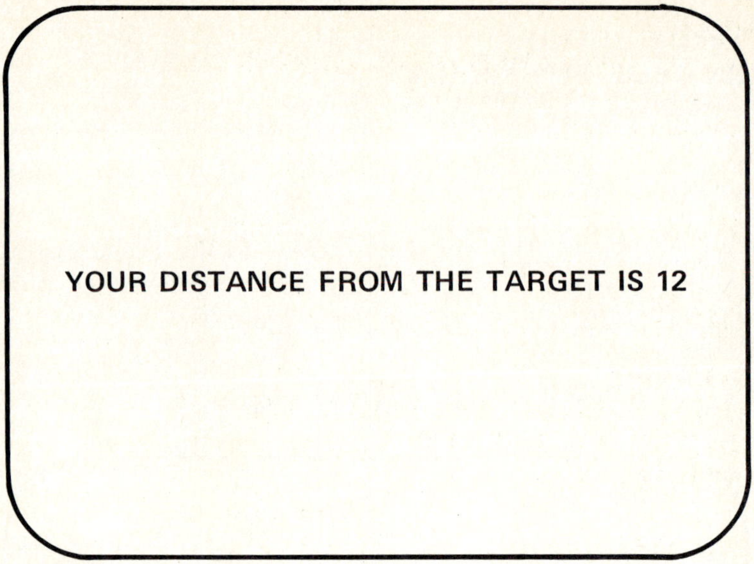

Figure 8-4.

Here is a listing of our program.

```
10 PRINT "BLIND TARGET SHOOT"
20 PRINT "TO BEGIN GAME, TYPE "READY"
30 INPUT A$
40 IF A$="READY" THEN 90 ELSE 10
90 CLS
100 POKE 16919,0:'SET CLOCK SECONDS TO 0
110 PRINT CHR$(15):'MOMENTARILY TURN CURSOR OFF
120 X(0)=RND(128)-1:'CHOOSE RANDOM COLUMN
130 Y(0)=RND(64)-1:'CHOOSE RANDOM ROW
140 SET(X(0),Y(0))
150 IF PEEK(16919)=2 THEN 200 ELSE 160
160 GOTO 150 : WAIT 2 SECONDS
200 RESET (X(0),Y(0)):'TURN OFF TARGET
210 PRINT CHR$(14): 'TURN CURSOR BACK ON
220 PRINT CHR$(28):'HOME CURSOR
300 POKE 16919,0:'SET CLOCK SECONDS TO 0
310 X=0,Y=0: (X,Y) ARE COORDINATES OF CURSOR
400 A$=INKEY$:'READ KEYBOARD
500 IF A$="E" THEN 510 ELSE 600:'CURSOR UP
510 IF X>1 THEN 520 ELSE 1000
520 PRINT CHR$(27)
```

```
530 X=X-1
540 GOTO 1000
600 IF A$="X" THEN 610 ELSE 700:'CURSOR DOWN
610 IF X<24 THEN 620 ELSE 1000
620 PRINT CHR$(26)
630 X=X+1
640 GOTO 1000
700 IF A$="D" THEN 710 ELSE 800:'CURSOR RIGHT
710 IF X<127 THEN 720 ELSE 1000
720 PRINT CHR$(25)
730 X=X+1
740 GOTO 1000
800 IF A$="S" THEN 810 ELSE 1000:'CURSOR LEFT
810 IF Y>1 THEN 820 ELSE 1000
820 PRINT CHR$(24)
830 Y=Y-1
840 GOTO 1000
1000 IF PEEK(16919)=10 THEN 1100 ELSE 400
1100 T=ABS(X-X(0))+ABS(Y-Y(0)):'T=DIST. TO TARGET
1105 CLS
1110 PRINT "YOUR DISTANCE FROM THE TARGET IS",T
1120 IF T=0 THEN PRINT "CONGRATULATIONS!"
1130 IF T=0 THEN PRINT "YOU HIT THE TARGET."
1140 SC=100
1150 IF D>0 THEN SC=SC-10
1160 IF D>2 THEN SC=SC-20
1170 IF D>5 THEN SC=SC-20
1180 IF D>10 THEN SC=SC-20
1190 IF D>15 THEN SC=SC-20
1200 IF D>20 THEN SC=SC-10
1300 PRINT "YOUR SCORE IS", SC
1400 INPUT "DO YOU WISH TO PLAY AGAIN(Y/N)";B$
1410 IF B$="Y" THEN 20 ELSE 1500
1500 END
```

EXERCISES

1. Experiment with the above program by making the time of target viewing shorter or longer than one second.
2. Experiment with the above program by making the time for target location shorter or longer than ten seconds.

3. Modify the program to keep a running total score for a sequence of ten games.
4. Modify the program to allow for two players, keeping a running total score for a sequence of ten games. At the end of ten games, the computer should announce the total scores and declare the winner.

Answer to Test Your Understanding 1.1

See line 800 of the listing.

8.2 TIC-TAC-TOE

In this section, we present a program for the traditional game of tic-tac-toe. We will not attempt to let the computer execute a strategy. Rather, we will let it be fairly stupid and choose it's moves randomly. Moreover, we use the random number generator to "flip" for the first move. Throughout the program, you will be "O" and the computer will be "X". Here is a sample game.

```
LOAD "TICTAC"
READY
RUN
```

Figure 8-5.

```
TIC TAC TOE
YOU WILL BE O;THE COMPUTER WILL BE X
THE POSITIONS OF THE BOARD ARE NUMBERED
AS FOLLOWS:
          1          2          3
          4          5          6
          7          8          9
THE COMPUTER WILL TOSS FOR FIRST.
YOU GO FIRST.
WHEN READY TO BEGIN TYPE 'R'
R
```

Figure 8-6.

Test Your Understanding 2.1

How can the computer toss to see who goes first?

The computer now draws a TIC-TAC-TOE board. See Figure 8-7.

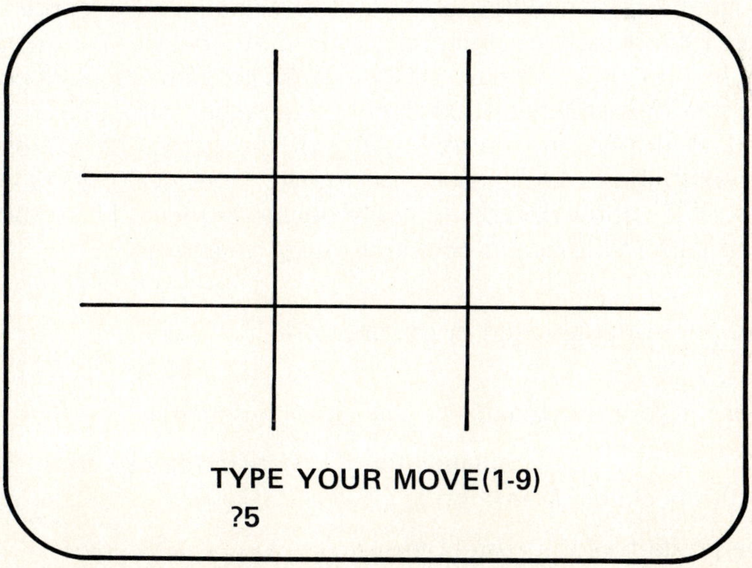

Figure 8-7.

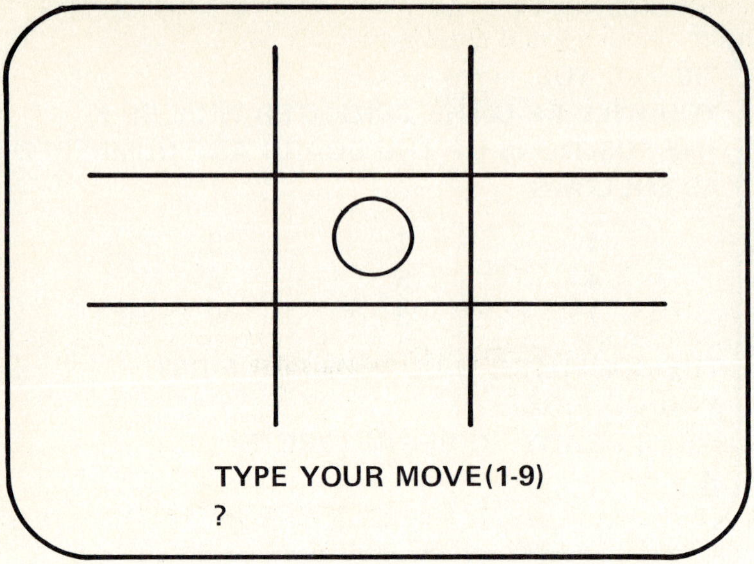

Figure 8-8.

The computer now displays your move and makes a move of its own. See Figure 8-8. The computer will now make its move and so on until someone wins or a tie game results.

The program below makes use of much of what we have learned. First of all, we used the graphics command SET to draw the TIC-TAC-TOE board, beginning in line 2000. We have structured the program so that it consists of a series of subroutines. Lines 2000–2999 contain the instructions to draw the board and to display the current status of the game. Lines 3000–3999 contain a subroutine which inputs your move. Lines 4000–4999 contain a subroutine which allows the computer to decide its move. Lines 5000–5999 process the current move and decide if the game is over.

Here are the variables used in the program.

Z = 0 if it's your move and =1 if it's the computer's

A$(J) (J=1, 2, . . . , 9) contain either O, X, or the empty string, indicating the current status of position J

S = the position of the current move

M = the number of moves played (including the current one)

We used a video display worksheet to lay out the board and to determine the coordinates for the lines and the X's and O's.

Here is a listing of our program.

```
10 DIM A$(9)
20 DIM B$(3,3,3)
30 CLS
40 PRINT "TIC TAC TOE"
50 PRINT "YOU WILL BE O; THE COMPUTER WILL BE X"
60 PRINT "THE POSITIONS ON THE BOARD ARE NUMBERED"
70 PRINT "AS FOLLOWS"
80 PRINT 1,2,3
90 PRINT 4,5,6
100 PRINT 7,8,9
110 PRINT "THE COMPUTER WILL TOSS FOR FIRST"
120 IF RND(0)>.5 THEN 130 ELSE 160
130 PRINT "YOU GO FIRST"
140 LET Z=0
150 GOTO 180
160 PRINT "I'LL GO FIRST"
170 LET Z=1
180 PRINT "WHEN READY TO BEGIN TYPE 'R' "
190 INPUT C$
200 IF C$="R" THEN 210 ELSE 180
210 GOSUB 2000
300 FOR M=1 TO 9: 'M=MOVE #
310 IF Z=0 THEN GOSUB 3000
320 IF Z=1 THEN GOSUB 4000
330 Z=1-Z: REM Z=1 MEANS NEXT MOVE IS COMPUTER
340 REM DECIDE IF GAME IS ENDED
350 IF W=1 THEN 400 ELSE NEXT M
360 PRINT "THE GAME IS TIED"
400 END
2000 REM DRAW TIC TAC TOE BOARD
2010 CLS
2020 FOR J=1 TO 2
2030 FOR K=0 TO 127
2040 SET (K,16*J)
2050 NEXT K
2060 NEXT J
2070 FOR J=1 TO 2
2080 FOR K=0 TO 47
```

```
2090 SET (40*J,K)
2100 NEXT K
2110 NEXT J
2115 REM DISPLAY CURRENT GAME STATUS
2120 PRINT @138,A$(1)
2121 PRINT @159,A$(2)
2122 PRINT @180,A$(3)
2123 PRINT @458,A$(4)
2124 PRINT @480,A$(5)
2125 PRINT @500,A$(6)
2126 PRINT @842,A$(7)
2127 PRINT @864,A$(8)
2128 PRINT @884,A$(9)
2130 RETURN
3000 PRINT @960,"TYPE YOUR MOVE (1–9)"
3010 INPUT S
3020 A$(S)="O"
3030 GOSUB 2000
3040 GOSUB 5000
3050 RETURN
4000 LET S=RND(9)
4010 IF A$(S)="" THEN 4060 ELSE 4000
4060 A$(S)="X"
4070 GOSUB 2000
4080 GOSUB 5000
4090 RETURN
5000 IF Z=0 THEN C$="O" ELSE C$="X"
5010 IF A$(1)=A$(2) THEN 5011 ELSE 5020
5011 IF A$(1)=A$(3) THEN 5900
5020 IF A$(1)=A$(4) THEN 5021 ELSE 5030
5021 IF A$(1)=A$(7) THEN 5900
5030 IF A$(1)=A$(5) THEN 5031 ELSE 5040
5031 IF A$(1)=A$(9) THEN 5900
5040 IF A$(2)=A$(5) THEN 5041 ELSE 5050
5041 IF A$(2)=A$(8) THEN 5900
5050 IF A$(3)=A$(6) THEN 5051 ELSE 5060
5051 IF A$(3)=A$(9) THEN 5900
5060 IF A$(4)=A$(5) THEN 5061 ELSE 5070
5061 IF A$(4)=A$(6) THEN 5900
5070 IF A$(7)=A$(8) THEN 5071 ELSE 5080
5071 IF A$(7)=A$(9) THEN 5900
5080 IF A$(3)=A$(5) THEN 5081 ELSE 5990
```

```
5081 IF A$(3)=A$(7) THEN 5900 ELSE 5990
5900 PRINT C$, "WINS THIS ROUND":W=1
5990 RETURN
```

EXERCISES

1. Modify the above program so that you and the computer may play a series of ten games. The computer should decide the champion of the series.
2. Modify the above program to play 4 × 4 Tic-Tac-Toe.

Answer to Test Your Understanding 2.1

See lines 120–170 of the listing.

9

Programming For Scientists

In this chapter, we will discuss some aspects of Model III programming of interest to scientists, engineers, and mathematicians. In particular, we will introduce the library of mathematical functions which can be used in Model III BASIC.

9.1 SINGLE AND DOUBLE PRECISION NUMBERS

Up to this point, we have used the computer to perform arithmetic without giving much thought to the level of accuracy of the numbers involved. However, when doing scientific programming, it is absolutely essential to know the number of decimal places of accuracy of the computations. So let's begin this chapter by discussing the form in which BASIC stores and utilizes numbers.

Actually, BASIC recognizes three different types of numeric constants: integer, single precision, and double precision.

An *integer* numeric constant is an ordinary integer (positive or negative) in the range −32768 to +32767. Here are some examples of integer numeric constants:

7, 58, 3712, −15, −598

Integer numeric constants may be stored very efficiently in RAM. Moreover, arithmetic with integer numeric constants takes the least time. Therefore, in order to realize these efficiencies, the Model III recognizes integer numeric constants and handles them in a special way.

A *single-precision* constant is a number having seven or fewer digits. Some examples of single precision constants are:

5.135, −63.5785, 1234567, −1.467654E12

Note that a single-precision constant may be expressed in "scientific" or "floating point" notation, as in the final example. In such an expression, however, you are limited to seven or fewer digits. In Model III BASIC, single-precision constants must lie within the ranges: Between -1×10^{38} and -1×10^{-38}; Between 1×10^{-38} and 1×10^{38}. This is a limitation that is seldom much of a limitation in practice. After all, 1×10^{-38} equals

.00000000000000000000000000000000000001

(37 zeros followed by a 1), which is about as small a number as you are ever likely to encounter! Similarly, 1×10^{38} equals

100,000,000,000,000,000,000,000,000,000,000,000,000

(a 1 followed by 38 zeros), which is large enough for most practical calculations.

A *double-precision* numeric constant is a number containing more than 7 digits. Here are some examples of double-precision numbers:

2.0000000000, 3578930497594, −3946.635475495

Scientific notation may also be used to represent double-precision numbers: use the letter D to precede the exponent. For example, the number

2.7575757575D-4

equals the double-precision constant:

.00027575757575

The number

1.3145926535D15

equals the double-precision constant:

1,314,159,265,350,000

A double-precision constant may have up to 17 digits. Double-precision constants are subject to the same range limitations as single-precision constants.

Single-precision constants occupy more RAM than do integer constants. Moreover, arithmetic with single-precision constants proceeds more slowly than integer arithmetic. Similarly, double-precision constants occupy even more memory and arithmetic proceeds even more slowly than with single-precision constants. The Model III is programmed to recognize each of the three types of numerical constants and to use only as much arithmetic power as necessary.

Here are the rules for determining the type of a numerical constant:

1. Any integer in the range −32768 and 32767 is an integer constant.
2. Any number having seven or fewer digits and is not an integer constant is a single-precision constant. Any number in scientific notation using an E before the exponent is assumed to be a single-precision constant. If a number has more than 7 digits in scientific notation but uses an E, it will be truncated after the seventh digit. For example, the number

   1.23456789E15

   will be interpreted as the single-precision constant

   1.234567E15
3. A number having more than seven digits will be interpreted as a double-precision constant. If more than 17 digits are specified, then the number will be truncated after the l7th digit and written in scientific notation. For example, the number

   123456789123456789

   will be interpreted as the double-precision constant

   1.2345678912345678D18

The type of numeric constant may be specified by means of a *type declaration tag*. For instance, a numeric constant followed by % will be interpreted as an integer constant. Any fractional part of the number will be truncated. For example, the constant

25.87%

will be interpreted as the constant:

25

(If the constant is too large to be an integer constant, an OVERFLOW error will occur.) A numeric constant followed by ! will be interpreted as single-precision and truncated accordingly. For example, the constant

1.23456789!

will be interpreted as:

1.234567

The constant

1234567 89!

will be truncated to seven significant digits and written in scientific notation:

1.234567E9

A # serves as a type declaration tag to indicate a double-precision constant. For example, the constant

1.2#

will be interpreted as the 17-digit double-precision constant

1.2000000000000000

In scientific notation, the letters E and D serve as type declaration tags.

Test Your Understanding 1.1

Write out the decimal form of the following numbers:

(a) −7.5%

(b) 4.589234501836 49E12

(c) 270D-2

(d) 12.55#

(e) −1.62!

A type declaration tag supersedes the rules 1–4. in determining the type of a numeric constant.

Let's now discuss the way BASIC performs arithmetic with the various constant types. The variable type of the result of an arithmetic operation is determined from the variable types of the data entering into the operation. For example, the sum of two integer constants will be an integer constant, provided that the answer is within the range of an integer constant. If not, the sum will be a single-precision constant. Arithmetic operations among single-precision constants will always yield single-precision constants. Arithmetic constants among double-precision constants will yield a double-precision result. Here are some examples of arithmetic:

5% + 7%

The computer will add the two integer constants 5 and 7 to obtain the integer constant 12.

4.21! + 5.2!

The computer will add the two single-precision constants 4.21 and 5.2 to obtain the single-precision result 9.41.

3/2

Here the two constants 3 and 2 are of the integer type. However, since the result, 1.5, is not an integer, it is assumed to be of single-precision type. Similarly, the result of

1/3

is the single-precision constant .3333333. Similarly, the result of the double-precision calculation

1#/3#

is the double-precision constant .3333333333333333.

Test Your Understanding 1.2

What result will the computer obtain for the following problems?

(a) 2/5 + 1/3

(b) (2/5)% + (1/3)%

(c) (2/5)# + (1/3)#

(d) (2/5)! + (1/3)!

It is important to realize that if a number does not have an exact decimal representation (such as 1/3 = .333 . . .) or if the number has a decimal representation which has too many digits for the constant type being used, then the computer will be working with an approximation to the number rather than the number itself. The built-in errors caused by the approximations of the computer are called *round-off errors*. For example, consider the problem of calculating:

1/3 + 1/3 + 1/3

As we have seen above, 1/3 is stored as the single-precision constant .3333333. The computer will form the sum as

.3333333 + .3333333 + .3333333 = .9999999.

So the sum has a round-off error of .0000001.

Note that BASIC makes up for these round-off errors by displaying only six digits for single-precision constants. These digits are obtained by rounding off the seven digits contained in the computer. In the case of the problem just considered, the computer will take the answer .9999999, round it off to six places to give 1.000000, which is the value which will be displayed. By calculating with seven digits and displaying only six, the computer guarantees that any single arithmetic operation will be accurate to six digits. This does not mean that you will never see round-off errors. Rather, you will not see them if their effect is confined to the seventh digit. If the effect of round-off error spills over into the sixth digit or beyond (as might be the case if many operations are performed, with each contributing its own round-off error), then the displayed answer will contain some round-off error. (See the exercises.)

Just as single-precision constants are rounded off to six digits for display purposes, double-precision constants are rounded off to 16 digits. For a single arithmetic operation, the computer's design guarantees that a double-precision answer will be accurate to 16 digits. Of course, if you perform many such operations, it is possible that cumulative round-off error will make the 16th or earlier digits inaccurate.

Test Your Understanding 1.3

What answer will be displayed for each of the problems (a) through (d) of Test Your Understanding 1.2?

EXERCISES (answers on 295)

For each of the constants below, determine the number stored by the computer.

1. 3
2. 2.37
3. 5.78E5
4. 2#
5. 3!
6. −4.1!
7. −4.1%
8. 3500.6847586958658!
9. 2.176D2

10. −5.94E12
11. 3.5869504003837265374
12. −234542383746.21
13. −2.367D20
14. 4570000000000000000!

For each of the arithmetic problems below, determine the number as stored by the computer.

15. 1 + 45
16. 2/4
17. 3#/5#
18. 3!/5! + 1
19. 2#/3#
20. 2#/3# + .53#
21. 2/3
22. 2/3 + .53
23. .5E4 − .37E2
24. 1.75D3 − 1.0D-5
25. For each of the exercises 15–24, determine how the computer will display the result.
26. Calculate 1/3 + 1/3 + 1/3 + . . . + 1/3 (10 1/3's) using single-precision constants. What answer is displayed? Is this answer accurate to 6 digits? If not, explain why not.
27. Answer the same question as 26, but use double-precision constants and 17 digits.

Answers to Test Your Understanding 1.1-1.3

1.1: (a) −7

(b) 4,589,234,000,000

(c) 2.7000000000000000

(d) 12.550000000000000

(e) −1.620000

1.2: (a) .7333333

(b) 0

(c) .7333333333333333

(d) .7333333

1.3: (a) .733333

(b) 0

(c) .7333333333333333

(d) .733333

9.2 VARIABLE TYPES

In the previous section, we introduced the various types of numerical constants: integer, single-precision, and double-precision. There is a parallel set of types for variables.

A variable *of integer type* takes on values which are constants of integer type. A variable of integer type is indicated by the symbol % after the variable name. Thus, for example, here are some variables of integer type:

A%, BB%, A1%

In setting the value of a variable of integer type, the computer will truncate any fractional parts to obtain an integer. For example, the instruction

10 LET A%=2.54

will set the value of A equal to the integer constant 2. Variables of integer type are useful when keeping track of integer quantities, such as line numbers in a program.

A variable of *single-precision type* is one whose value is a single-precision constant. A variable of single-precision type is indicated by the symbol ! after the variable name. Here are some examples of single-precision variables:

K!, W7!, ZX!

In setting the value of a single-precision variable, all digits beyond the seventh are truncated. Thus, for example, the instruction

20 LET A!=1.23456789

will set A! equal to 1.234567.

If a variable is used without a type designator, then the computer will assume that it is a single-precision variable. Thus, all of the variables we have used until now have been single-precision variables. These are, by far, the most commonly used variables.

A double-precision variable is a variable whose value is a double-precision constant. Such variables are useful in computations where great numerical accuracy is required. A double-precision variable is indicated by the tag # after the variable name. Here are some examples of double-precision variables:

B#, CI#, E#

In setting values of double-precision variables, all digits after the seventeenth are truncated.

Note that the variables A%, A!, A#, and A$ are four distinct variables. You could, if you wish, use all of them in a single program.

Test Your Understanding 2.1

What values are assigned to each of these variables?

(a) A# = 1#

(b) C% = 5.22%

(c) BB! = 1387.5699

Using type declaration tags %, !, and # is a bit of a nuisance since they must be included whenever the variable is used. There is a way around this tedium, however. The instructions **DEFINT, DEFSNG,** and **DEFDBL** may be used to define the types of variables for an entire program, so that type declaration tags need not be used. For example, consider the instruction:

100 DEFINT A

It specifies that every variable which begins with the letter A (such as A, AB, A1) should be considered as a variable of integer type. Here are two variations of this instruction:

200 DEFINT A,B,C
300 DEFINT A-G

Line 200 defines any variables beginning with A,B, or C to be of integer type. Line 300 defines any variables beginning with any of the letters A through G to be of integer type. The **DEFINT** instruction is usually used at the beginning of a program so that the resulting definition is in effect throughout the program.

The instruction **DEFSNG** works exactly like **DEFINT** and is used to define certain variables to be single-precision. The instructions **DEFDBL** and **DEFSTR** also work the same way for double-precision and string variables, respectively.

Note that type declaration tags override the **DEF** instructions. Thus, for example, suppose that the variable A was defined to be single-precision via a **DEFSNG** instruction at the beginning of the program. It would be legal to use A# as a double-precision variable, since the type declaration tag # would override the single-precision definition.

WARNING. Here is a mistake that is easy to make. Consider the following program:

```
10 LET A#=1.7
20 PRINT A#
30 END
```

This program seems harmless enough. We set the double-precision variable A# to the value 1.7 and then display the result. You probably expect to see the display:

1.700000000000000

If you actually try it, the display will read:

1.700000047683716

What went wrong? Well, it has to do with the way the internal logic of the computer works and the way in which numbers are represented in binary notation. Without going into details, let us merely observe that the computer interprets 1.7 as a *single-precision constant.* When this single-precision constant is converted into a double-precision constant (an operation which makes use of the binary representation of 1.7), the result coincides in its first 16 digits with the number given above. Does this mean that we must worry about such craziness? Of course not! What we really should have done in the first place is to write 1.7# instead of 1.7. Then the display will be exactly as we expected it to be.

EXERCISES (answers on 296)

Calculate the following quantities in single-precision arithmetic:

1. (5.87 + 3.85 − 12.07)/11.98
2. (15.1 + 11.9)[4/12.88
3. (32485 + 9826)/(321.5 − 87.6[2)

4.–6. Rework exercises 1.–3. using double-precision arithmetic.

7. Write a program to determine the largest integer less than or equal to X, where the value of X is supplied in an INPUT statement.

Determine the value assigned to the variable in each of the following exercises.

8. A% = −5
9. A% = 4.8
10. A% = −11.2
11. A! = 1.78
12. A# = 1.78#
13. A! = 32.653426278374645237
14. A! = 4.25234544321E21
15. A! = −1.23456789E-32
16. A# = 3.283646493029273646434
17. A# = −5.74#

Answers to Test Your Understanding 2.1

(a) 1.0000000000000000

(b) 5

(c) 1387.569

9.3 MATHEMATICAL FUNCTIONS IN BASIC

In performing scientific computations, it is often necessary to make use of a wide variety of mathematical functions, including the natural logarithm, the exponential, and the trigonometric functions. The Model III has a wide range of such functions "built-in." In this section, we will describe these functions and their use.

All mathematical functions in BASIC work in a similar fashion. Each function is identified by a sequence of letters (SIN for sine, LOG for natural logarithm, and so forth). To evaluate a function at a number X, we write X in parentheses after the function name. For example, the natural logarithm of X is written **LOG(X).** The program will use the current value of the variable X and will evaluate the natural logarithm of that value. For example, if X is currently 2, then the computer will calculate **LOG(2).**

Instead of the variable X, we may use any variable of any type: integer, single-precision, or double-precision. Or we may use a numerical constant of any type, for example, **SIN(.435678889658595)** asks for the sine of a double-precision numerical constant. Note, however, that with only a few exceptions (see below), all BASIC functions return a single-precision result, accurate to six digits. Thus, for example, the above value of the sine function will be computed as:

SIN(.435678889658595) = .422026

BASIC allows you to evaluate a function at any expression. For example, consider the expression X[2 + Y[2 − 3*X. It is perfectly acceptable to call for calculations such as:

SIN(X[2 + Y[2 − 3*X)

The computer will first evaluate the expression X[2 + Y[2 − 3*X using the current values of the variables X and Y. For example, if X = 1 and Y = 4, then X[2 + Y[2 − 3*X = $1^2 + 4^2 - 3*1$ = 14. The above sine function will be evaluated as SIN(13) = .420167.

Trigonometric Functions

Model III has the following trigonometric functions available.

SIN(X) = THE SINE OF THE ANGLE X
COS(X) = THE COSINE OF THE ANGLE X
TAN(X) = THE TANGENT OF THE ANGLE X

Here the angle X is expressed in terms of radian measure. In this measurement system, 360 degrees equals 2π radians. Or one degree equals .017453 radians and one radian equals 57.29578 degrees. So if you want to calculate trigonometric functions with the angle X expressed in degrees, use these functions:

SIN(.017453*X)
COS(.017453*X)
TAN(.017453*X)

The three other trigonometric functions, namely **SEC(X), CSC(X),** and **COT(X),** may be computed from the formulas:

SEC(X) = 1/COS(X)
CSC(X) = 1/SIN(X)
COT(X) = SIN(X)/COS(X)

Here, as above, the angle X is in radians. To compute these trigonometric functions with the angle in degrees, replace X by

.017453*X

Model III BASIC includes only one of the inverse trigonometric functions, namely the arctangent, denoted **ANT(X).** This function returns the angle whose tangent is X. The angle returned is expressed in radians. To compute the arctangent with the angle expressed in degrees, use the function

57.29578*ATN(X)

Test Your Understanding 3.1

Write a program which calculates sin 45°, cos 45°, and tan 45°.

Logarithmic and Exponential Functions

BASIC allows you to compute e^X via the exponential function

EXP(X)

Furthermore, you may compute the natural logarithm of X via the function

LOG(X)

You may calculate logarithms to base b using the formula:

$$\mathrm{LOG}_b(X)=\mathrm{LOG}(X)/\mathrm{LOG}(b)$$

Example 1. Prepare a table of values of the natural logarithm function for values X = .01, .02, .03, . . . , 100.00. Output the table on the printer.

Solution. Here is the desired program. Note that we have prepared our table in two columns, with a heading over each column.

```
10 LPRINT "X", "LOG(X)"
20 J=.01
30 LPRINT J, LOG(J)
40 IF J=100.00 THEN END ELSE 50
50 J =J+.01
60 GOTO 30
100 END
```

Test Your Understanding 3.2

Write a program which evaluates the function $f(x) = \sin x/(\log x + e^x)$ for $x = .45$ and $x = .7$.

Example 2. Carbon dating is a technique for calculating the age of ancient artifacts by measuring the amount of radioactive carbon-14 remaining in the artifact, as compared with the amount present if the artifact were manufactured today. If r denotes the proportion of carbon-14 remaining, then the age A of the object is calculated from the formula:

A = −(1/.00012)*LOG(r)

Suppose that a papyrus scroll contains 47% of the carbon-14 of a piece of papyrus just manufactured. Calculate the age of the scroll.

Solution. Here r = .47 so we use the above fomula:

```
10 LET R=.47
20 LET A=-(1/.00012)*LOG(R)
30 PRINT "THE AGE OF THE PAPYRUS IS", A, "YEARS"
40 END
```

Powers

Model III BASIC has a square-root function, denoted SQR(X). As with all the functions considered so far, this function will accept an input of any type and will output a single-precision constant. For example, the instruction

10 LET Y=SQR(2.0000000000000000)

will set Y equal to 1.414214, only six digits of which can be displayed.

Actually, the exponentiation procedure which we learned in Chapter 2 will work equally well for fractional and decimal exponents and therefore provides an alternative method for extracting square roots. Here is how to use it. Taking the square root of a number corresponds to raising the number to the 1/2 power. So we may calculate the square root of X as

X[(1/2)

Note that the square-root function SQR(X) operates with greater speed and hence is preferable. The alternate method is more flexible, however. For instance, we may extract the cube root of X as

X[(1/3)

or we may raise X to the 5.389 power as follows:

X[5.389

Greatest Integer, Absolute Value, and Related Functions

Here are several functions which are extremely helpful. The greatest integer less than or equal to X is denoted **INT(X).** For example, the largest integer less than or equal to 5.46789 is 5, so

INT(5.46789) = 5

Similarly, the largest integer less than or equal to −3.4 is −4 (on the number line, −4 is the first integer to the left of −3.4). Therefore,

INT(−3.4) = −4

Note that the INT function throws away the decimal part of a positive number, although this description does not apply to negative numbers. To throw away the decimal part of a number, we use the function **FIX(X).** For example,

FIX(5.46789) = 5,

FIX(−3.4) = −3

The absolute value of X is denoted **ABS(X).** Recall that the absolute value of X is X itself if X is positive or 0 and equals −X if X is negative. Thus,

ABS(9.23) = 9.23,

ABS(0) = 0,

ABS(−4.1) = 4.1

Just as the absolute value of X "removes the sign" of X, the function **SGN(X)** throws away the number and leaves only the sign. Thus, for example,

SGN(3.4) = +1,

SGN(−5.62) = −1

Conversion Functions

Model III BASIC includes functions for conversion of a number from one type to another. For example, to convert X to integer type, use the function **CINT(X).** This function will truncate the decimal part of X. Note that the resulting constant must be in the integer range −32768 to 32767. Otherwise an error will be produced.

To convert X to single-precision, use the function **CSNG(X).** If X is of integer type, then **CSNG(X)** will cause the appropriate number of zeroes to be appended to the right of the decimal point to convert X to a single-precision number. If X is double-precision, then X will be rounded to seven digits.

To convert X to double-precision, use the function **CDBL(X).** This function appends the appropriate number of zeros to X to convert it into a double-precision number.

EXERCISES (answers on 297)

Calculate the following quantities:

1. $e^{1.54}$
2. $e^{-2.376}$
3. log 58
4. log .0000975
5. sin 3.7

6. cos 45
7. arctan 1
8. tan .682
9. arctan 2 (express in degrees)
10. $\log_{10}$ 18.9
11. Make a table of values of the exponential function e^x for $x = -5.0, -4.9, \ldots, 0, .1, \ldots, 5.0$.
12. Evaluate the function

$$3x^{1/4}\log(5x) + e^{(-1.8x)}\tan x$$

for x = 1.7, 3.1, 5.9, 7.8, 8.4 and 10.1.
13. Write a BASIC program to graph the function y = sin x for x from 0 to 6.28. Use an interval of .05 on the x-axis.
14. Write a BASIC program to graph the function y = ABS(x).
15. Write a program to calculate the fractional part of x. (The fractional part of x is the portion of x which lies to the right of the decimal point.)

Answers to Test Your Understanding

3.1:
```
10 LET A=57.2958
20 PRINT SIN(45*A), COS(45*A) , TAN(45*A)
30 END
```

3.2:
```
10 DATA .45,.7
20 FOR J=1 TO 2
30 READ A(J)
40 PRINT SIN(A(J))/(LOG(A(J))+EXP(A(J)))
50 NEXT J
60 END
```

9.4 DEFINING YOUR OWN FUNCTIONS (DISK USERS ONLY)

In mathematics, functions are usually defined by specifying one or more formulas. For instance, here are formulas which define three functions f(x), g(x) and h(x):

$f(x) = (x^2 - 1)^{1/2}$

$g(x) = 3x^2 - 5x - 15$

$h(x) = 1/(x - 1)$

Note that each function is named by a letter, namely f, g, and h, respectively. Disk BASIC allows you to define functions like these and to use them by name throughout your program. To define a function, you use the **DEF FN** instruction. This instruction is used before the first use of the function in the program. For example, to define the function f(x) above, we could use the instruction:

```
10 DEF FNF(X)=(X[2-1)[(1/2)
```

To define the function g(x) above, we use the instruction:

```
20 DEF FNG(X)=3*X[2-5*X-15
```

Note that in each case, we use a letter (F or G) to identify the function. Suppose that we wish to calculate the value of the function F for X = 12.5. Once the function has been defined, this calculation may be described to the computer as FNF(12.5). Such calculations may be used throughout the program and save the effort of retyping the formula for the function in each instance.

You may use function names from A to Z. Moreover, in defining a function, you may use other functions. For example, if FNF(X) and FNG(X) are as defined above, then we may define their product by the instruction:

```
30 DEF FNC(X)=FNF(X)*FNG(X)
```

All of the functions above were functions of a single variable. However, BASIC allows functions of several variables as well. They are defined using the same procedure as above. For example, to define the function A(X,Y,Z,) = $X^2 + Y^2 + Z^2$, the instruction:

```
40 DEF FNA(X,Y,Z)=X[2+Y[2+Z[2
```

You may even allow one of the variables to be a string variable. For example, consider the following function:

```
50 DEF FNB(A$)=LEN(A$)
```

This function computes the length of the string A$.

Finally, functions may produce a string as a function value. The name for such a function must end in $. For example, consider the following function:

```
60 DEF FND$(A$,J)=LEFT(A$,J)
```

This function of the two variables A$ and J will compute the string consisting of the J leftmost characters of the string A$. For example, suppose that A$ = "computer" and J = 3. Then

FND$(A$,J)="com"

EXERCISES (answers on 298)

Write instructions to define the following functions:

1. $x^2 - 5x$
2. $1/x - 3x$
3. $5e^{-2x}$
4. $x \log(x/2)$
5. $\tan x/x$
6. $\cos(2x) + 1$
7. The string consisting of the right 2 characters of C$.
8. The string consisting of the 4 middle characters of A$ beginning with the Jth character.
9. The middle letter of the string B$. (Assume that B$ has an odd number of characters.)
10. Write a program which tabulates the value of the function in exercise 3 for x = 0, .1, .2, .3, .4, . . . , 10.0.

10

COMPUTER-GENERATED EXPERIMENTS

10.1 SIMULATION

Simulation is a powerful analysis tool by means of which you can use your computer to perform experiments to solve a wide variety of problems which might be too difficult to solve otherwise.

To describe what simulation is, let us proceed from a concrete example. Suppose that you own a dry cleaning store. At the moment, you have only one sales person behind the counter, but you are considering adding a second. Your question is: Should you hire the extra person? Being an analytical person, you have collected the following data. Traffic through your store varies by the hour. However, you have kept a log for the past month and are able to estimate the average number of potential customers arriving in the shop, according to the following table:

7–8 A.M.	30
8–9	15
9–10	6
10–11	3
11–12	8
12–1 P.M.	25
1–2	9
2–3	8
3–4	12
4–5	12
5–6	35
6–7	22

You have observed that you are currently paying a penalty for not having a second salesperson: If there is too long a wait, then a customer will go somewhere else to have their clothes cleaned! In your observations, you have noted that, on the average, of people entering the shop, a certain percentage will leave, depending on the size of the line. The likelihood that a person leaves depends on whether it is a drop-off or a pick-up. Those picking up clothes are more likely to wait in line. Here are the results of your observations:

line size	% leaving (drop-off)	% leaving (pick-up)
0	0	0
1–3	15	5
4–6	25	15
7–10	60	35
11–15	80	50

The average time to wait on a person is four minutes and the size of the average cleaning bill is $5.75. The cost of hiring the new salesperson is 200 dollars per week. Assuming that the salespersons work continuously while the shop is open, what action should you take?

This problem is fairly typical of the problems which arise in business. It is characterized by data accumulated from observations and unpredictable events. (When will a given customer arrive? Will he encounter a long line? Will he be the impatient sort who walks out?) Nevertheless, you must make a decision based on the data you have. How should you proceed?

One technique is to let your computer "imitate" your shop. That is, let the computer play a game which consists of generating customers at random times. These customers enter the "shop" and, on the basis of the current line, decide whether or not to stay. The computer will keep track of the line, the number of customers who leave, the revenue generated, and the revenue lost. The computer will keep up the simulated traffic for an entire "day" and present you with the results of the daily activity. But, you might argue, the computer data might not be valid. Suppose that it generates a "non-typical" day. Might not its data be biased? This could, indeed, happen. In order to avoid this pitfall, we run the program for many simulated days and average the results. The process we have just described is called *simulation*.

In the remainder of this chapter, we will provide a glimpse of the power of simulation and provide you with enough of an idea to build simple simulations of your own.

First, however, let us handle some of the mathematical ideas we will need in the next section. The required notions center around the following question: How do we make the computer imitate an unpredictable event? Consider, for example, the irate customer who arrives to drop off cleaning and encounters a line of four people ahead of him. According to the above table, the customer will leave 25% of the time and remain in line 75% of the time. How do you let the computer make the decision for the customer?

Easy! Just use the random number generator. Recall that RND(0) generates a random number between 0 (included) and 1(excluded). Suppose we ask how often RND(0) is larger than .25. If, indeed, the numbers produced by the random number generator show no biases, approximately 75% of the numbers produced will lie in the given interval since this interval occupies 75% of the length of the interval from 0 to 1. Thus, we let our customer decide as follows: If RND(0) > .25 then the customer joins the line; otherwise, the customer walks out in a huff. We will employ this simple idea several times in designing our simulation.

10.2 SIMULATION OF A DRY CLEANER

Let us build a simulation to solve the problem stated in the preceding section. We must decide on techniques for imitating each of the important aspects of the problem.

Since the problem calls for analysis of actions as time passes, we must, somehow measure the passage of (simulated) time. To do this, we will use the variables TH (time-hours) and TM (time-minutes) to keep track of the current time. In order to avoid a problem with AM and PM, let's use the military time system, in which the PM hours are denoted 13 through 24. Thus, for example, 1:15 PM is denoted 13:15. As our unit of simulated time, let's use four minutes, the time it takes to serve one customer. Then our program will look at time in four minute segments. During each 4 minute segment, it will take certain actions and then advance to the next time segment by adjusting TH and TM. Let us do the time advance in a subroutine at line 1000. Here is the subroutine:

```
1000 REM TIME ADVANCE
1010 LET TM=TM+4
1020 IF TM >=60 THEN 1030 ELSE 1100
1030 TM=TM-60: TH=TH+1
1100 RETURN
```

Let us store the statistical data on customer arrivals in the array A(J) (J = 7,8, . . . , 18). That is A(7) will equal the number of customers arriving between 7 and 8 AM, A(8) the number arriving between 8 and 9 AM, . . . , A(18), then number arriving between 6 and 7 PM. The first action of the program is to set up this array:

```
10 DIM A(18)
20 DATA 30,15,6,3,8,25,9,8,12,12,35,22
30 FOR J=7 TO 18
40 READ A(J)
50 NEXT J
```

The next step will be to read in the customer "impatience data." Let B(K) be the percentage of drop-off customers who leave when the line is K people long. Let C(K) be the corresponding statistic for pick-up customers. Here is the portion of the program which sets up these arrays.

```
100 DIM B(20), C(20)
110 DATA 0,0,.15 ,.05,.25,.15,.60,.35,.80,.50
115 READ B(0),C(0)
120 READ B(1),C(1)
130 B(2)=B(1): B(3)=B(1)
140 C(2)=C(1): C(3)=C(1)
150 READ B(4), C(4)
160 B(5)=B(4): B(6)=B(4)
170 C(5)=C(4): C(6)=C(4)
180 READ B(7), C(7)
190 B(8)=B(7): B(9)=B(7): B(10)=B(7)
200 C(8)=C(7): C(9)=C(7): C(10)=C(7)
210 READ B(11), C(11)
220 FOR J=12 TO 15
230 B(J)=B(11): C(J)=C(11)
240 NEXT J
```

The next step in our program is to set the clock at the beginning of a day. Moreover, the length of the waiting line, indicated by the variable L, is set equal to 0, the total of lost cash, indicated by the variable LC, and the total sales for the day, indicated by the variable CF (cash flow) are both set equal to 0.

```
300 TH=7: TM=0
310 L=0
320 LC=0
330 CF=0
```

At the beginning of each hour, the program will schedule the arrival of the customers. Namely for the Jth hour, it will schedule the arrival of A(J) customers. Each customer will be given a time of arrival, in minutes past the hour. The computer will choose this arrival time using the random number generator. In the absence of any other information, let's assume that the customers spread themselves out in a random, but uniform manner, over the hour. The way we will handle things inside the computer is as follows. At the beginning of each simulated hour, we set up an array D(T) with 15 entries, one for every four minute period in the hour. This array will indicate how many customers arrive in each four minute interval. For example, if D(10) = 4, then four customers will arrive between 36 and 40 minutes past the hour (that is, in the tenth four minute interval in the hour). The program will randomly place each of the A(J) customers in four minute intervals using the random number generator. Our program will test the time for the beginning of an hour. If so, it will go to a subroutine at 1200 which schedules the arrival of the customers for the hour.

```
11 DIM D(15)

410 IF TM=0 THEN GOSUB 1200

1200 FOR S=1 TO 15
1210 D(S)=0
1220 NEXT S
1230 FOR I=1 TO A(TH)
1240 X=RND(15)
1250 D(X)=D(X)+1
1260 NEXT I
1270 RETURN
```

The program now progresses through the simulated hour in four minute segments. For the Tth four minute segment, it causes D(T) customers to arrive at the shop. Let's assume that of these customers, half are drop-off and half are pick-up. The computer lets these customers each look at the line and decide whether to leave or stay. If a customer decides to stay, then he is added to the line. If the customer decides to go, the computer makes a note of the $5.75 cash flow lost. The lost cash flow will be stored in the variable LC. After the customers are either in line or have left, the salesperson services a customer (remember, one customer is serviced every 4 minutes) and $5.75 is added to the cash flow, which is tallied in the variable CF. Finally, the time is updated and the entire procedure is repeated for the next four minute segment. Let's be rather hard-hearted. If there are any customers left in line at closing time, we do not wait on them and add their business to that lost. This rather odd way of doing business is appropriate since we are analyzing the need for more personnel and any overtime should be considered in that analysis. Here is the portion of the program which accomplishes these tasks of the simulation.

```
420 T=TM/4+1:T=# OF 4 MIN. SEGMENT
430 FOR J=1 TO D(T)
440 LET C=RND(2):'1=DROP-OFF, 2=PICK-UP
450 IF C=1 THEN 500 ELSE 600
490 REM 500-560 DOES DROP-OFF CUST. STAY?
500 IF RND(0) > B(L) THEN 550 ELSE 510
510 LC=LC+5.75: 'CUSTOMER LEAVES
520 GOTO 690
550 L=L+1:'CUSTOMER JOINS LINE
560 GOTO 690
590 REM 600-660 DOES PICK-UP CUST. STAY?
600 IF RND(0) > C(L) THEN 640 ELSE 610
610 LC=LC+5.75:'CUSTOMER LEAVES
620 GOTO 690
640 L=L+1:'CUSTOMER JOINS LINE
690 NEXT J
700 IF L=0 THEN 710 ELSE 701:'THERE WERE NO CUSTOMERS
701 L=L-1:'WAIT ON CUSTOMER
705 CF=CF+5.75 : 'TAKE CUSTOMER'S MONEY
710 GOSUB 1000 : 'UPDATE TIME
720 IF TH=19 THEN 1500 ELSE 800
730 REM TH=19 IS THE END OF THE DAY
800 GOTO 400:'GO TO NEXT 4 MINUTE SEGMENT
1500 PRINT "END OF DAY STATISTICS"
1510 PRINT "BUSINESS LOST", LC+L*5.75
1520 PRINT "CASH FLOW", CF
1530 PRINT "LINE AT CLOSING", L
200 END
```

Our program simulates the activities of a single day. In order to average the statistics over a number of days let's set up a loop which repeats the above program for a certain number of days. Let's make an arbitrary choice of ten days repetition. Let the variable D denote the day number. Let the variable TL denote the total amount of business lost and let TF denote the total cash flow. These two variables will be updated at the end of each day. Let us denote the day number by E then our change of day will be controlled by a loop in lines 290 and 1700:

```
290 FOR E=1 to 10
1700 NEXT E
```

As statistics, let us compute the average of the revenue lost (LC), cash flow (CF), and the line length at closing (L). We keep the totals of these three variables for all the days up to the present in the variables L1, C1, and CL, respectively. We modify lines 1500-1530 as follows:

```
1500 LET L1=LC+L1+L*5.75
1510 LET C1=CF+C1
1520 LET CL=L+CL
```

Lines 1800–1850 compute the averages of L1, C1, and CL and display the results.

```
1800 LET L1=L1/10
1810 LET C1=C1/10
1820 LET CL=CL/10
1830 PRINT "AVERAGE CASH LOST PER DAY", L1
1840 PRINT " AVERAGE CASH FLOW PER DAY", C1
1850 PRINT "AVERAGE LINE LENGTH AT CLOSING",L
```

Finally, let us make sure that the random number generator is started at a random point by inserting a **RANDOM** instruction at the beginning of the program.

```
5 RANDOM
```

This completes the construction of our program. We have carried out the construction of the program in detail so you could see how a reasonable lengthy program is developed. However, our program is in a rather poor form to read, so let's recopy it in order.

```
5 RANDOM
10 DIM A(18)
11 DIM D(15)
20 DATA 30,15,6,3,8,25,9,8,12,12,35,22
30 FOR J=7 TO 18
40 READ A(J)
50 NEXT J
100 DIM B(20), C(20)
110 DATA 0,0,.15,.05,.25,.15,.60,.35,.80,.50
115 READ B(0), C(0)
120 READ B(1),C(1)
130 B(2)=B(1): B(3)=B(1)
```

```
140 C(2)=C(1): C(3)=C(1)
150 READ B(4), C(4)
160 B(5)=B(4): B(6)=B(4)
170 C(5)=C(4): C(6)=C(4)
180 READ B(7), C(7)
190 B(8)=B(7): B(9)=B(7): B(10)=B(7)
200 C(8)=C(7): C(9)=C(7): C(10)=C(7)
210 READ B(11), C(11)
220 FOR J=12 TO 15
230 B(J)=B(11): C(J)=C(11)
240 NEXT J
290 FOR E=1 TO 10
300 TH=7: TM=0
310 L=0
320 LC=0
330 CF=0
410 IF TM=0 THEN GOSUB 1200
420 T=TM/4+1
430 FOR J=1 TO D(T)
440 LET C=RND(2):'1=DROP-OFF, 2=PICK-UP
450 IF C=1 THEN 500 ELSE 600
490 REM 500-560 DOES DROP-OFF CUST. STAY?
500 IF RND(0) > B(L) THEN 550 ELSE 510
510 LC=LC+5.75: 'CUSTOMER LEAVES
520 GOTO 690
550 L=L+1:'CUSTOMER JOINS LINE
560 GOTO 690
590 REM 600-660 DOES PICK-UP CUST. STAY?
600 IF RND(0) > C(L) THEN 640 ELSE 610
610 LC=LC+5.75:'CUSTOMER LEAVES
620 GOTO 690
640 L=L+1:'CUSTOMER JOINS LINE
690 NEXT J
700 IF L=0 THEN 710 ELSE 701:'THERE WERE NO CUSTOMERS
701 L=L-1:'WAIT ON CUSTOMER
705 CF=CF+5.75 : 'TAKE CUSTOMER'S MONEY
710 GOSUB 1000 : 'UPDATE TIME
720 IF TH=19 THEN 1500 ELSE 800
730 REM TH=19 IS THE END OF THE DAY
800 GOTO 400:'GO TO NEXT 4 MINUTE SEGMENT
1000 REM TIME ADVANCE
1010 LET TM=TM+4
1020 IF TM = 60 THEN 1030 ELSE 1100
```

```
1030 TM=TM-60: TH=TH+1
1100 RETURN
1200 FOR S=1 TO 15
1210 D(S)=0
1220 NEXT S
1230 FOR I=1 TO A(TH)
1240 X=RND(15)
1250 D(X)=D(X)+1
1260 NEXT I
1270 RETURN
1500 LET L1=LC+L1+L*5.75
1510 LET C1=CF+C1
1520 LET CL=L+CL
1700 NEXT E
1800 LET L1=L1/10
1810 LET C1=C1/10
1820 LET CL=CL/10
1830 PRINT "AVERAGE CASH LOST PER DAY", L1
1840 PRINT "AVERAGE CASH FLOW PER DAY", C1
1850 PRINT "AVERAGE LINE LENGTH AT CLOSING", L
2000 END
```

In order to see what is happening at our hypothetical dry cleaning establishment, we run our program. Below are the results of five program runs.

RUN #1

```
AVERAGE CASH LOST PER DAY       258.75
AVERAGE CASH FLOW PER DAY       805.00
AVERAGE LINE AT CLOSING              9
```

RUN #2

```
AVERAGE CASH LOST PER DAY       270.25
AVERAGE CASH FLOW PER DAY       793.50
AVERAGE LINE AT CLOSING              3
```

RUN #3

```
AVERAGE CASH LOST PER DAY       264.50
AVERAGE CASH FLOW PER DAY       799.25
AVERAGE LINE AT CLOSING              4
```

RUN #4

AVERAGE CASH LOST PER DAY	270.83
AVERAGE CASH FLOW PER DAY	792.93
AVERAGE LINE AT CLOSING	6

RUN #5

AVERAGE CASH LOST PER DAY	287.50
AVERAGE CASH FLOW PER DAY	776.25
AVERAGE LINE AT CLOSING	4

We note several interesting facts about the output. First of all note that the runs are not all identical. This is because the **RANDOM** instruction creates new random customer arrival patterns for each run. Second, note the small percentage error in the data from the various runs. We seem to have discovered a statistical pattern which persists from run to run.

Finally, and most significantly, note that we are losing several hundred dollars per day in business because of our inability to service customers. At 200 dollars per week, the additional salesperson is a bargain! Even a single day's lost sales is enough to pay the salary. It appears as if we should add the extra salesperson. Actually, a bit more caution is advisable. We were dealing with cash flow rather than profit. In order to make a final decision, we must compute the profit generated by the additional sales. For example, if our profit margin on plant costs (exclusive of sales) is 40% then the profit generated by the extra sales will clearly amount to more than $200 per week and the extra salesperson should be hired.

The above example is fairly typical of the way in which simulation may be applied to analyze even fairly complicated situations in a small business. We will present some further refinements in the exercise set.

EXERCISES

1. Run the above program for ten consecutive runs and record the data. Does your data come close to the data presented above? (Remember: Due to the RANDOM instruction, you cannot expect to duplicate the given results exactly. Only within statistical error.)
2. Suppose that customers become more impatient and the likelihood of leaving is doubled in each case. Redo the experiment to determine the lost cash flow in this case.

3. Suppose that customers become more patient and the likelihood of leaving is cut in half in each case. Redo the experiment to determine the lost cash flow in this case.
4. Consider the original set of experimental data. However, now assume that the second salesperson has been hired. Redo the experiment to determine the average lost cash flow and the average line at closing.
5. Modify the program given so that you may calculate the average waiting time for each customer.

11

Some Other Applications of Your Computer

In this chapter, we will discuss several additional applications of your computer. We shall content ourselves with an overview of these applications since a complete discussion would carry us well beyond the scope of this book. However, these applications are extremely important and you should be aware of them.

11.1 COMPUTER COMMUNICATIONS

At some point, you will want to connect your computer to external devices (called *peripheral devices*). There are many such devices available and more are being introduced at a frightening pace. At the moment, such devices include graphics screens, light pens, plotters, voice synthesizers, music synthesizers, and temperature probes, to mention only some of the possibilities. Moreover, you will want the capability of connecting your computer to other computers, so that you may interchange programs and data with other users.

In this section, we present some of the fundamentals of computer communications. Our purpose is not to make you an expert, but rather to introduce you to the ideas and the vocabulary so that you may read and understand the articles in the various computer journals.

In most cases, it is not possible to connect two electronic devices directly to one another. Rather, it is necessary to have an intermediate device which translates the electronic signals of one into a form intelligible to the other. Such an intermediate device is called an *interface*; the task of electronically mating the devices is called *interfacing*. For microcomputer interfacing, there is a standard interface device called an *RS232-C* interface. This device allows two devices to communicate with one another via a 25 wire cable, with each of the wires carrying a signal having a standardized meaning. You may purchase an RS232-C interface for your Model III computer at your local Radio Shack Computer Center. Using this interface, you can connect your Model III to a wide variety of peripheral equipment, sold by Radio Shack and by outside vendors as well.

Before we go any further, a word of caution: Many devices are advertised as having a built-in RS232-C interface or as being "RS232-C compatible." It may require some hard work to make them operate with your computer! There are several reasons for this: Although all RS232-C interfaces utilize a 25 wire cable, not all the wires are necessarily used. Therefore, your computer (or rather your programs) may require a signal which is not being sent or is not sending a signal required at the other end. A further problem lies in the confusion of connecting data sets to data terminals. There are two conventions for wiring RS232-C interfaces—one for data terminals and one for data sets. (Never mind what these are.) In order to connect two devices via an RS-32-C interface, one must be a data terminal and one must be a data set. If both are of the same variety (say both computers), then it will be necessary to connect the interfaces on the devices by means of a special cable. The moral of all this is: when purchasing peripheral devices to connect to your computer, proceed with caution. Be sure your supplier is willing to help you or at least to exchange the device if you cannot make it work.

Our purpose in this section is to introduce you to some of the ideas and the vocabulary of computer communications. To begin with, let's discuss in somewhat greater detail the form in which the computer stores data.

A binary number is a string of 0's and 1's. Here is a typical example of a binary number:

1011101101110101000000011111

A binary digit (that is, a 0 or a 1) is called a *bit*. A string of 8 consecutive bits is called a *byte*. Here are examples of two bytes:

10011001   11100011

Within the computer, all data and instructions are written in terms of binary numbers, with each byte corresponding to a character. (Except for rather specialized applications, you do not need to concern yourself with the precise manner in which characters are translated into binary.) Because the basic unit of data within your machine consists of 8 bits, it is called an *8 bit computer*. Larger computers (often-called *main frames*) operate with 32 or 64 bits at a time. The added efficiency thus achieved accounts, in part, for their increased speed.

There are two fundamental types of computer communications: parallel and serial. In parallel communications, a byte is transmitted all 8 bits at a time. This is achieved by sending the byte over 8 wires. A signal on the wire corresponds to a 1 and the absence of a signal corresponds to a 0. The Radio Shack printers utilize parallel communications. In serial communications, the various bits are transmitted in sequence over a single wire. Many printers utilize serial communications. In addition, serial communications are used to transmit computer data to another computer via telephone lines. The interfaces required by parallel and serial communications are quite different. Your Model III is equipped with a parallel interface into which you may plug your printer. However, if you wish to use serial communications, it will be necessary to add the RS232-C interface.

In establishing a computer communications link, there are a number of different variables which must be considered. First, there is the speed of the communications. The standard measure of communications speed is the *baud rate*. Old fashioned teletypes communicate at 110 baud (about 12 characters per second). Data transmission rates from your computer to a printer range from 300 to 1200 baud. High speed data transmission rates range up to 9600 baud. You may set the baud rate of your RS232-C interface via a computer command.

All communications links are subject to noise caused, primarily, by static on the lines. It is essential that computer data communications be accurate. Imagine the havoc that could be created by the erroneous transmission of a few digits of a financial report! In order to guard against errors, many data transmission links utilize an extra bit which is tacked on to each byte. This extra bit is called a *parity bit*. It is agreed in advance whether this bit will always be set to 0 (even parity) or 1 (odd parity). The receiving device checks the parity bit to determine its correctness. If an error is detected, then a retransmission is usually requested. All this happens quite automatically. However, you must adjust your transmissions to match the parity expected. This can be done via computer command to the RS232-C interface.

Finally, it is sometimes necessary to have a *communications protocol*. In some situations, it is useful to transmit the data at a speed higher than the receiver can accept. To do this, your computer sends the data in "bursts." Your computer can utilize the waiting time between bursts to perform other chores. At the receiving end, each burst is temporarily stored in a memory called a *buffer*. This memory holds the burst of data until the receiver has a chance to look at it. In this scheme of data transmission, it is necessary to have a pair of signals that the sender and receiver exchange. Namely, the sender must tell the receiver that more data is on the way and the receiver must tell the sender that it may send more data. Such an exchange of signals is called a *communications protocol*. There are a number of different protocols in common use. Just what they are is not important. However, it is crucial that the sender and receiver use the *same* protocol. You may select among the most common protocols via a computer command. Note that it is necessary to use a communications protocol only in situations in which the data transmission rate is too fast for the receiver. Typically, it is not necessary to use a communications protocol with a printer at 300 baud or less. However, to get the top printing speed out of a daisy wheel printer, it is necessary to go to 1200 baud.

Further information on the operation of the RS232-C interface may be found in your Model III reference manual.

11.2 INFORMATION STORAGE AND RETRIEVAL

In this book, we have presented the rudiments of file construction and maintenance. What we have said will carry you through if your requirements are reasonably modest. However, if your files become very large or if you wish the ability to sort through them and compile complex management reports, then you will need more elaborate programs than anything we have discussed.

There are a large number of data retrieval systems which you can consider for your particular purposes. In fact, there are appearing now specialized programs which are structured for the needs of a particular profession (lawyer, doctor, architect). If your accounting and information management needs go beyond what we have discussed (or if you do not want to bother writing your own programs), you should investigate the various packages which are commercially available.

11.3 ADVANCED GRAPHICS

Computer graphics has become an incredibly sophisticated field in only a few years. Your Model III can be used to obtain an introduction to computer graphics principles. However, you can go only so far. If you wish to go further, you might want to consider adding the Radio Shack Color Computer to your personal computer center. This computer attaches to your own color television. Using it, you can create color displays of a much higher degree of resolution than is present on your Model III. Moreover, the Color Computer has a *graphics language* by means of which you can draw even reasonably complex graphics displays with little effort. For example, there are one line commands to draw lines and circles, to set colors, paint regions of the screen, and so forth.

Many printers have a graphics mode whereby you can produce hard copies of screen graphics. This is usually accomplished via "dot printing" with a high resolution of dots. To obtain even finer hard copy graphics, there are available a number of plotters which (at their most sophisticated) can faithfully produce blueprints, weather maps, etc.

The microcomputer user can even add a graphics tablet. This is a device which allows you to input a picture to the computer by essentially tracing the picture on a special board using an electronic "pencil." The picture is transformed into a series of dots and transmitted to the computer via a communications interface.

To survey the latest in computer devices, you should attend one of the many computer shows which are taking place with increasing regularity all over the country. Also, a good written source is BYTE magazine, available at many computer stores.

11.4 CONNECTIONS TO THE OUTSIDE WORLD

You may connect your Model III to the outside world! In order to do so you must have an RS232-C interface and a special communications device called a *modem*.

A modem converts the electronic signals of your computer into signals which may be transmitted via telephone lines. A modem is connected to your computer via the RS232-C interface. To set up a telephone connection with another computer, your first dial the number of the outside computer. Once a connection has been made, you rest the telephone receiver in the cradle of the modem. (Your RS232-C should be turned on and waiting.) You have now established a communications link between you and the outside world.

You may use this communications link in many ways. First, you may communicate with other microcomputer users. You can play games, exchange data, program ideas, and so forth. You may even use the computer as an "electronic mail service." In fact, this application of computer communications promises to revolutionize the office in the next decade. Instead of sending paper memos and printed reports, you will send such data via computer communications. If the information is to be held confidential, then access will be regulated either by password or encoding. Just think! No more delayed mail delivery, lost letters, or other problems. As a microcomputer user, you can be one of the first to use such a system.

You may use computer communications to connect your operations to a time sharing system to which you have access. This will give you access to the greater capabilities of a larger machine as well as the program library of the time sharing system.

Finally, there are a number of computer information networks being developed which you can plug your system into. Such networks provide the latest stock market quotations, news, and other data. In addition, they provide a library of programs on which you may call. Such information services are in their infancy and are sure to grow in number and sophistication over the next few years. Radio Shack is currently part of one such service. For details, inquire at your local Computer Center.

12

Where To Go From Here

In this book, we have attempted to provide you with a working knowledge of the Radio Shack Model III computer and its associated BASIC language. Of course, we have only scratched the surface of the field of computer science and the applications in which your computer can be used. In this final chapter, let's say a few words about some of the subjects we will not have a chance to discuss in depth and point out some directions for further study.

12.1 ASSEMBLY LANGUAGE PROGRAMMING

All of our programming has been carried out in the language BASIC. However, there is a much more primitive language which underlies your Model III, namely Z80 machine language. Actually, BASIC is *itself* a program which is written in machine language. Indeed, many complex commercial programs are written directly in machine laguage.

Machine language consists of the instructions which the Z80 chip can execute. These instructions tend to be much more primitive than the instructions of a higher level language such as BASIC. In a certain sense, this is unfortunate since you are forced to look at a program in very fine steps. However, the resulting programs will generally be much more efficient and will run much more quickly than programs written in BASIC. In addition, you will better understand what is going on inside the Z80 chip in response to your instructions.

After you have become proficient in BASIC, your next step can be a study of machine language. In order to help you get started, let's spend a short time discussing how machine language works. As we have previously said, the internal workings of the computer are all carried out in binary. This includes machine language commands. However, it is extremely difficult to write a program which is nothing but a long string of 0's and 1's. To ease this tremendous burden, you write machine language commands in terms of *mnemonics*, which are similar to instruction designations used in BASIC. The program, written in terms of mnemonics is called the *source code*.

The next step in preparing a machine language program is to translate the mnemonics into binary. This is done using a program called an *assembler*. The resulting program is called the *object code* or *machine code*. You may list the object code but it is extremely difficult to read since it consists of a seemingly endless string of 0s and 1s. To ease this burden, computer scientists use a notational system consisting of 16 symbols, namely 0-9 and A-F. This system is called the *hexadecimal* system and may be used to list the object code of a program. Moreover, all memory addresses are specified in terms of hexadecimal notation. Because of its direct relationship to binary, hexadecimal notation is directly intelligible to the computer.

In the process of running the assembler, you must decide where in memory your program is to be stored. This is a complication that you do not worry about in BASIC programming. BASIC finds memory space and keeps track of where the various parts of the program are located. However, in machine language programming, all that internal bookkeeping is your responsibility.

Once your program is assembled, you are ready to load and run it.

You might wonder if machine language programming is really worth the effort described above. Probably not in the case of a program you plan to use once or twice. However, if you are planning a program which you will be using often, perhaps as a subroutine in many different BASIC programs, then it will probably be worth the invested time to write the program in machine language. First of all, your program will run much faster. Second, you will be able to make the screen, keyboard, and printer perform actions which may be clumsy or downright impossible to specify in BASIC.

Here are two excellent references on machine language programming for the TRS-80:

How to Program the Z80 by Rodnay Zaks, SYBEX Inc., 1980; Radio Shack Catalog No.62-2066

TRS-80 Assembly Language by Hubert S. Howe, Jr., Prentice-Hall, Inc., 1981

12.2 OTHER LANGUAGES AND OPERATING SYSTEMS

BASIC is only one of several hundred different computer languages. And it is only one of the possible languages which is available to run on your Model III. Mastering one or more of these other languages is another possible area for further study.

As microcomputers have become more common, many of the languages designed to run on large computer systems have been configured for microcomputers. Any list of available languages will probably be incomplete by the time this book goes to press. Nevertheless, let's mention some of the most common languages which either are available or will soon be available for the Model III.

The old standard of computing languages is FORTRAN. This is a powerful language especially useful in scientific and engineering applications.

FORTRAN is a *compiler*, whereas Model III BASIC is an *interpreter*. This is an important distinction. With an interpreter, you type in the program directly as it will be executed. In order to execute a particular instruction, the computer refers to a machine language subroutine to "interpret" the intent. With a compiler, you type in the program in much the same manner as with an interpreter. However, you must *compile* the program prior to running it. That is, you must run a special routine which translates the various typed instructions into machine language. It is the machine language version of the program which you actually run. A compiled program is much more efficient than a program written with an interpreter. Depending on the program, the compiled program will run from 5 to 50 times faster!

You may supplement your BASIC interpreter with a BASIC compiler. This will allow you to program in a language you already know (you must still learn the intricacies of the compiler version) and yet achieve the efficiencies of compiled programs.

COBOL and PASCAL are two very popular languages. COBOL is probably the most commonly used language for business programs. It is designed to allow ease in preparing management and financial reports. PASCAL is an extremely powerful language which may be used for general programming. It allows you to write complex programs in very few commands.

In purchasing languages for your computer, it is important to recognize that the particular version you purchase must be compatible with your operating system. The Radio Shack disk operating system is TRSDOS. In order to make use of other languages or other programs, you may wish to add another operating system. The most likely candidate is CP/M, the most common microcomputer operating system.

Answers to Selected Exercises

CHAPTER 2

Section 2.2 (pages 22 and 23)

1.
```
10 PRINT 57+23+48
20 END
```

2.
```
10 PRINT 57.83*(48.27−12.54)
20 END
```

3.
```
10 PRINT 127.86/38
20 END
```

4.
```
10 PRINT 365/.005+1.02[5
20 END
```

5.
```
10 PRINT 2[1,2[2,2[3,2[4
20 PRINT 3[1,3[2,3[3,3[4
30 PRINT 4[1,4[2,4[3,4[4
40 PRINT 5[1,5[2,5[3,5[4
50 PRINT 6[1,6[2,6[3,6[4
60 END
```

6.
```
10 PRINT "CAST REMOVAL",45
20 PRINT "THERAPY", 35
30 PRINT "DRUGS",5
40 PRINT
50 PRINT "TOTAL",45+35+5
60 PRINT "MAJ MED", .8*(45+35+5)
70 PRINT "BALANCE", .2*(45+35+5)
80 END
```

7.
```
10 PRINT "THACKER", 698+732+129+487
20 PRINT "HOVING", 148+928+246+201
30 PRINT "WEATHERBY",379+1087+148+641
40 PRINT "TOTAL VOTES",698+732+129+487+148+928
   +246+201+379+1087+148+641
50 END
```

Note that line 40 extends over two lines of the screen. To type such a line just keep typing and do not hit a carriage return until you are done with the line. The maximum line length is 255 characters.

8. −2

9.
```
SILVER  GOLD  COPPER  PLATINUM
327     448   1052    2
```

10.
```
     GROCERIES  MEAT   DRUGS
MON  1,245      2,348  2,531
TUE    248      3,459  2,148
```

11. 2.3E7

12. 1.7525E2

13. −2E8

14. 1.4E-4

15. −2.75E-10

16. 5.342E16

17. 159,000

18. −20,345,600

19. −.000000000007456

20. .0000000000000000239456

Section 2.3 (pages 30 and 31)

1. 10

2. 0

3. 50

4. 9   −7   18

5. JOHN JONES   AGE   38

6. 22
   57

7. A can only assume numeric constants as values.

8. Nothing

9. A$ can only assume string contants as values.

10. No line number. String constant not in quotes.

11. Only two letters allowed in variable name.

12. Variable name must begin with a letter.

13.
```
10 LET A=2.3758:B=4.58321:C=58.11
20 PRINT A+B+C
30 PRINT A*B*C
40 PRINT A[2+B[2+C[2
50 END
```

14.
```
10 LET A$="Office Supplies":B$="Computers":C$="Newsletters"
20 LET RA=346712:RB=459321:RC=376872
30 LET EA=176894:EB=584837:EC=402195
40 PRINT ,A$,B$,C$
50 PRINT "REVENUE",RA,RB,RC
60 PRINT "EXPENSES",EA,EB,EC
70 LET PA=RA-EA:PB=RB-EB:PC=RC-EC
80 PRINT "PROFIT",PA,PB,PC
90 PRINT
100 PRINT "TOTAL PROFIT EQUALS",PA+PB+PB
```

Section 2.4 (page 41)

1.
```
10 LET S=0
20 FOR J=1 TO 25
30 LET S=S+J[2
40 NEXT J
50 PRINT S
60 END
```

2.
```
10 LET S=0
20 FOR J=0 TO 10
30 LET S=S+(1/2)[J
40 NEXT J
50 PRINT S
60 END
```

3.
```
10 LET S=0
20 FOR J=1 TO 10
30 LET S=S+J[3
40 NEXT J
50 PRINT S
60 END
```

4.
```
10 LET S=0
20 FOR J=1 TO 100
30 LET S=S+1/J
40 NEXT J
50 PRINT S
60 END
```

5.
```
10 PRINT "J","J[2","J[3","J[4"
20 FOR J=1 TO 12
30 PRINT J,J[2,J[3,J[4
40 NEXT J
50 END
```

6.
```
10 PRINT "MONTH","INTEREST","BALANCE"
20 B=4000,P=125.33
30 FOR J=1 TO 12
40 LET I=.01B:'I=THE INTEREST FOR MONTH
50 LET R=P-I:'R=REDUCTION IN BALANCE FOR MONTH
60 LET B=B-R: NEW BALANCE
70 PRINT J,I,B
80 NEXT J
90 END
```

7.
```
10 PRINT "END OF YEAR", "BALANCE"
20 B=1000
30 FOR J=1 TO 15
40 B=B+1000+.10*B :'ADD DEPOSIT AND INTEREST
50 PRINT J,B
60 NEXT J
70 END
```

8.
```
10 LET S=3.5E7: P=5.54E6
20 PRINT "END OF YEAR", "SALES", "PROFITS"
30 FOR J=1 TO 3
40 LET S=1.2*S: P=1.3*P
50 PRINT J,S,P
60 NEXT J
70 END
```

Section 2.6 (pages 57 and 58)

1.
```
10 J=1
20 IF J[2>45000 THEN 100 ELSE 30
30 PRINT J,J[2
40 J=J+I
50 GOTO 20
100 END
```

2.
```
10 PI=3.14159
20 R=1
30 IF PI*R[2<=5000 THEN 40 ELSE 100
40 PRINT R,PI*R[2
50 R=R+1
60 GOTO 30
100 END
```

3.
```
10 PRINT "SIDE OF CUBE","VOLUME"
20 S=1
30 V=S[3
40 IF V3<175000 THEN 50 ELSE 100
50 PRINT S,V
60 S=S+1
70 GOTO 30
100 END
```

4.
```
10 FOR J=1 TO 10 : 'LOOP TO GIVE 10 PROBLEMS
20 INPUT "TYPE TWO 2-DIGIT NUMBER"; A,B
30 INPUT "WHAT IS THEIR PRODUCT";C
40 IF A*B=C THEN 200
50 PRINT "SORRY. THE CORRECT ANSWER IS",A*B
60 GO TO 500 : 'GO TO THE NEXT PROBLEM
200 PRINT "YOUR ANSWER IS CORRECT! CONGRATULATIONS"
210 LET R=R+1 : 'INCREASE SCORE BY 1
220 GO TO 500 : 'GO TO THE NEXT PROBLEM
500 NEXT J
600 PRINT "YOUR SCORE IS",R,"CORRECT OUT OF 10"
700 PRINT "TO TRY AGAIN, TYPE RUN"
800 END
```

5.
```
10 FOR J=1 TO 10 : 'LOOP TO GIVE 10 PROBLEMS
15 PRINT "CHOOSE OPERATION TO BE TESTED:"
16 PRINT "ADDITION (A), SUBTRACTION (S),
   OR MULTIPLICATION (M)"
17 INPUT A$
```

```
20 INPUT "TYPE TWO 2-DIGIT NUMBERS"; A,B
21 IF A$="A" THEN 30
22 IF A$="S" THEN 130
23 IF A$="M" THEN 230
30 INPUT "WHAT IS THEIR SUM";C
40 IF A+B=THEN 400
50 PRINT "SORRY. THE CORRECT ANSWER IS",A+B
60 GO TO 500 : 'GO TO NEXT PROBLEM
130 INPUT "WHAT IS THEIR DIFFERENCE";C
140 IF A-B=C THEN 400
150 PRINT "SORRY. THE CORRECT ANSWER IS",A-B
160 GO TO 500 : 'GO TO THE NEXT PROBLEM
230 INPUT "WHAT IS THEIR PRODUCT";C
240 IF A*B=C THEN 400
250 PRINT "SORRY. THE CORRECT ANSWER IS",A+B
260 GO TO 500 : 'GO TO THE NEXT PROBLEM
400 PRINT "YOUR ANSWER IS CORRECT! CONGRATULATIONS"
410 LET R=R+1 : 'INCREASE SCORE BY 1
420 GO TO 500 : 'GO TO THE NEXT PROBLEM
500 NEXT J
600 PRINT "YOUR SCORE IS",R,"CORRECT OUT OF 10"
700 PRINT "TO TRY AGAIN, TYPE RUN"
800 END
```

6. See 8.

7. See 9.

8.
```
10 INPUT "NUMBER OF NUMBERS";N
20 FOR J=1 TO N
30 INPUT A
40 IF J=1 THEN B=A
50 IF A>B THEN B=A
60 NEXT J
70 PRINT "THE LARGEST NUMBER INPUT IS",B
80 END
```

9. Replace line 50 in 8. by:
```
50 IF A<B THEN B=A
```

10.
```
10 A0=5782:A1=6548:B0=4811:B1=6129:C0=3865:C1=4270
20 D0=7950:D1=8137:E0=4781:E1=4248:F0=6598:F1=7048
30 FOR J=1 TO 6
40 IF J=1 THEN A=0:B=A1
50 IF J=2 THEN A=B0:B=B1
```

```
60 IF J=3 THEN A=C0:B=C1
70 IF J=4 THEN A=D0:B=D1
80 IF J=5 THEN A=E0:B=E1
90 IF J=6 THEN A=F0:B=F1
100 I=B-A
110 IF 1>0 THEN PRINT "CITY",J,"HAD AN INCREASE OF", I
120 GOTO 200
130 IF I<0 THEN PRINT "CITY",J,"HAD A DECREASE OF",A-B
140 GOTO 300
200 IF 1>500 THEN PRINT "CITY",J,"MORE THAN 500 INCREASE"
300 NEXT J
400 END
```

11.

```
10 PRINT "THIS PROGRAM SIMULATES A CASH REGISTER"
20 PRINT "AT THE QUESTION MARKS, TYPE IN THE PURCHASE"
30 PRINT "AM'TS. TYPE -1 INDICATE THE END OF THE ORDER"
40 INPUT "TYPE 'Y' IF READY TO BEGIN"; A$
50 IF A$='Y' THEN 60 ELSE 10
60 CLS
70 INPUT "ITEM"; A
80 IF A=-1 THEN 200 ELSE 90
90 T=T+A: T IS RUNNING TOTAL
100 GOTO 70
200 PRINT "THE TOTAL IS", T
210 S=.05*T:'S=SALES TAX
220 PRINT "SALES TAX", S
230 PRINT "TOTAL DUE", S+T
240 INPUT "PAYMENT GIVEN";P
250 PRINT "CHANGE DUE", P-(S+T)
300 END
```

12.

```
INPUT "CASH ON HAND"; C1
20 PRINT "INPUT ACCOUNTS EXPECTED TO BE RECEIVED IN NEXT
MONTH."
30 PRINT "TO INDICATE END OF ACCOUNTS TYPE -1."
40 INPUT "ACCOUNT RECEIVABLE";A
50 IF A=-1 THEN 100
60 C2=C2+A:'C2=RUNNING OF ACCOUNTS RECEIVABLE
70 GOTO 40
100 PRINT "INPUT ACCOUNTS EXPECTED TO BE PAID IN NEXT
    MONTH."
110 PRINT "TO INDICATE END OF ACCOUNTS TYPE -1."
120 INPUT "ACCOUNT PAYABLE";A
130 IF A=-1 THEN 200
```

```
140 C3=C3+A:'C3=RUNNING TOTAL OF ACCOUNTS PAYABLE
150 GOTO 120
200 PRINT "CASH ON HAND",C1
220 PRINT "ACCOUNTS RECEIVABLE",C2
230 PRINT "ACCOUNTS PAYABLE",C3
240 PRINT "NET CASH FLOW",C1+C2-C3
300 END
```

CHAPTER 3

Section 3.1 (pages 74 and 75)

1. DIM A(5)
2. DIM A(2,3)
3. DIM A$(3)
4. DIM A(3)
5. DIM A$(4),B(4)
6.
```
10 DIM A$(3),B(3,3),C$(3)
20 PRINT ,,"RECEIPTS"
30 C$(1)="STORE #1",C$(2)="STORE #2",C$(3)="STORE #3"
40 A$(1)="1/1-1/10",A$(2)="1/11-1/20",A$(3)="1/21-1/31"
50 B(1,1)=57385.48,B(1,2)=89485.45,B(1,3)=38,456.90
60 B(2,1)=39485.98,B(2,2)=76485.49,B(2,3)=40387.86
70 B(3,1)=45467.21,B(3,2)=71494.25,B(3,3)=37983.38
100 PRINT ,C$(1),C$(2),C$(3)
200 FOR J=1 TO 3
220 PRINT A$(J),B(J,1),B(J,2),B(J,3)
230 NEXT J
300 END
```
7. Add the instructions:
```
5 DIM D(3)
240 FOR J=1 TO 3
250 D(J)=B(1,J)+B(2,J)+B(3,J)
260 NEXT J
270 PRINT "TOTALS",D(1),D(2),D(3)
```
8. Move the END to 400 and add the following instructions.
```
6 DIM E(3)
300 FOR J=1 TO 3
```

```
310 E(J)=B(J,1)+B(J,2)+B(J,3)
320 NEXT J
330 PRINT
340 PRINT "PERIOD", "TOTAL SALES"
350 FOR J=1 TO 3
360 PRINT A$(J) , E(J)
370 NEXT J
400 END
```

9.
```
10 DIM A$(4), B$(5), C(5,4)
20 A$(1)="STORE #1",A$(2)="STORE #2", A$(3)="STORE #3"
21 A$(4)="STORE #4"
30 B$(1)="REFRIG.",B$(2)="STOVE",B$(3)="AIR COND."
40 B$(4)="VACUUM", B$(5)="DISPOSAL"
50 PRINT "INPUT THE CURRENT INVENTORY"
60 FOR J=1 TO 4
70 PRINT A$(J)
80 PRINT
90 FOR I=1 TO 5
100 PRINT B$(I)
110 INPUT C(I,J)
120 NEXT I
130 NEXT J
200 REM REST OF PROGRAM IS FOR INVENTORY UPDATE
210 PRINT "CHOOSE ONE OF THE FOLLOWING"
220 PRINT "RECORD SHIPMENTS(R) "
230 PRINT "DISPLAY CURRENT INVENTORY(D)"
240 INPUT "TYPE R OR D";D$
250 IF D$="R" THEN 300
260 IF D$="D" THEN 600 ELSE CLS:GOTO 200
300 CLS
310 PRINT "RECORD SHIPMENT"
320 INPUT "TYPE STORE#(1-4)";J
330 PRINT "ITEM SHIPPED"
340 PRINT "REFRIG=1,STOVE=2,AIR
COND.=3,VACUUM=4,DISPOSAL=5"
350 INPUT I
360 INPUT "NUMBER SHIPPED";S
370 B(I,J)=B(I,J)-S
380 GOTO 200
600 CLS
610 PRINT A$(1),A$(2),A$(3),A$(4)
620 FOR I=1 TO 5
```

```
630 FOR J=1 TO 4
640 PRINT B(I,J);
650 NEXT J
660 NEXT I
670 GOTO 200
1000 END
```

Note that this program is really an infinite loop. For this type of program this is a good idea. You do not want to accidentally end the program thereby erasing the current inventory figures! End this program using the BREAK key.

Section 3.2 (pages 80 and 81)

1. A(1) = 2, A(2) = 4, A(3) = 6, A(4) = 8, A(5) = 10, A(6) = 12, A(7) = 14, A(7) = 16, A(8) = 18, A(9) = 20
2. A(0) = 1.1, A(1) = 3.3, A(2) = 5.5, A(3) = 7.7, B(0) = 2.2, B(1) = 4.4, B(2) = 6.6, B(3) = 8.8
3. A(0) = 1, A(1) = 2, A(2) = 3, A(3) = 4, B(0) = "A", B(1) = "B", B(2) = "C", B(3) = "D"
4. A(0) = 1, B(0) = 2, A(1) = 3, B(1) = 4, A(2) = 1, B(2) = 2, A(3) = 3, B(3) = 4
5. A(1,1) = 1, A(1,2) = 2, A(1,3) = 3, A(1,4) = 4, A(2,1) = 5, A(2,2) = 6, A(2,3) = 7, A(2,4) = 8, A(3,1) = 9, A(3,2) = 10, A(3,3) = 11, A(3,4) = 12
6. A(1,1) = 1, A(2,1) = 2, A(3,1) = 3, A(1,2) = 4, A(2,2) = 5, A(3,2) = 6, A(1,3) = 7, A(2,3) = 8, A(3,3) = 9, A(1,4) = 10, A(2,4) = 11, A(3,4) = 12
7. Out of Data in Line 30
8. Type Mismatch in Line 30 (Attempt to set numeric variable equal to string)
9. Set F(J) equal to the Federal withholding for employee J, N(J) = the net pay; and add the following lines:

```
280 PRINT "EMPLOYEE", "WITHHOLDING","NET PAY"
290 FOR J=1 TO 5
300 IF D(J)<=200 THEN F(J)=0
310 IF D(J)<=210 THEN F(J)=29.10
320 IF D(J)<=220 THEN F(J)=31.20
330 IF D(J)<=230 THEN F(J)=33.80
```

```
340 IF D(J)<=240 THEN F(J)=36.40
350 IF D(J)<=250 THEN F(J)=39.00
360 IF D(J)<=260 THEN F(J)=41.60
370 IF D(J)<=270 THEN F(J)=44.20
380 IF D(J)<=280 THEN F(J)=46.80
390 IF D(J)<=290 THEN F(J)=49.40
400 IF D(J)<=300 THEN F(J)=52.10
410 IF D(J)<=310 THEN F(J)=55.10
420 IF D(J)<=320 THEN F(J)=58.10
430 IF D(J)<=330 THEN F(J)=61.10
440 IF D(J)<=340 THEN F(J)=64.10
450 IF D(J)<=350 THEN F(J)=67.10
500 N(J)=D(J)-E(J)-F(J)
600 PRINT B$(J),F(J),N(J)
700 NEXT J
```

10.
```
5 DIM A(25)
10 DATA 10,10,9,9,8,11,15,18,20,25,31,35,38,39,40,40,42,38
20 DATA 33,27,22,18,15,12
30 FOR J=0 TO 23
40 READ A(J)
50 S=S+A(J)
60 NEXT J
70 PRINT "AVERAGE 24 HOUR TEMP.", S/24
100 PRINT "TO FIND THE TEMPERATURE AT ANY PARTICULAR
    HOUR"
110 PRINT "TYPE THE HOUR IN 24-HOUR NOTATION:
    0-12=AM"
120 PRINT "13-24=PM"
130 PRINT "TO END THE PROGRAM, TYPE 25"
140 INPUT "DESIRED HOUR";A
150 IF A=25 THEN 200
160 PRINT "THE QUERIED TEMPERATURE WAS",A(J),"DEGREES"
170 GOTO 100
200 END
```

Section 3.3 (page 89)

2.
```
5 CLS
10 PRINT TIME$
20 END
```

3. 5 CLS
   10 PRINT TIME$
   20 LET Y=PEEK(16919)
   30 IF Y=PEEK(16919)+1 THEN 10 ELSE 40
   40 GOTO 30
   50 END

4. Same as 3. except replace 16919 everywhere by 16920

6. Add the following program lines. Hours will be measured on a 24-hour clock.
   305 FOR H=1 TO 24
   400 IF B(J)=Y THEN 450:'IS APPT. FOR RIGHT DAY?
   450 IF C(J)=H THEN 500:'IS APPT. FOR HOUR H?
   600 NEXT H

7. Add the following program lines.
   1 PRINT "CHOOSE LEVEL OF DIFFICULTY"
   2 PRINT "EASY(E),MODERATE(M),HARD(H),WHIZ KID(W)"
   3 INPUT A$
   4 IF A$="E" THEN X=120
   5 IF A$="M" THEN X=30
   6 IF A$="H" THEN X=15
   7 IF A$="W" THEN X=8
   40 POKE 16920,0
   41 POKE 16919,0
   50 IF PEEK(16919)+60*PEEK(16920)=X THEN GOTO 100

8. Modify program of exercise 6. as follows. Delete lines 200–250 and replace them by the following:
   200 X=F(1):Y=F(0):H=F(3)
   600 IF PEEK(16922)=H+1 THEN 700 ELSE 610
   610 GOTO 600
   700 CLS
   710 GOTO 300

Section 3.4 (pages 97 and 98)

1. 10 PRINT "THE VALUE OF X IS",5.378
   20 END

2. 10 PRINT "THE VALUE OF X IS";TAB(22) 5.378
   20 END

3.
```
10 PRINT "DATE";TAB(6) "QTY";TAB(12) "@";TAB(17) "COST";
20 PRINT TAB(25) "DISCOUNT";TAB(37) "NET COST"
30 END
```

4.
```
10 X=6.753:Y=15.111:Z=111.850:W=6.702
20 PRINT USING ###.### X
30 PRINT USING ###.### Y
40 PRINT USING ###.### Z
50 PRINT USING ###.### W
60 PRINT "_____"
70 PRINT USING ###.### X+Y+Z+W
80 END
```

5.
```
10 X=12.82:Y=117.58:Z=5.87:W=.99
20 PRINT USING $###.## X
30 PRINT USING $###.## Y
40 PRINT USING $###.## Z
50 PRINT USING $###.## W
60 PRINT USING $###.## W
70 PRINT "_____"
80 PRINT USING $###.## X+Y+Z+W+W
90 END
```

6.
```
10 PRINT TAB(46) "DATE";TAB(53) "3/18/81"
20 PRINT
30 PRINT "PAY TO THE ORDER OF";
40 PRINT TAB(27) "WILDCATTERS, INC."
50 PRINT
60 PRINT "THE SUM OF";TAB(41) "*********$89,385.00"
```

7.
```
10 X=5787:Y=387:Z=127486:W=38531
20 PRINT USING ###,###; X
30 PRINT USING ###,###; Y
40 PRINT USING ###,###; Z
50 PRINT ###,###; W
60 PRINT "_____"
70 PRINT USING ###,###;X+Y+Z+W
80 END
```

8.
```
10 X=385.41:Y=17.85
20 PRINT USING $$###.##;X
30 PRINT "-";
40 PRINT USING $$###.##;Y
50 PRINT "__________"
60 PRINT USING $$###.##;X-Y
70 END
```

9.
```
10 INPUT "NUMBER TO BE ROUNDED";X
20 PRINT USING ######;X
30 END
```

10. Modify the program of Exercise 11 of Section 2.6 by substituting PRINT USING $####.## statements.

11. Put the computer into 32 character per line mode by typing SHIFT and [↓]. Then RUN the program of exercise 6.

Section 3.5 (pages 104 and 105)

1. 100*RND(0)
2. 100+RND(0)
3. RND(50)
4. 3+RND(77)
5. 2*RND(25)
6. 50+50*RND(0)
7. 3*RND(9)
8. 1+3*RND(7)

10. Add the following instructions:
```
132 IF C(J)>A(J) THEN 135 ELSE 140
135 PRINT "BET INVALID:NOT ENOUGH CHIPS PURCHASED"
137 C(J)=0
139 GOTO 120
```

11. Change line 132 in exercise 10 to read:
```
132 IF C(J)>A(J)+100 THEN 135 ELSE 140
```

12.
```
10 PRINT "CHOOSE OPERATION TO BE TESTED"
20 PRINT "ADDITION(A),SUBTRACTION(S),MULTIPLICATION(M)"
30 INPUT A$
40 A=RND(10)-1:B=RND(10)-1
50 IF A$="A" THEN 100
60 IF A$="B" THEN 200
70 IF A$="C" THEN 300
100 CLS
110 PRINT "WHAT IS ";A;"+";B;"?"
120 INPUT C
130 D=A+B
```

```
140 GOTO 400
200 CLS
210 PRINT "WHAT IS ";A;"-";B;"?"
220 INPUT C
230 D=A-B
240 GOTO 400
300 CLS
310 PRINT "WHAT IS ";A;"X";B;"?"
320 INPUT C
330 D=A*B
340 GOTO 400
400 IF C=D THEN 410 ELSE 420
410 PRINT "YOUR ANSWER IS CORRECT"
415 GOTO 430
420 PRINT "INCORRECT.THE CORRECT ANSWER IS", D
430 INPUT "ANOTHER PROBLEM(Y/N)";B$
440 IF A$="Y" THEN 10
450 END
```

13. Combine the ideas of Exercise 7 of Section 3.3 with those of Exercise 12 above.

14. Put your names in a series of DATA statements located in lines 1000–1010.

```
2 CLEAR 200
5 DIM A$(10)
10 FOR J=1 TO 10
20 READ A$(J)
30 NEXT J
40 FOR J=1 TO 4
50 PRINT A$(RND(10))
60 NEXT J
70 END
```

Section 3.6 (page 112)

1.
```
10 FOR J=.1 TO .5 STEP .1
20 GOSUB 100
30 PRINT X
40 END
100 X=5*J[2=3*J
110 RETURN
```

2.
```
1000 C(J)=100*(B(J)-A(J))/A(J)
```

3.
```
2000 M=C(1)
2010 FOR J=2 TO 6
2020 IF M<C(J) THEN M=C(J)
2030 NEXT J
2040 K=1
2050 IF M=C(K) THEN 2100 ELSE 2060
2060 K=K+1
2070 GOTO 2050
2100 RETURN
```

5. Let D(J) = 4 mean that J bets on 1st 12, D(J) = 5 that J bets on 2nd 12, D(J) = 6 that J bets on 3rd 12. In all such bets B(J) will be 0. Corresponding to the new values of D(J), there will be three new subroutines, starting in lines 4000, 5000, and 6000, respectively. Modify lines 121 to 125 as follows:

```
121 PRINT "BET TYPE:1=NUMBER BET,2=EVEN,3=ODD,4=1st
    12"
122 PRINT "5=2nd 12, 6=3rd 12"
123 INPUT "BET TYPE(1–6)";D(J)
124 IF D(J)>1 THEN 125 ELSE 130
125 INPUT "AMOUNT";C(J)
126 GOTO 180
```

Replace lines 320–330 by:

```
320 ON D(J) GOSUB 1000,2000,3000,4000,5000,6000
```

Finally, here are the three new subroutines.

```
4000 FOR K=1 TO 12
4010 IF X=K THEN 4100 ELSE 4020
4020 PRINT "PLAYER";"J;"LOSES"
4030 A(J)=A(J)C(J)
4050 RETURN
4100 PRINT "PLAYER";J;"WINS";2*C(J);"DOLLARS"
4110 A(J)=A(J)+2*C(J)
4120 RETURN
```

The subroutines in 5000 and 6000 are identical, except for the lines:

```
5000 FOR K=13 TO 24
6000 FOR K=25 TO 36
```

CHAPTER 4

Section 4.1 (pages 120 and 121)

1. 4Sq
2. 4Sq, 1D
3. I538

4. H
5. Hit Backspace 8 times
6. Hit 3 followed by Spacebar.
7. L
8. 4S0, 1C1
9. 8Sa, 1D
10. Q
11. 1S, 1D
12. 1SE 3C TEP
13. 1S2 1C3 1S5 1C2
14. Backspace to . in .5 then 2D I −1.5 SHIFT and [↓]
15. E : Y=M+1

Section 4.2 (page 124)

1.

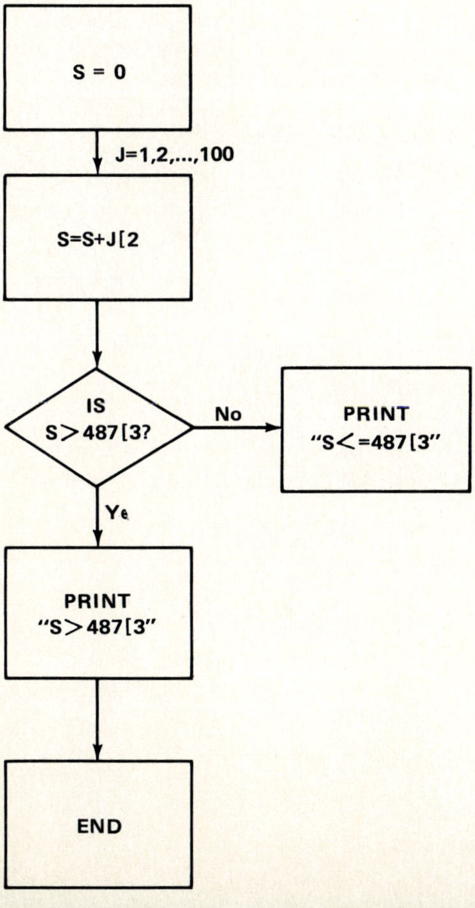

2.

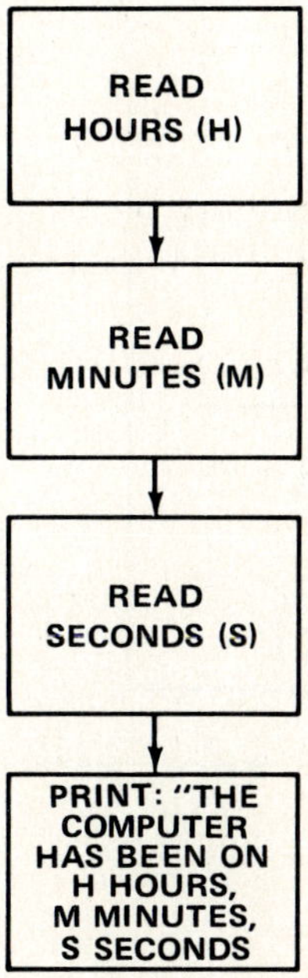

3.

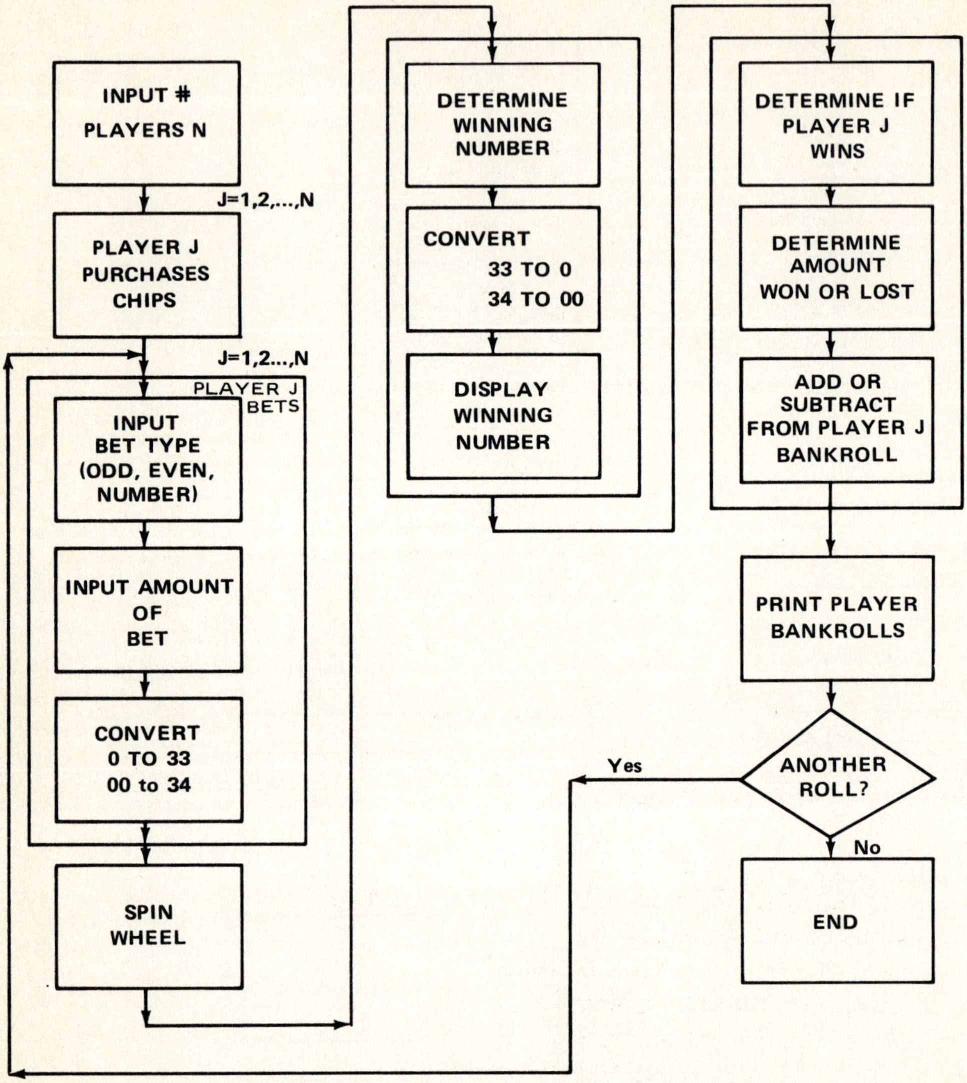
INPUT #
PLAYERS N
J=1,2,...,N
PLAYER J
PURCHASES
CHIPS
J=1,2...,N
PLAYER J
BETS
INPUT
BET TYPE
(ODD, EVEN,
NUMBER)
INPUT AMOUNT
OF
BET
CONVERT
0 TO 33
00 to 34
SPIN
WHEEL
DETERMINE
WINNING
NUMBER
CONVERT
33 TO 0
34 TO 00
DISPLAY
WINNING
NUMBER
DETERMINE IF
PLAYER J
WINS
DETERMINE
AMOUNT
WON OR LOST
ADD OR
SUBTRACT
FROM PLAYER J
BANKROLL
PRINT PLAYER
BANKROLLS
ANOTHER
ROLL?
Yes
No
END

4.

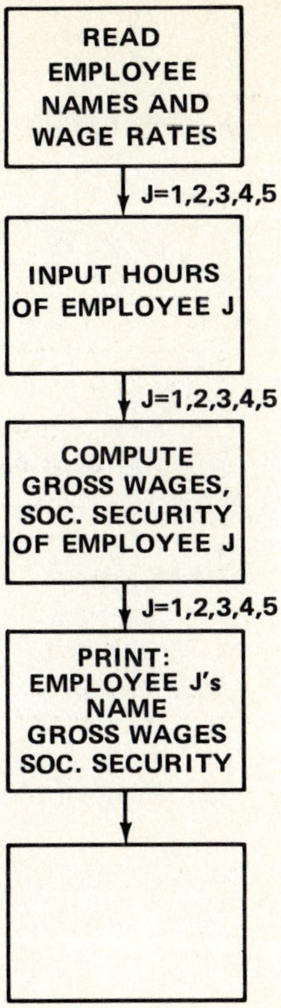

Section 4.3 (pages 127 and 128)

1. Here are the errors:
   TYPE MISMATCH in line 10: "0" should be 0
   line 30: J(2 should be J[2
   line 80: NXT T should be NEXT T
   line 90: should be deleted
   line 100: ST should be S*T
   line 110: "THE ANSWER IS"
2. line 30 should read: PRINT "THE FIRST N EQUALS",N
   Need line 40: GOTO 200

CHAPTER 5

Section 5.2 (page 136)

1. 10 DATA 5.7,−11.4,123,485,49
   20 FOR J=1 TO 5

```
30 READ A
40 PRINT #−1 A
50 NEXT J
60 END
```

2.
```
10 FOR J=1 TO 5
20 INPUT #−1 A
30 PRINT A
40 NEXT J
50 END
```

3. Position cassette to end of data file and execute the following program.
```
10 DATA 5,78,4.79,−1.27
20 FOR J=1 TO 4
30 READ A
40 PRINT #−1 A
50 NEXT J
60 END
```

4. Position the cassette to the beginning of the file and execute the following program.
```
10 FOR J=1 to 9
20 INPUT #−1 A
30 PRINT A
40 NEXT J
50 END
```

5. Let the program accommodate 500 checks. Let A denote the check numbers, B$ the date, C$ the payee, D the amount, and E$ any explanation.
```
10 CLEAR 1000
20 PRINT "TYPE DATA FOR CHECK"
30 INPUT "CHECK #";A
40 INPUT "DATE XX/XX/XX";B$
50 INPUT "PAYEE";C$
60 INPUT "AMOUNT"; D
70 INPUT "EXPLANATION";E$
80 PRINT #−1 A,B$,C$,D,E$
90 PRINT "ANOTHER CHECK?(Y/N)"
100 INPUT F$
110 IF F$="Y" THEN 120 ELSE 200
120 CLS
130 GOTO 20
200 PRINT #−1 −1000
210 END
```

6. Position cassette to beginning of file.

```
10 INPUT #-1 A
20 IF A=-1000 THEN 200 ELSE 30
30 INPUT B$,C$,D,E$
40 S=S+D
50 GOTO 10
200 "TOTAL OF ALL CHECKS IS", S
300 END
```

7. Make the last item in the data file the word "END". When reading the data file, you may then look for the occurrence of this item to signify the end of the file. For Example 1, add the lines:

```
90 IF G$="Y" THEN 10 ELSE 100
100 PRINT #-1 "END"
110 END
```

For example 2, add the lines:

```
20 INPUT #-1 A$
30 IF A$="END" THEN 150 ELSE 35
35 INPUT #-1 B$,C$,D$,E$,F$
```

Section 5.3 (pages 143 and 144)

1. OTTO.SKUNK:0
2. SHIRLEY/BAS:1
3. Too long
4. Does not begin with a letter
5. Does not begin with a letter
6. valid
7. valid
8. valid
9. valid
10. extension too long, password must begin with a letter
11. password too long
12. valid

Section 5.4 (pages 148 and 149)

1. (a)
```
10 S=0
20 FOR J=1 TO 50
30 S=S+J[2
40 NEXT J
50 PRINT S
60 END
```
   (b) Type MERGE "SQUARES"

2. (a)
```
100 S=0
110 FOR J=1 TO 30
120 S+S+J[3
130 NEXT J
140 PRINT S
150 END
```
   (b) Type MERGE "SQUARES"
   (c) Type LIST
   (d) DELETE 60 (This is the END of SQUARES.) Type RUN.
   (e) Type SAVE "COMBINED",A (The A is optional.)

3. Type LOAD "COMBINED"

4. Type KILL"SQUARES"

5. Insert diskette into drive 0 (assuming you have two drives) and type BACKUP. (If you are in BASIC, you must return to the system level first by typing CMD "S".)

6. Type FORMAT and follow instructions given.

Section 5.5 (pages 157 and 158)

1.
```
10 DATA 5.7,-11.4,123,485,49
20 OPEN "O",1,"NUMBERS"
30 FOR J=1 TO 5
40 READ A
50 PRINT #1,A
60 NEXT J
70 CLOSE 1
80 END
```

2.
```
10 OPEN "I",1,"NUMBERS"
20 FOR J=1 TO 5
```

```
30 INPUT #1,A
40 PRINT A
50 NEXT J
60 CLOSE 1
70 END
```

3.
```
10 OPEN "I",1,"NUMBERS"
20 OPEN "O",2,"TEMP"
30 FOR J=1 TO 5
40 INPUT #1,A
50 PRINT #2,A
60 NEXT J
70 DATA 5,78,4.79,-1.27
80 FOR J=1 TO 4
90 READ A
100 PRINT #2,A
110 NEXT J
120 CLOSE
130 OPEN "O",1,"NUMBERS"
140 OPEN "I",2,"TEMP"
150 FOR J=1 TO 9
160 INPUT #2, A
170 PRINT #1, A
180 NEXT J
190 CLOSE
200 END
```

4. Use same program as 2. except change 5 to 9.

5.
```
5 ON ERROR GOTO 500
10 CLEAR 500
20 PRINT "TYPE CHECK DATA ITEMS REQUESTED."
30 PRINT "FOLLOW EACH ITEM BY A CARRIAGE RETURN."
40 OPEN "0",1,"CHECKS"
50 INPUT "CHECKS #";A
60 INPUT "DATE";B$
70 INPUT "PAYEE";C$
80 INPUT "AMOUNT(NO $)";D
90 INPUT "EXPLANATION";E$
100 PRINT #1,A,B$,C$,D,B$
110 INPUT "ANOTHER CHECK(Y/N)";F$
120 CLS
130 IF F$="Y" THEN 20
```

```
140 CLOSE
150 GOTO 1000
500 RESUME 80
1000 END
```

6.
```
10 OPEN "I",1,"CHECKS"
20 ON ERROR GOTO 500
30 INPUT #1, A,B$,C$,D,B$
40 S=S+D
50 GOTO 30
100 CLOSE
110 PRINT "TOTAL OF CHECKS IS",S
120 GOTO 1000
500 RESUME 100
1000 END
```

CHAPTER 6

Section 6.1 (pages 168 and 169)

1.
```
10 FOR J=0 TO 127
20 SET(J,38)
30 NEXT J
40 END
```

2.
```
10 FOR J=0 TO 47
20 SET(17,J)
30 NEXT J
40 END
```

3.
```
10 FOR J=0 TO 127
20 SET(J,23)
30 NEXT J
40 FOR J= 0 T0 47
50 SET(64,J)
60 NEXT J
70 END
```

4.
```
10 CLS
20 FOR J=1 TO 2
30 FOR K=0 TO 127
40 SET(K,16*J)
50 NEXT K
60 NEXT J
```

```
70 FOR J=1 TO 2
80 FOR K=0 TO 47
90 SET(40*J,K)
100 NEXT K
110 NEXT J
120 END
```

5.
```
10 FOR J=0 TO 24
20 SET(30,J)
30 SET(31,J)
40 NEXT J
50 END
```

6.
```
10 FOR J=0 TO 47
20 SET(J,J)
30 NEXT J
40 END
```

7.
```
10 FOR J=0 TO 127
20 SET(J,32)
30 NEXT J
40 FOR K=0 TO 3
50 SET(24+K*25,31)
60 SET(24+K*25,33)
70 NEXT K
80 END
```

8.
```
10 FOR J=0 TO 47
20 SET(60,J)
30 NEXT J
40 FOR J=0 TO 4
50 SET(59,7+8*J)
60 NEXT J
70 END
```

9. Suppose that the name to be displayed is "JOHN JONES".
```
10 PRINT @475,"JOHN JONES"
20 FOR J=409 to 422
30 PRINT @J, "*"
40 NEXT J
50 FOR J=537 to 550
60 PRINT @J, "*"
65 NEXT J
70 PRINT @473,"*"
80 PRINT @486,"*"
90 END
```

10.
```
10 FOR J=0 TO 127
20 SET(J,32)
25 NEXT J
30 FOR J=0 TO 10
40 SET (10*J,31)
50 SET (10*J,33)
60 PRINT @772+5*J,10*J
70 NEXT J
80 END
```

11.
```
10 INPUT "ASCII GRAPHICS CODE";A
20 PRINT CHR$(A)
30 END
```

12.
```
10 PRINT @0, "COST"
20 PRINT @64,"PRICE"
30 PRINT @128,"INDEX"
100 DIM B$(12)
110 DATA "J","F","M","A","M","J","J","A","S","O"
120 DATA "N","D"
130 FOR J=1 TO 12
140 READ B$(J)
150 NEXT J
160 FOR J=1 TO 12
170 PRINT @ 902+4*J, B$(J):'MONTH LABELS
180 NEXT J
190 PRINT @0, "PROFIT"
200 FOR J=0 TO 40
210 SET(14,J):'VERTICAL AXIS
220 NEXT J
230 FOR J=0 TO 36 STEP 4
240 SET(13,J) : ' TICK MARKS
250 NEXT J
260 FOR J=14 TO 111
270 SET (J,40): ' HORIZONTAL AXIS
280 NEXT J
300 PRINT @960, "MONTH"
```

Section 6.2 (pages 176 and 177)

2. Delete lines 20–30. Change line 50 to read: INPUT A(M)

3. Type in numbers A(M) as prompted. (Remember: No commas or dollar signs.)

4. Mil. $ should be printed at position 64. There is no room for vertical labels 1.0 and .9. Print .8, .7, . . . , .1, respectively, at positions 128, 256, 320, 364, 512, 576, 640, 768. The alignment is not perfect, but is as close as we can come given the resolution of the screen.

Section 6.3 (pages 183 and 184)

4.
```
10 FOR J=10 TO 117
20 SET(J,3)
30 SET(J,44)
40 NEXT J
50 FOR J=3 TO 44
60 SET(10,J)
70 SET(117,J)
80 NEXT J
300 GOTO 310
310 GOTO 300
400 END
```

5. Add to the program of Exercise 4 the instruction:
```
65 SET(63,J)
```

6.
```
10 FOR J=5 TO 125
20 SET(J,3)
30 NEXT J
40 FOR J=30 TO 75
50 SET (J,28)
60 NEXT J
70 FOR J= 40 TO 125
80 SET(J,15)
90 NEXT J
100 FOR J=65 TO 125
110 SET(J,22)
120 NEXT J
130 K=3 TO 44
140 SET(5,K)
150 NEXT K
160 FOR K=15 TO 28
170 SET(40,K)
180 NEXT K
190 FOR K= 22 TO 28
200 SET(65,K)
210 NEXT K
```

```
220 FOR K=3 TO 15
230 SET(125,K)
240 NEXT K
250 FOR K=22 TO 44
260 SET(125,K)
270 NEXT K
280 END
```

Section 6.4 (page 186)

2. The entire screen will be white.

CHAPTER 7

Section 7.2 (pages 196 and 197)

3. Change 80 to 64 in lines 30, 50 and 60.

4. Add the following line:
   2 INPUT "DESIRED LINE LENGTH";Z
   Change 80 to Z in lines 30, 50, 60.

5.
```
10 A$="15+48+97=160"
20 B$(1)=LEFT$(A$,2)
30 B$(2)=MID$(A$,4,2)
40 B$(3)=MID$(A$,7,2)
50 B$(4)=RIGHT(A$,3)
60 FOR J=1 TO 4
70 B(J)=VAL(B$(J))
80 NEXT J
90 FOR J=1 TO 3
100 PRINT USING ###, B(J)
110 NEXT J
120 PRINT "____"
130 PRINT USING ###, B(4)
140 END
```

6.
```
10 A$="$6718.49": B$="$4801.96"
20 A1$=RIGHT(A$,7):B1$=RIGHT(B$,7)
30 A2=VAL(A1$): B2=VAL(B1$)
40 PRINT USING $####.##, A2
50 PRINT USING $####.##, B2
60 PRINT "____"
70 PRINT USING $####.##,A2+B2
80 END
```

Section 7.4 (page 206)

2.
```
10 FOR J=1 TO 15
20 PRINT CHR$(26)
30 NEXT J
40 END
```

3.
```
10 FOR J=1 TO POS(0)
20 PRINT CHR$(24)
30 NEXT J
40 END
```

CHAPTER 9

Section 9.1

1. 3.000000
2. 2.370000
3. 578,000.0
4. 2.00000000000000000
5. 3.000000
6. −4.100000
7. −4
8. 3500.685
9. 217.60000000000000
10. −5,940,000,000,000
11. +3.586950
12. −2.34542E10
13. −236,700,000,000,000,000,000
14. 4570000000000000000
15. 46.00000
16. .5000000
17. .60000000000000000
18. 1.600000
19. .66666666666666667

20. 1.1966666666666667

21. .6666667

22. 1.196667

23. 4963.00

24. 1749.9999900000000

25. 46, .5, .6#, 1.6#, .6666666666666667, 1.1966666666666667, .666667, 1.19667, 4963, 1749.99999#

26. 3.33333, accurate to 6 digits.

27. 3.3333333333333330, round-off error occurs in the 17th place.

Section 9.2 (page 235)

1.
```
10 PRINT (5.87+3.85−12.07)/11.98
20 END
```
2.
```
10 PRINT (15.1+11.9[4)/12.88
20 END
```
3.
```
10 PRINT (32485+9826)/(321.5−87.6[2)
20 END
```
4. −6. Place # after all constants in the above programs.

7.
```
10 INPUT X%
20 IF X%<0 THEN X%=X%−1
30 PRINT X%
40 END
```
8. −5

9. 4

10. −11

11. 1.780000

12. 1.7800000000000000

13. 32.65342

14. 4.252345E 21

15. −1.234567E−32

16. 3.2836464930292736

17. −5.7400000000000000

Section 9.3 (pages 240 and 241)

1.
```
10 PRINT EXP(1.54)
20 END
```
2.
```
10 PRINT EXP(−2.376)
20 END
```
3.
```
10 PRINT LOG(58)
20 END
```
4.
```
10 PRINT LOG(9.75E−5)
20 END
```
5.
```
10 PRINT SIN(3.7)
20 END
```
6.
```
10 PRINT COS(57.29578*45)
20 END
```
7.
```
10 PRINT ATN(1)
20 END
```
8.
```
10 PRINT TAN(.682)
20 END
```
9.
```
10 PRINT 57.2958*ATN(2)
20 END
```
10.
```
10 PRINT LOG(18.9)/LOG(10)
20 END
```
11.
```
10 FOR X=−5.0 TO 5.0 STEP .1
20 PRINT X, EXP(X)
30 NEXT X
40 END
```
12.
```
10 DATA 1.7, 3.1, 5.9, 7.8, 8.4, 10.1
20 FOR J=1 TO 6
30 READ X
40 PRINT X, 3*X[(1/4)*LOG(5*X)+EXP(−1.8*X)*TAN(X)
```
13.
```
10 CLS
20 FOR J=0 TO 127
30 SET (J,23)
40 NEXT J
50 FOR J=0 TO 46
60 SET (1,J)
70 NEXT J
```

```
80 FOR J=1 TO 127
90 SET(J, -23*SIN(.05*(J-1))+23)
100 NEXT J
110 GOTO 120
120 GOTO 110
130 END
```

14.
```
10 CLS
20 FOR J=0 TO 127
30 SET (J,23)
40 NEXT J
50 FOR J=0 TO 46
60 SET(63,J)
70 NEXT J
80 FOR J=0 TO 127
90 SET(J,23*ABS((J-63)/5)-23): VERT SCALE–1BLK=5 UNITS
100 NEXT J
110 GOTO 120
120 GOTO 110
130 END
```

15.
```
10 INPUT X
20 PRINT "THE FRACTIONAL PART OF",X,"IS", X–INT(X)
30 END
```

Section 9.4 (page 243)

1. 10 DEF FNA(X)=X[2-5*X
2. 10 DEF FNA(X)=1/X-3*X
3. 10 DEF FNA(X)=5*EXP(-2*X)
4. 10 DEF FNA(X)=X*LOG(X/2)
5. 10 DEF FNA(X)=TAN(X)/X
6. 10 DEF FNA(X)=COS(2*X)+1
7. 10 DEF FNA$(C$)=RIGHT$(C$,2)
8. 10 DEF FNA$(A$,J)=MID$(A$,J,4)
9. 10 DEF FNA$(B$)=MID$(B$,INT(LEN(B$)/2)+1,1)
10.
```
10 DEF FNA(X)=5*EXP(-2*X)
20 FOR X=0 TO 10 STEP .1
30 PRINT X, FNA(X)
40 NEXT J
50 END
```

Index